THE
FILM
THAT
CHANGED
MY
LIFE

**30
DIRECTORS
ON
THEIR
EPIPHANIES
IN THE
DARK**

Robert K. Elder

CHICAGO
REVIEW
PRESS

An A Cappella Book

Library of Congress Cataloging-in-Publication Data

Elder, Robert K.
The film that changed my life : 30 directors on their epiphanies in the dark
/ Robert K. Elder.
  p. cm.
Includes index.
ISBN 978-1-55652-825-5
1. Motion pictures. 2. Motion picture producers and directors—Interviews.
I. Title.
 PN1995.E5585 2011
 791.43'75—dc22

2010038581

Cover and interior design: Visible Logic, Inc.

Published by Chicago Review Press, Incorporated
814 North Franklin Street
Chicago, Illinois 60610
ISBN 978-1-55652-825-5
Printed in the United States of America

To my mom, Tina, who weathered the storm of insomnia-driven movie marathons—and even sat down to watch a few films with me (though she never developed a taste for Monty Python). Thanks for the love and support.

Contents

Introduction

Movies are personal touchstones. They provide soundtracks and wallpaper for our memories, and sometimes they become part of our own histories. For these directors, the films in this book are much more. They provided a spark that illuminated the rest of their lives. They inspired whole careers and, as the book title suggests, changed lives.

What made this project so entertaining wasn't just talking about film—although I, like most cinema lovers, can do that endlessly. The best parts of these interviews are not just about the movies themselves but also about the impact they had on each director's life. For instance, John Woo's story of how Martin Scorsese's *Mean Streets* almost made him a Catholic. Or how Kevin Smith was convinced, *convinced* that no other movie but *Slacker* could have made him a director. In these many conversations, I found not one but two directors who told me about their adolescent quest to find brief cinematic nudity on arts channels—only to have their lives transformed by the movies *Persona* and *L'âge d'or* (hint: both directors are Canadian). Still other interviews took unexpected turns—including Michel Gondry's thoughts about death and how he'd like to die, given that his cinematic hero was killed while working on a film.

There are great stories of directors meeting their heroes, as in Kimberly Peirce's tale of meeting Francis Ford Coppola, and these connections turning into enduring friendships. We hear of Michael Polish loving *Once Upon a Time in America* so much that he later hired one of the film's stars—James Woods—to star in his own masterpiece.

Throughout this project, I was able to gather directors from across the cinematic landscape. Oscar-winners include Danny Boyle, animator Peter Docter, and documentarian Alex Gibney. I've also tried to reach across genres and generations, with conversations with veteran filmmakers such as Arthur Hiller and Peter Bogdanovich, and relative newcomers such as Brian Herzlinger and Jay Duplass. Some were long-winded, others pithy, but almost everyone wanted to keep talking about their love of the films that shaped them. Only two filmmakers refused to stick with one movie. You (and the table of contents) know who you are.

I learned as much about these directors by their choice of films as I did from their own work. Perhaps John Landis says it best: "It's extremely important to know . . . that how you appreciate a movie has everything to do with your life experience at the moment when you see it, how you see it, and where you see it."

He continues, "People who see *2001* on DVD, on an eighteen-inch TV, letterboxed or not, that movie is not going to have the impact it did when you saw it in a Cinerama theater in 70mm. It's just not, it's a different experience. . . but that space station set to 'Blue Danube' is still one of the most powerful images ever. And it's just, how old were you when you saw it? Where were you? How did you see it? Movies are subjective."

And that's why we keep coming back. Movies are not just movies, they are mirrors of ourselves, our society, and our dreams—even if we're not quite ready for them. They make us laugh, cry, ponder our humanity, and escape from it entirely.

And, for a few, movies make them want to go out and make more movies.

A Brief P.S.

Almost every director asked me this question, so here's the answer:

The film that changed my life—that made me want to write about film—was Quentin Tarantino's *Reservoir Dogs*. Specifically, it was the scene in which an undercover cop learns how to be an undercover cop.

Spoiler alert: It's Tim Roth. His character learns a cover story—in this case, the story of a marijuana deal. We see him learning the story, scene by scene, practicing it over time. Then, he tells the story with increasing detail and finesse *to* gangsters he's infiltrating. In the next beat, Tarantino puts his character in the story he's telling. We see him walk into a bathroom with a bag of weed to find himself in the company of policemen and their drug-sniffing dog.

And the dog starts barking.

And then our hero, the undercover cop, begins talking inside the story he's telling—shaping the details of the story as he's in the bathroom, a drug dog barking at him and his black bag of marijuana.

It's an amazing sequence, a piece of virtuosic directing—not a story within a story, but a single story told by a character learning the story, telling it and then—knowing it so well—living that lie.

For me, a seventeen-year-old high school student, it was the first time I was overwhelmed by cinema, when the form did something unexpected, literary. In this instance, Tarantino's sleight-of-hand storytelling could only be done with the medium of film. Moreover, it was the first time I felt the presence of the director, a full-on personality and force of style imposed on the movie. Tarantino's DNA was on each frame of celluloid.

That, in a way, is the fix I'm constantly chasing—to find the directors inside their work. To hear and see and feel that personality connect with an audience.

Even if that audience is just me.

When you find it, it takes the wind out of you.

1

Edgar Wright
An American Werewolf in London

Edgar Wright was probably a little too young to see John Landis's *An American Werewolf in London*, even when he attempted to watch it on TV with his family. Even before he saw the film, he was enamored with it, particularly by images in fan magazines.

American Werewolf was a forbidden fruit made sweeter by Wright's adolescent pursuit to see it. But once he did, the impact was lasting. Compare it with Wright's own zombie-horror romantic comedy, *Shaun of the Dead*, and it's easy to see the inspiration, the attitude, the humor, and the humanity shared by both films.

Here, the director talks about Landis's masterpiece, a well-executed update of the horror-comedy formula. "It can probably never be replicated—nor should it," Wright says.

Edgar Wright, selected filmography:
A Fistful of Fingers (1995)
Shaun of the Dead (2004)
Hot Fuzz (2007)
Scott Pilgrim vs. the World (2010)

An American Werewolf in London
1981
Directed by John Landis
Starring David Naughton, Griffin Dunne, Jenny Agutter, and Frank Oz

How would you describe the film to someone who has never seen it?

Wright: Well, *An American Werewolf in London,* for my money, is like the best horror-comedy of all time. You've got lots of comedies that are very similar, and you have lots of horror films that are very similar. But very few horror-comedies are exactly the same, and *An American Werewolf in London* is really defined by its tone. And it's one of the few horror-comedies that's really funny.

It was directed by John Landis, coming off a run of very successful comedies. People didn't know how to take it because they were really scared by it, and because it was coming from the director of *Animal House.* And the fact that the poster said, "From the director of *Animal House* . . . A different kind of animal," people should've considered that they had fair warning with that tagline. [*laughs*]

In reality, it was the first script he ever wrote, and he wrote the script in the late '60s. And he shot three or four other films before he did *An American Werewolf in London.* It was obviously a real passion project for him. It's about two American guys in their early twenties hiking across the Yorkshire moors. And both of them get attacked by a werewolf. One of them survives and the other one doesn't. The one who does survive becomes a lycanthrope, a werewolf.

Why did you choose this particular film to talk about?

Wright: *An American Werewolf in London* was way ahead of its time as a postmodern film, taking its own inspiration from the Abbott and Costello horror films and the Bob Hope films.

The thing in *An American Werewolf in London* that really marks it out from everything—even now—is how scary the horror is and how visceral it is. I honestly think there are not many other films that really come close. There are other films that I like—*Evil Dead II* or Peter Jackson's *Braindead* [a.k.a. *Dead Alive* in the United States]. But both of those are a little more cartoonish and campy.

Whereas in *An American Werewolf in London,* it's very funny; it's also very real. The scene-setter on the moors where Griffin Dunne and David Naughton get attacked, or even before they get attacked, is absolutely terrifying. It's the stuff of nightmares. Tonally, it's a really interesting film. I think it's both hugely influential and, strangely, kind of underrated in a weird way.

Can you tell me about when you saw it and under what circumstances?
WRIGHT: I had a very interesting circumstance of seeing it, having to do with very bad parental decision-making. I think it was showing on British network TV in 1984, so maybe I was nine when it was actually on TV.

It was a real entry-level film into more adult films because both I and my brother had grown up on genre films and *Star Wars*—Spielberg and Lucas specifically. And through magazines like *Starburst* and *Starlog*, we definitely had an interest in films with effects in them. It is really only a skip and a jump from *Star Wars* and *The Thing* to *An American Werewolf in London* just on the basis of creature effects.

And I remember vividly, when it first came out, there used to be a British magazine called *Starburst*, which Alan Jones edited. During his tenure years as editor, it briefly went really gory for a magazine that was just selling at regular newsagents in Britain. There were massive complaints. One of the issues I had, which I would flip through ravenously, was the one with *American Werewolf* on the cover.

It had a photo of David Naughton smiling, surrounded by the people he's killed. And you see them all completely drenched in blood, which always struck me, because it was a crew photo essentially. It was like a production still; it wasn't stripped from the film.

And I think that, straightaway, just struck me as odd because it wasn't like a standard horror film shot. I remember reading everything about it and then actually it was on TV. It was on BBC 1, maybe nine o'clock at night, quite early. And my parents, because they knew we were so insanely keen to see it—we were allowed to stay up and watch it. So we were only nine and allowed to stay up past nine o'clock to watch *An American Werewolf in London*. And I couldn't be more excited watching it.

About forty minutes in, after Naughton has been attacked on the moors and his friend is dead, he's in the hospital having these very vivid nightmares and daydreams. There's a scene where he's back at home and the door gets kicked down and his Jewish family gets wiped out by Nazi monsters. They shoot his sister, shoot his brother and his parents. Then there's an extremely gory Rick Baker makeup job wherein Naughton's throat gets slit in close-up by a Nazi monster.

At that point, my mom and dad said, "OK, that's enough! Bed!" and sent us both to bed. So I wasn't allowed to watch the end of the film. That was a rash decision by my parents. They were trying to protect my innocence, but all that meant is that I had no resolution, didn't see the end of the film, and all I was left with was these images of the nightmares.

And so I was plagued by that for the next couple of weeks: the Nazi monsters and the moors attack itself—all the really scary parts in the early part of the film continued to plague me. So I don't think I actually saw it for another couple of years.

Did that make it even sweeter fruit because it was forbidden?
WRIGHT: Absolutely! And every time I see it, it just really strikes me. It's a special film for me. It's just really unique. I don't think anything else comes close to hitting the particular recipe of ingredients that film has.

Have you ever met anyone associated with the film?
WRIGHT: The other day I actually took part in like a documentary for a Blu-ray DVD that's coming out, and I've been very lucky to get to know some of the people who have been involved, like John Landis and Eric Baker. I even met Griffin Dunne and George Folsey Jr., who produced it. So I've met a lot of the people involved in the film.

In fact, the crowning part of that was: I had a festival in 2007 where I curated the new Beverly Cinema in Los Angeles. And one of the films I showed was *An American Werewolf in London* with John Landis, doing a Q&A with him.

Let me ask you this then: Landis has said he was trying to make a contemporary version of an old movie. He still believes it is not a comedy. Did you reconcile that at all with him?
WRIGHT: It's definitely a horror-comedy. It's frequently very funny.

I think what happened is that he made a horror film, but he's such a naturally funny person. The scenes in between the horror are just very funny. It's not arch at all—you care about the characters. You care what happens to them, which is very unusual for any horror film. When Griffin Dunne gets killed within fifteen minutes, it's shocking. Because even in just the first fifteen minutes, he establishes himself as incredibly engaging and funny.

Landis set out to make a horror film, and then his comedy instincts, which are amazing, just kind of shined through throughout the film. But what really sells *An American Werewolf in London* is the horror elements, which are really vivid and really work. It's properly scary and properly gory and full-blooded.

It is just as interesting that he wrote it when he was a teenager because it does feel like—and this is probably one of the reasons I liked it so much at a young age—it feels so much like the ultimate sixteen-year-old film. And I mean this so much as a compliment.

He actually said this to me when I did the Q&A with him. Some of the dialogue in the film—particularly the monologue by Jenny Agutter just before she sleeps with Naughton, when she says, "I've had seven lovers" [*laughs*]—Landis said, "Oh, that was like the teenage me speaking." And I said, "I don't care; I love it! It worked for me."

Well, anytime you have a female character be that open . . .
WRIGHT: Yes. It's interesting that he brought that up as being something that didn't work for him. But it's funny. I've just seen it so many times. Obviously when you're a preteen or teenager, you're thinking, "Oh my God, he's kissed Jenny Agutter. This is amazing! Things aren't that bad! His friend's dead; he's a werewolf. But he gets to go home with the ultimate English rose straight out of hospital. It's not a bad game!" [*laughter*]

How much impact did *An American Werewolf in London* have on *Shaun of the Dead*, your own horror-comedy?
WRIGHT: The tone of it very much influenced *Shaun of the Dead*. One of the things that we made as a rule for ourselves in *Shaun of the Dead* is that—with very few exceptions—all the humor came from the reactions and the context. And nobody said anything in dialogue that they wouldn't be able to come up with on the spot.

Now, a lot of '90s horror-comedies are written with more stylized dialogue, you know, where people are being very witty about things that are going on. People are coming up with zingers about the situation. And I think the thing that really makes *An American Werewolf in London* feel very real is that the reactions of all the characters—even though they're kind of incredulous sometimes—they feel kinda real.

The comedy helps the realism of the piece, if that makes sense. When they're on the moors and they know they're in trouble, and they're lost, and it's raining, and there's a wolf howling—they start nervously laughing about it. It's moments like that where they're joking around because you get into that slight kind of hysteria. Like where you're shit-scared and you're trying to take your mind off of it by joking with each other. And it really nails that aspect.

I think there's just a real alchemy to this film. John knew exactly what he was doing. It was the film that he really wanted to make even before *Animal House* and *The Blues Brothers*. This was his real passion project, and he had ten years to think about it and build up to it.

Well, Edgar, the title of the book is *The Film That Changed My Life*, so can you tell me how it changed your life?
WRIGHT: I've always been fascinated by horror films and genre films. And horror films harbored a fascination for me and always have been something I've wanted to watch and wanted to make. Equally, I'm very fascinated by comedy. I suppose the reason that this film changed my life is that very early on in my film-watching experiences, I saw a film that was so sophisticated in its tone and what it managed to achieve.

It really changed my life. It's informed both *Shaun of the Dead* and *Hot Fuzz*. There have been moments of verbal comedy, physical comedy, and tonal comedy. And extreme violence, somehow. Something like *An American Werewolf in London*, the idea of having this mix of socially awkward comedy preceded by incredibly vivid Oscar-winning horror, was just astonishing—is really astonishing. Horror films never get considered for Academy Awards; it's kind of incredible that *An American Werewolf in London* won the first ever makeup Oscar.

Tell me about your favorite scene.
WRIGHT: I've got so many favorite scenes in that film. Well, the werewolf transformation scene prominently features my favorite shot. The transfor-

mation sequence is obviously, rightly famous for John's decision to do it in bright light. Every previous werewolf transformation had always been done in the dark and kind of obscured or using montage.

But the bit I love is that cutaway to a Mickey Mouse figure in the middle of the scene, and the Mickey Mouse is kind of just observing this transformation. And I never entirely understood it. I don't really know why it's there, other than that it's just a cutaway. But it always makes me laugh. It's just absurd and surreal.

Tell me about first encountering that transformation scene. In addition to winning the Oscar, it's one of the most memorable sequences in film history.

WRIGHT: That was probably the element of the film I was most aware was gonna be in it. I'd read everything about the film, certainly seen lots of stills of that scene.

The transformation is preceded by David Naughton sort of puttering around the flat, bored. You have a whole sequence where he flips through British TV. You've got this whole sequence then set to Creedence Clearwater Revival's "Bad Moon Rising" and him just puttering around, and you know it's coming.

And then when it finally comes, Sam Cooke's version of "Blue Moon" kicks in, and it just starts—it's not in a dramatic scene. In fact, every other werewolf transformation prior to that in film occurs at some dramatic moment. You know, the lycanthrope is in human form and being chased by villagers. Or it's in the middle of a confrontation with somebody. Or a revelation.

Even in something like *The Howling*, released the same year, there's a werewolf transformation in the middle of a sex scene. And in *An American Werewolf in London* it starts off with Naughton sitting on the couch reading a book, then suddenly it's like "Jesus Christ!" It starts.

Every cliche setup from horror films is subverted with the mundanity of the situation. It keeps putting these extraordinary scenes and really vivid, graphic scenes in everyday settings. That's what really makes that film.

You mentioned the music, so let's talk about the soundtrack.

WRIGHT: The thing that I think is really amazing in *An American Werewolf in London*—I think it has to take its place in being one of the most influential films—is the use of music in the film. It's got a jukebox soundtrack. You've got *Easy Rider*. You've got *American Graffiti, Mean Streets*. And before you get to *Reservoir Dogs* in the early '90s, *An American Werewolf in London* has to stand out as one of the great soundtrack films ever.

And also probably the best—the film with the best soundtrack that never had a soundtrack LP. There's no soundtrack album for *An American Werewolf in London* for reasons that John Landis will go into very entertaining detail about. But the whole postmodern sort of conceit was taking all the songs with "Moon" in the title and making that your soundtrack. And using different versions of "Blue Moon." To have Bobby Vinton's "Blue Moon" scored over the foggy moors as your hero shows up, in the beginning of the film, in a truck full of lambs to the slaughter—it's just amazing!

It's got one of the best cuts to the end credits, when the Marcels' doo-wop version of "Blue Moon" kicks in. It's so brilliantly edited; it's something about the cut to the end credits that always gets me so excited.

I had *An American Werewolf in London* taped straight from right off the TV, and then I made an audiotape of all the songs, because there was no soundtrack LP. And because it was coming off the film, usually you had bits of the sound just before. So I sometimes had sound effects. It's funny because I had the Marcels' version of "Blue Moon" taken straight off the VHS—it always was preceded by Jenny Agutter crying.

This is going to sound so geeky; I'm really revealing myself right now. But even when I saw it in 2007 with John Landis and it got to that end scene with Jenny Agutter crying, I knew exactly when the music was going to cut in because I knew she goes [*imitates her whimper, then the intro to the Marcels' song*]. I know this film by heart.

When he was filming the movie, Landis talked about really wanting people to see it in London because of the Piccadilly Circus sequence, where the werewolf runs wild in the busy part of town. What was it like for you, a native, to see that?
WRIGHT: The next time I went to London after having seen *An American Werewolf in London*, my school friend and I, we went on a school trip to

London. I guess we were really like fourteen, fifteen, and the first thing we did when we had some time off is we tried to find the porno theater in Piccadilly Circus where the film was shot, which by that time didn't exist. I couldn't figure out where the entrance was.

John Landis achieved some location work in London that wasn't done again for a very long time. It's extraordinary what they managed to achieve in night shoots in London—having shot in London myself and knowing how restrictive that is of a location. When you watch that scene it's just incredible. There's a lot of location work in the film, which would be very difficult to do today. Like the Trafalgar Square stuff, the London Zoo stuff. You know, even the scene on the tube. All the location work is so vivid, those locations are forever linked with *An American Werewolf in London*. Like the Tottenham Court Road tube station, where the commuter is being pursued.

There were odd lines in that film that would just kind of, like, really resonate with me and my friends. We would constantly do impressions of the commuter before he starts getting chased and he's standing on the platform alone, which to be honest would be very rare at Tottenham Court Road, where it's strange to see one person alone any time of day or night.

Tell me about lines. What was the impression?
WRIGHT: Oh, the line that the commuter says is [*in a high, indignant voice*]: "Hello? Is there someone there? I can assure you that this is not in the least bit amusing." It's not one of the funniest lines in the film, but it's one of these lines that everybody always remembers. Like, "Beware the moon" and "Stay on the road." There are too many favorite bits in this film. I'm not sure I could pick favorites.

Another classic—and this is where John Landis's theory about it not being a comedy falls down—is in the scene where David Naughton wakes up in the wolf cage naked and has to escape the London Zoo. And so there's the young school boy with some balloons and Naughton is hiding behind the bush and says to the little kid, "Hey, kid. Little boy with the balloons! Come over here! If you come over here, I'll give you a pound. Two pounds."

The kid goes, "I don't know who you are." And Naughton says, "I'm the famous balloon thief," and then walks out, stark naked, takes his balloons and then runs off. So that's pretty funny itself.

And then the deadpan punch line, when the little kid goes up to his mom and says, "A naked American man stole my balloons." That's the line. That's one for all time.

The line from Griffin Dunne that people quote back to him all the time is . . .
WRIGHT: "Have you ever talked to a corpse? It's boring."

Yes! For me, the delivery is the best part of that line. Because you expect something else.
WRIGHT: His performance in that scene is amazing. When Griffin first comes into the hospital, his makeup is astonishing. And it's so gory. He has that little flap of skin that's kind of like flapping away through the entire scene, which always seems to draw everybody's eye. When I showed it in 2007, I mentioned the flap of skin, and everybody really reacted to that. But he has some funny lines in that scene.

He has the whole bit about his own funeral and talking about Debbie Klein, the girl that he fancied, you know, and he says, "She's so grief-stricken, she runs to find solace in Mark Levine's bed." He starts talking about the reactions to his death.

He does an amazing thing in that he really kind of walks the tightrope between little wisecracks and being this impish figure who comes to warn David: "Kill yourself, before you kill others." It gets very serious and there is something that really is bittersweet about it. It's funny, but it's also really painful because you like that character. You don't want to see him like that. It's upsetting. It's as upsetting to us as it is to David.

Griffin Dunne went off to star in *After Hours* and then *Who's That Girl*. And David Naughton didn't do much afterward, nothing as high profile. For me, the film is in one of those weird categories where it's a classic but the people associated with it did not go on to great acclaim, like the actors in Stanley Kubrick's *2001: A Space Odyssey*.
WRIGHT: I totally agree. In both cases I'm kind of surprised. What's interesting is that in the UK *An American Werewolf in London* is probably a much bigger film than it is in the States.

And even as a kid, I used to say to myself, Griffin Dunne should've been bigger. I mean, he's an amazing comic actor. And David Naughton! I used to think aloud, "Why didn't David Naughton do more?" David Naughton was so good in that.

I wasn't aware that maybe he had any baggage from those Dr Pepper commercials or that disco hit. He had that hit called "Makin' It."

Really? [*laughs*]

WRIGHT: I only found this out later, but David Naughton was in a network sitcom that was essentially a rip-off, spin-off of *Saturday Night Fever*, where he was playing a sitcom version of Tony Manero. And he had a hit single called "Makin' It." He's almost the film version of a one-hit wonder in terms of being in that film and not really being in a great deal else. Griffin Dunne is great in the film, but David Naughton I think is brilliant in it.

It's too easy, unfortunately, to gloss over his contribution. But for the film to work in any way at all, it's gotta drip down from the leading man. Something's gotta hold it together. And he does hold it together. And he's an incredibly sympathetic lead, and he goes a long way to making the tone of it work, which is not easy. You totally sympathize with him. He's very funny. He's very sweet.

But the scene of his I think is absolutely brilliant—and always gets me— is the scene where he rings his sister. Once he realizes that he's killed as a werewolf, he's going to commit suicide.

I love that scene where David Naughton rings to speak to his parents to tell them how much he loves them. But he gets his kid sister on the line and only his kid sister is there, and he's saying, "And please don't forget what I told ya about Mom and Dad: that I love them." And obviously as a kid she's not taking it seriously, and he's trying to get what's going to be his last words across to the family. You only hear Naughton's end of the conversation. I love that scene.

I feel slightly emotional when I watch it. It's because there are these elements to the film that feel . . . it really feels unique. It can probably never be replicated—nor should it. I can't imagine that anything else will come close to it, since it's such a unique place in somebody's career like John Landis's, when a director has a degree of success and puts all of his or her good will and financial clout into a passion project. And *An American Werewolf in London* is absolutely that film. And especially considering the subject matter, it's sort of very personal. And I think that's what really makes it just extraordinary. I'm always reminded every time I watch it of how dear it is to me and how much it means to me.

2

Rian Johnson
Annie Hall

Writer and director Rian Johnson is a romantic. A softy. But, like most of us, he's a slightly cynical softy—which is why *Annie Hall* seemed like the perfect film to spur him to cinematic action.

"It's magical to me," he says. "To this day, I can watch the film and try to analyze it and try to figure out how this little movie works, and it's almost impossible. I just end up getting lost. . . . For me, watching the film is like a kid watching a magic trick."

Johnson also has an affinity for playing with—and sometimes breaking—cinematic forms, which explains why he cast his first feature, *Brick*, as a noir murder mystery set in a high school. This, perhaps, explains why *Annie Hall* has been so attractive to him in its playfulness with (and outright disregard for) movie conventions.

"I'd put it up there with *8½* in terms of a film that personally redefined for me what film was capable of," Johnson says. "This was one of the first films I saw that played with form in a brave way, and it paid off."

Rian Johnson, selected filmography:
Brick (2005)
The Brothers Bloom (2008)

Annie Hall
1977
Directed by Woody Allen
Starring Woody Allen, Diane Keaton, Tony Roberts, Carol Kane, Paul Simon, and Shelley Duvall

How would you describe the film to someone who hasn't seen it?
JOHNSON: *Annie Hall* is a neurotic romantic comedy about a comedian named Alvy Singer, who's played by Woody Allen. It's a fragmented chronicle of his failed relationship with this woman, Annie Hall, who is played by Diane Keaton. It's told in a very nonlinear way, hopping around to various points in the relationship, from when they first meet to when they eventually break up. It's a bittersweet, subjective memory of a relationship.

Can you tell me when you saw the film and how you saw the film?
JOHNSON: I think most people saw the film in theaters. I have an experience that approximated that, even though I'm too young to know Woody Allen through his wackier comedies and then be hit by this, which is how most people had it. I grew up in high school watching *Bananas* and *Sleeper*; those happened to be the Woody Allen films my dad had on his shelf. It was only when I got to film school that I watched *Annie Hall* for the first time. It's one of a couple films that I can vividly remember exactly how it affected me when it was done. I watched it in film school at this horrible place—well, it was a wonderful place—but, looking back on it now, it was pretty terrible. They called it the "Cinema Study Center," and it was basically thirty televisions with LaserDisc machines and VCRs hooked up to them in this little basement. You were crowded in these little cubicles next to thirty other smelly film students, and that's where I first saw *Annie Hall*.

I remember sitting there after the final notes of the song go away and that shot of the empty street cuts off. I was in a state of suspended animation after that. That, for me, is the big thing with *Annie Hall* to this day. There's so many technical things you can say about it in terms of how it uses nonlinear storytelling or in terms of the photography. Even more than that it's the emotional impact brought about by this variation on traditional storytelling.

Even Woody Allen recognizes this as a departure. He says, "I finally had the courage to abandon just clowning around, and the safety of complete broad comedy." There's also the influence of Ingmar Bergman's *The Passion of Anna* here, because the actors in that film stop and explain their actions and roles to the audience.

JOHNSON: Absolutely. It's obvious that this is the first time he let himself indulge. One of the first scenes of the film is the two characters in line at an art house. They're waiting to see *Persona*. They end up going to see *The Sorrow and the Pity* after they can't get into *Persona*—remember they miss the credits?

Annie Hall is one of those legends of film lore that originally the film was written, made, and cut as a completely different film. Originally, it was a little less audacious in its storytelling, and it had more of a narrative hook. I've read that it was supposed to be a murder mystery. I'm blanking on what the name of it was. . . .

It was originally titled *Anhedonia*, which means the inability to experience pleasure.
JOHNSON: Right, right. Originally, it was a much more traditionally structured film. The legend goes that while working with his editor, Allen threw out half the movie, patched it together, and made it into a much more impressionistic, subjective canvas of memories. It's interesting watching the film if you're aware of that, because you can see the glue. You can hear the lines that stitch one scene to another, but it works. It doesn't end up detracting from it. If anything, it makes it even more amazing that they were able to create one statue, shatter that statue, and from those fragments build a completely different statue that left me stunned in the Cinema Study Center.

It's neither here nor there, but I often hear the opposite story: that it was Gordon Willis, his cinematographer. Allen credits Willis by saying, "My maturity in film came when I met Gordon Willis." Willis helped him discard and keep certain gags. Some of the more Bergmanesque, surrealistic scenes were cut. There's one scene where he and Shelley Duvall go to the Garden of Eden to discuss the female orgasm.
JOHNSON: Right, and there's one where he goes to hell, which is eventually in *Deconstructing Harry*.

Yeah, and there's a great quote from that, "Layer 5: For Organized Crime, Fascist Dictators, and People Who Don't Appreciate Oral Sex."

[*laughter*] So there is a tug-of-war historically. I haven't been able to ferret out which is true, and the book *Woody Allen on Woody Allen* wasn't able to do it for me.

JOHNSON: Unlike so many things today, this has never been seen. Usually you hear about legendary stuff, and everything has gotten out there. Even the most legendary material is on YouTube. This is the stuff of legend for film fanatics.

Let me reel back just a little bit. You've called this—

JOHNSON: A neurotic romantic comedy?

Yeah, and that was its tagline: "A Nervous Romance." But how exactly did you experience it? So you were expecting what other people had expected to see: *Sleeper, Bananas,* and his film before this, *Love and Death.* How did it meet and change your expectations?

JOHNSON: I had some context sitting down for it. I knew this was entirely different. I wasn't prepared for how it would strike me. It takes a complete left turn from those films in terms of tone. It's unafraid to linger. Whereas in *Love and Death* and *Sleeper* there isn't a frame of film where there isn't a visual gag happening or rapid-fire dialogue. The pacing is very much like a Marx Brothers film. It's striking how much it lingers even in the scenes that are built around a gag; there's a dryness to them. There's something bare about them. Like the scene with the mother and the doctor when he's a kid—rewatching that I was struck by the quietness of it, and how it doesn't play like a sketch. There's something that feels like a bare lightbulb. So tonally that's the big thing.

Finally, I'd come back to the emotional resonance of it. All of the style—and there's quite a bit of style in the film—is focused toward emotionally engaging you with these two people and this relationship. That, for me, is a big departure. Because there are love stories in *Love and Death* and *Sleeper,* but the fact that it hits you hard emotionally in this film is a big difference.

You picked this film because it changed your life. How exactly did it change your life? How did it influence your filmmaking?

JOHNSON: In terms of filmmaking, I'd put it up there with *8½* in terms of a film that personally redefined for me what film was capable of. This was one of the first films I saw that played with form in a brave way, and it paid off. It completely worked in the back end. It wasn't like a [Jean-Luc] Godard film where it was about "getting it" at the end of the film. It wasn't like, an "Oh wow, I see what they're doing, and that's incredibly clever. I can analyze it this way and that way write a paper in film school about it."

This was a film that broke so many rules in terms of film narrative, and it moved me in a way that very few other films have moved me. That's something that, I pray to God, if I am able to keep making movies, I can only hope, twenty years down the line maybe, I'll be able to approach. It's magical to me. To this day, I can watch the film and try to analyze it and try to figure out how this little movie works, and it's almost impossible. I just end up getting lost. It's not the sort of thing that I can analyze. For me, watching the film is like a kid watching a magic trick.

You talked about the film breaking rules. What rules did it break, and to what effect?

JOHNSON: First of all, traditional narrative. Just in terms of the timeline of the film, it hops around and is incredibly subjective. There's direct address at points, but the point at which those things come seems almost random. It doesn't seem, on the surface at least, to have any rules. All of a sudden you cut to an animated sequence, with the evil queen.

At one point he approaches random people on the street, and then he approaches a horse that a cop is riding and starts talking to the horse. That's one of the huge contrasts that to this day astounds me that it works so well and feels so cohesive. If you watch the stuff that's happening in it, it's just as chaotic and wacky as anything in *Love and Death* or *Sleeper,* but tonally it manages to have realism that feels very grounded. That's a lot of what buys it that emotional payoff at the end.

Let's talk about a couple of the reasons why that might be. *Annie Hall,* **of course, the name comes from Diane Keaton, because her real last name is Hall; it's written for her. Gordon Willis was the cinematographer for**

The Godfather, and this film comes after Keaton starred in the first two *Godfathers.* This is Allen and Keaton's fourth film together (after *Play It Again Sam, Love and Death,* and *Sleeper*), and they had a romantic history. He is essentially directing his ex-girlfriend.

JOHNSON: [*laughter*]—in a film about their relationship.

Maybe not about their relationship explicitly, but about a failed relationship. Did you know that going in?

JOHNSON: I know that now, but when I first watched it I didn't. It's hard to try, as a viewer, to attribute the genuineness of the film to that, and I'm sure that's there. At the same time, it's such a swamp to get into—to try to and attribute the success of the film to whatever personal contexts you as a film viewer or as a reader think you have. The reality of the situation between them, the reality of how much of [Keaton and Allen's] relationship was in there. On a basic level it's hard to imagine that he had a history with her and they were broken up at the time. Also, it's hard to watch her performance and not feel like there's something genuine at work there—not feel like he's tapping into something that's fundamentally her.

What scene sticks with you most?

JOHNSON: There's a lot because this film, almost more than any other, is presented as a series of tableaus, as a series of scenes. There's the second scene when she sings at the cabaret. In the first one they're on their first date, and it was awkward because she sang and nobody listened to her.

Then, in the second scene, you see her commanding the crowd through her performance on the stage, and through the ambience of the cabaret. The fact that it's quiet and people are listening—through that you see more than you could in any other way. I can't imagine a stronger way to portray her growth as a human being from that first scene to the second scene. And, at the same time, realizing what that means for their relationship, in the context of what the whole film is about—their relationship. It's a very powerful thing, especially when you think in our own lives about how we get into relationships with people, and then people grow. How it's wonderful for them, but that line about a relationship being like a shark. It has to be constantly moving forward, otherwise it dies.

Or it dies and you have a dead shark.
JOHNSON: "And I think what we got on our hands is a dead shark." The opposite can also be true, too. She's moving, growing, and going forward, and he's flopping in the water. We're aware of their relationship, while she is giving this beautiful, strong performance on the stage, and with that context it becomes much more than that. It becomes something very sad, at least for me.

It's because she's singing "Seems Like Old Times."
JOHNSON: Exactly, which brings me to the other moment, which is the end montage of the film, set to the exact same song. It ends with this very bittersweet moment when they're each with another person, and they're on a street corner. It's shot very distant from across the street. You see them meet up with each other and pass. That's a beautiful sequence for me, because it contextualizes the relationship in a way that, on the surface, seems to marginalize it. It's about as far from the ending of a traditional romantic comedy as you can get. It almost brushes it off. We start the film with Woody Allen speaking directly to the camera and our perspective is very immediate; it's as though he's just broken up with this woman. His head is still swimming with everything. At the end of the film, he has perspective on a relationship that ended years ago.

There is a reading of the film that says he wins her. In a certain way, she is his shiksa, but he can't change her to fit into his worldview no matter how many books about death he buys her. She ultimately changes; how does she change him?
JOHNSON: In a way it feels like fundamentally she doesn't change. There's the line, "Alvy, you're incapable of enjoying life, you know that? I mean you're like New York City. . . . You're like this island unto yourself."

Well, first of all, it's more complicated than that. I think that's one of the reasons why the film works. I don't think you can point directly and say, "She changed, he didn't, that was the problem, and that's why the relationship didn't work." If you look at it, they were fundamentally mismatched from the beginning. All of our relationships—it's hard for me to point to a relationship in my life that wasn't a fundamental mismatch. That's what creates the beauty of it, the bittersweet memories of the relationship. I think it was near the start of the relationship when they're in the bookstore, and she wants to buy the cat book and he wants to get her these books on death.

On this point, I'd like to contend that Alvy does not have the capacity to change, that it's really Annie that has the capacity to change, and that's why the movie is named *Annie Hall* and not *Alvy Singer*. Film scholars later pointed out, and I think correctly, that after the relationship is over, he does change, because he becomes able to appreciate a woman who could love him. The movie begins with the Groucho Marx joke that he could never be a member of a club that would have him as a member. Basically, he's able to appreciate her as "a club that would have him as a member." That comes from Mary Nichols, a film writer.

JOHNSON: I can see shades of that, but I'm not sure if, at the end of the film, he met his equivalent. Then he would be able to have a successful relationship with her. It depends how you define change. His perspective on the relationship changed, but that might be another one of the reasons why the film lands so hard for me. I think we all feel like we've learned our lesson at the end of each relationship, and then we start the next one and fuck everything up again.

I think what Mary Nichols is saying is not that he's fixed and they can have a relationship. It's that he's able to appreciate her. That joke that he uses to explain his love life is unrivaled because he's able to actually understand that, "Oh, that's why she could love me."

JOHNSON: At the same time he's not with her. He's not able to be part of the club. He's developed a bittersweet appreciation for it. He's put it into context, and come to peace with it, which is growth. That may be the main type of growth that we're all capable of as human beings, to gain some perspective on a chapter in our lives. In terms of that joke unraveling to the point where he's somehow overcome the fundamental neurosis behind it, I'm not sure I agree with that. He's almost come to accept it, or not accept it, but be able to say it boldly, as a statement of how he is in life. I'm not sure I agree that he's overcome it by the end of it.

I don't think it's *overcome*, but *appreciate*.
JOHNSON: *Appreciate* I'd agree with.

It's a more generous word. Now, you were telling me about what you think is the saddest part of the movie. I'll tell you what mine is. It's a very quick scene, and it probably tells you more about me than anything else. It's the scene in which he's no longer with Annie and he's at a beach house someplace and he's trying to catch a lobster. He's trying to re-create this whimsical moment, and he's with a woman who just does not get him. [*laughter*] To me, that is so sad.
JOHNSON: Yeah, and the line with the smoking and the woman asking him, "Are you joking?"

What I love about the writing is it's so self-conscious. It's a joke at his expense that's extremely sad and revealing.
JOHNSON: It cuts right to the heart of what we were talking about before: his inability to change, to the point where he's actually trying to re-create a specific moment. Instead of growing forward with her, he's literally restaging—which is exactly what he's doing with the play that he's writing. Also, if you want to break these waves, it's what he's doing with this film, ostensibly. He's reliving it and trying to gain some sort of acceptance on it. Meanwhile, she's off in Los Angeles having personally grown.

Also, in terms of connecting with personal experience, anytime you're in the immediate aftermath of a breakup and you start dating—for some reason that scene cuts to the heart of my experience. Every single date you go on a month or two after a relationship ends, you're comparing, and they always pale in comparison.

Or not only that, but you have, "She would have loved this; she would have appreciated this." You end up haunting your own house at a certain point. You mentioned the play Alvy Singer writes, which is one of the great reveals. There's a great line, "You know how you're always trying to get things to come out perfect in art because it's real difficult in life." I realize you're still at the beginning of your career, but have you fallen prey to that in your own work?

JOHNSON: Oh God, are you kidding? That's what we do! [*laughter*] It's funny, but at the same time it's painful. It lays bare the deeply rooted motivation behind telling these stories, doing this work to frame moments and tell stories. That's another thing that I think is remarkable about the film. On the one hand, it gives the impression that it's outside of that; it's trying to genuinely be honest. It's like a frog dissecting itself on the table. It's being very brutal about a lot of moments.

At the same time, it gives me that romantic thrill, that romantic rush that a good romantic comedy does. It somehow manages to appear to be above that dishonesty of a traditional romantic comedy, but in the same way, it emotionally fulfills it. By the end, it leaves you very hopeful about love. In this particular relationship between these two particular people, it somehow manages to have them broken up by the end of it and yet leave you hopeful about love. Maybe that's as perfect as it can get in real life.

Historically this film is important for another reason. It took home four Academy Awards: Best Actress, Best Director, Best Original Screenplay, and Best Picture. Why do you think so few comedies win Best Picture?
JOHNSON: That invites speculation about what award shows tend to value in films, which I don't think I want to get into.

But that's what I'm interested in. What did this film overcome?
JOHNSON: I almost feel like this film was able to make people forget it's a comedy, even though it's very funny. It's about the feeling I was left with at the end; it wasn't a laugh at all. It was being genuinely moved, feeling laid bare. Maybe that gets to the heart of it: it moves you. Also, the craftsmanship of it is undeniable, along with the innovative nature of the way it told its story. It all adds up to a very effective love story. If it hadn't won those Oscars, it would have been seen as one of the great tragedy, mystery, shake-our-fists-at-the-Oscar-people moments in film history.

You talk about some of the other rules that it broke, and I want to point out a couple: the use of split screen. Not only the use of split screen, but the two halves of the screen interacting even when there are decades between them.

JOHNSON: Split screen itself was being used quite a bit in the '60s and the early '70s, but there was a way that Allen was using it tonally. There was a dryness, a matter-of-factness to it. Split screen is something that I identify with the wackier tone of his previous films.

It's a very audacious dash of style to use split screen. It was used in pedestrian scenes, like the one at the dinner table, and it was used almost intentionally imperfectly. It's not like the two sets line up exactly, and they cut somebody off halfway through. It almost feels offhanded. For some reason that helps to integrate it into the film, and make it seem less a gimmick and more a genuine use of film language to contrast these two different worlds.

When Woody Allen and Diane Keaton are talking to their therapists, and it's going back and forth between them, you don't feel the split screen as the point of the shot. It is a tool they are using to contrast what's happening in both of their heads.

And that's one of the best jokes, when their therapists ask, "How often do you sleep together?" He says, "Hardly ever! Three times a week!" And she says, "Constantly. Three times a week!" which is a very male/female perspective, I think. Speaking of which, do you have a favorite line?
JOHNSON: One of the funniest jokes, or the hardest I laughed in the whole film, is actually from his first wife, played by Carol Kane. He's talking about the Kennedy assassination and she says, "You're using this conspiracy theory as an excuse to avoid sex with me," and, "Oh my God! She's right!" There's something so deeply true, when you've been in a relationship for a while, about the layers of self-deception that are so obvious that you will still somehow fool yourself into not seeing. For some reason that line got the biggest belly laugh from me.

Talking about film tricks here, what effect does direct address have?
JOHNSON: It's that tightrope act that this movie pulls off. On the one hand it's an audacious, wacky, and self-conscious gambit. You can definitely see that he was drawing inspiration from Bergman, from that audacious use of film language, breaking the fourth wall. It manages to pull it off without feeling self-indulgent or like a wacky splash.

As a filmmaker it's the most terrifying thing in the world to try to do, because if you try it and it doesn't work, then it's pretentious. Everyone in the theater will roll their eyes at the same time. It's done so consistently throughout the film and it molds so well into the tone and the text of it.

For me, the key is that it's never done for the sake of itself. Like the conspiracy theory line, he turns and directly addresses the camera. That's not what I remember about that line. What I remember is the truth of it. He's not turning to the camera for a wacky aside; it's because of this fundamental truth about what he's doing in this relationship—that he's deceiving himself in order to avoid sleeping with her. The weight of it has just hit him, and it's snapped him out of the scene and caused this huge realization.

It's not done for the sake of a stylistic gimmick; it's done in the service of the moment and scene. Consistently you can point to most of the stylistic flourishes throughout the movie, and I think that's the reason that they work: they're always to an end, never for themselves.

How has this film aged? How has your experience with this film changed throughout the years?
JOHNSON: That's the amazing thing: very little. If anything it has grown in stature in my mind. What it achieved has become even more remarkable. I hate the tendency to say, "Films today don't do what they used to," because usually that's bullshit. In any generation, people are reticent to take the risks that this film does. One thing I'll say about today versus back then, the idea of taking the risks that this film took is frightening because there is less tolerance on the part of audiences today. I'm emotionally affected by it each time I see it. I appreciate what it pulled off.

3

Danny Boyle
Apocalypse Now

Danny Boyle's early exposure to Francis Ford Coppola's *Apocalypse Now* helped mold his own cinematic obsessions: people and societies in crisis, or at the edge of madness. Though he admits to an homage to Coppola's masterpiece in *The Beach*, Boyle has otherwise been reluctant to reference the film directly in his own work. *Apocalypse Now*'s scale and narrative form a kind of paradoxical, inimitable specter for Boyle, who remains loyal to the original 1979 version. He's not a fan of the recut, extended version Coppola released in 2001 as *Apocalypse Now Redux*. To him, the original film is logical and insane—flawed and yet perfect.

"If I had to nail one film on my heart, this would be the one."

Danny Boyle, selected filmography:
Shallow Grave (1994)
Trainspotting (1996)
A Life Less Ordinary (1997)
The Beach (2000)
28 Days Later (2002)
Millions (2004)
Sunshine (2007)
Slumdog Millionaire (2008)
127 Hours (2010)

Apocalypse Now
1979
Directed by Francis Ford Coppola

Starring Martin Sheen, Marlon Brando, Robert Duvall, Dennis Hopper, Frederic Forrest, Sam Bottoms, Laurence Fishburne, Albert Hall, and Harrison Ford

How would you describe this film to someone who has never seen it?
BOYLE: This movie is impossible to pigeonhole. It's the greatest war movie ever made. There are greater movies that condemn war, but no film captures our abhorrence of war and yet the pleasure we get from seeing it depicted in the movies. That's what's extraordinary about it. It's not just a war movie, it's about the nature of cinema and why we go and watch it—that journey we want to make in the cinema.

It's summed up obviously by Coppola, who appears in it himself, screaming at the guys to "keep going!" so he can get better pictures.

He plays a war documentarian and yells at the soldiers, "It's for television, just go through, go through!"
BOYLE: [*laughs*] And so it's not just a war movie. People make war movies and you feel the horror and the pity, but this is also about moviemaking because he went through such an extraordinary passage in order to make the film. And so to encapsulate it is virtually self-defeating in a way. That's what's extraordinary about it.

It is a master film. It's my own personal favorite; if I had to nail one film on my heart, this would the one. This would be it because it is unclassifiable.

Let's start with the basics, then. Preliminarily, it's based on Joseph Conrad's novella _Heart of Darkness_, and it's about Willard, played by Martin Sheen, who is sent to hunt down a rogue colonel, played by Marlon Brando. Existentially, it's about a guy sent to kill his darker self. Is that simplifying it too much?
BOYLE: I guess that's it, yeah. That's a good summation of it, really.

My relationship with it, and my relationship with most films that I love, is not really an intellectual one at all. It's a passionate, visceral, emotional one, and in a funny kind of way I learned to value and appreciate that more as I go on, really, rather than try to ever understand the films.

You saw this at what age?

BOYLE: I come from a place, a very small town outside of Manchester. I came to London—I guess I was twenty-one—and I moved to London to start my work, my career, whatever it turned out to be. I remember there were huge, anamorphic, black posters. [*laughs*] They just seemed to be the biggest posters I had ever seen and there was nothing on them other than "Apocalypse Now" and of course, "A Francis Ford Coppola film." It was obviously juggernaut publicity that was really concerned about how over-reaching the film was and the devastation that was caused by everyone who was involved with it.

Coppola rides two horses in the film; that is what pulls you toward the film of course, immediately. It's not just the sense you're going to see a successful film, like a product. You're going to see something that is beyond the film that has destroyed people's lives, that has bankrupted a genius. So it's a celebration of the destruction as well as a condemnation of its subject matter. It's the war in Vietnam. And when you consider that nobody wanted to make films about Vietnam, that America turned its back on it, here was this great boy genius, really.

Sure, sure, but it was after he had won Best Picture twice already, for the first two *Godfather* films.

BOYLE: It's obviously made at the absolute Everest of megalomania, the absolute peak of, "I can do nothing wrong, and I must just push myself." And that's, of course, one of the things celebrated in the film. You do see a film made at the absolute edge of sanity, really. In terms of the indulgence that movies can induce in people. But there's a great side to it as well because it is his ambition and it is about bigness, and I think that's something that we have lost.

We now watch big films in terms of impacts and scale. I'm sure we'll get it back, hopefully. But we really lost big films, these slightly overwhelming, overly ambitious big films. We've lost them, for whatever reason: confidence, marketing, whatever other factors you build into it. We do seem to have lost that ambitiousness, I think.

But tell me about that very first time you saw it. And what was your mind like as you left the theater?

BOYLE: [*laughs*] It had eviscerated my brain, completely. I was an impression-able twenty-one-year-old guy from the sticks. My brain had not been fed and watered with great culture, you know, as art is meant to do. It had been sand-blasted by the power of cinema. And that's why cinema, despite everything we try to do, it remains a young man's medium, really, in terms of audience.

That's why they are the loyal ones to go, because there's something about it that is particularly important to the intemperance, the impatience, of young men. And they want that feeling of their brains being sandblasted by the pure visceral power of cinema. At first, when you sort of discover that as a reflection, you kind of feel some shame about it. I don't feel shame of that at all. It's just: "That's what the art form is." And the much more reflective experience belongs to different art forms, I think.

Well, there are some films that do that; obviously this is a wild gener-alization. But it's true nonetheless. It sums up why the economic power of movies lies where it lies—in chasing the audience of young men.

Well, briefly, I want to get these details. Do you remember what theater you saw it at in London and what you did afterward?
BOYLE: I'm pretty sure it was on the Leicester Square Auditorium, which is the biggest cinema in Britain. I think I went to see it there because, again, that feel-ing. It was all built into it. If you're going to see it—this thing with the biggest posters in the world—you're going to see it in the biggest cinema in Britain.

Did you see it with friends?
BOYLE: Yes, a whole gang of us, young men all about the same age. I can't remember it all, but I was blown away. All the moments you think about, the famous sequences: the opening, "The Ride of the Valkyries," "Never get out of the boat"—I'm sure we just replayed those to each other. The film just has never left me.

I was so taken with it that after its initial run in London, I took my dad. My dad came down to London, and there was cinema called Prince Charles Cinema, which is a much smaller cinema. Actually, it was a porn cinema. It showed porn, but *Apocalypse Now* had a late run there when it had left the main cinemas. I remember taking him and telling him about it. And this is, of course, strange because he was in a war. And I wanted him to see it so much. I wanted to proselytize it to him. I remember sitting there, before it began. I do remember them running the porn trailers for what was going to be on in the following weeks. I was so embarrassed. [*laughs*] But then the film began and all was forgiven and forgotten.

And was your dad a World War II vet?
BOYLE: He was.

And what was his reaction?
BOYLE: I don't think he saw it in the way that I saw it. I think it's a really different depiction of war. It is about modern pop culture as much as it is about war and that first excitement and visceral stimulation. It's as much about that as it is actually about war. So he would personally find *Saving Private Ryan* a more appropriate picture of war, I think.

Whereas for us, that's why *Apocalypse Now* is so extraordinary, really. It's our war. The war we fight now, which is a battle between ourselves—in ourselves, between stimulation and yet somehow feeling morally you must condemn it.

Is there a particular scene or sequence that's remained powerful for you?
BOYLE: Well, I suppose, for any director, it's got to be "Ride of the Valkyries." Because it's too well known in a way; it's not the subtle one you should really point out. For me, it's a great washing machine scene. I call it a washing machine because he just throws all these ingredients into it: the savagery of what the Americans did, American culture, the surfing.

The Vietcong are holding a beachhead, and U.S. air cavalry raid it with dozens of helicopters. Robert Duvall commands the unit and plays this Wagner music to intimidate the Vietcong—which is an extraordinary idea, this fascist German composer being blasted out at the Vietcong as these twentieth-century machines ride in with destruction.

Duvall does take the beach, and he takes the beach partly because it's military imperative, but principally because on this beachhead the surf is really good and he loves to see his boys surf. Everybody is suddenly on the ground in the middle of the washing machine rather than protected by these swooping insects of destruction. Suddenly, when they are actually on the ground, they all look bewildered and scared. And he gives them two choices: You fight or you surf. Which one is it going to be? [*laughs*]

Coppola just piles everything into it. I think that's the sequence that Coppola appears in, and he just starts the washing machine, really. It's insane.

The guy's a genius, of course. When the girl runs out and puts the grenade in the helicopter—that punctuation of the grand opera—those kinds of observations are a great director at work. The guy sitting on his helmet because he doesn't want his balls blown off—those are punctuation marks. You are watching a grand opera, but it's not Brian De Palma; it's not Michael Bay. It's a genuine, genuine artist, inhabiting a butcher's abattoir of resources. But he's aware. He's aware he's in the abattoir because that's where we want him to be.

It's the boldness of the concept, the conception of it—that you will take part in this stunning physical attack, use the energy and the violence and cinema, and you play it to grand opera. That, itself, has become a type of pornography in a way.

There's a whole strand of cinema that inhabits that; you think of the films of Michael Bay. But Coppola is a filmmaker before all those guys existed; he is a filmmaker who knew that and anticipated it. He's not using it ironically. He's using it to give you intense pleasure, sheer physical pleasure as it streams across your irises. I think he knew that's what we were basically going to become. That's where visual stimulation in the cinema was taking us. I don't know if he knew it or not, but in his dementia, that's what he gave us. I'm sure that he knew it; that's why he gave it to us. That's why the film lasts for so long in a way. You watch any film, especially films that are about impact—visual, physical impact, aggressive energy—they date very, very quickly. This doesn't date. I can't think of a bit of this film that dates.

Oh, and the other sequence I like, which is a much more subtle sequence, is when they get out of the boat and they go for mangos. It's an extraordinary sequence of cinematography, just where he lights the jungle in these strips, like kind of photographic strips of light, and they're eventually jumped by a tiger.

That's a great metaphor from Conrad, which is, "Never get out of the boat." Sheen repeats it in voiceover. In Conrad, the river is a symbolic route of sanity, and the jungle is the unknown, insanity.

BOYLE: The film's use of voiceover, along with *Goodfellas*, is probably the greatest use of voiceover I've ever experienced. Because voiceover is normally criminal in a film, in a way, because it actually robs you of what you're meant to do. You're meant to be experiencing a visual journey. But it's so perfect, "Never get out of the boat, absolutely goddamn right."

It's the greatest use of voiceover.

I wanted to take a moment to step back and talk a little bit about the history. The film was originally called *The Psychedelic Soldier* and written by John Milius for George Lucas to direct.
BOYLE: Really?

Yes. Lucas abandoned it to go off and do *Star Wars*.
BOYLE: Yeah, in the [Peter] Biskind book *Easy Riders, Raging Bulls*, Lucas is a bit pissed off about that. [*laughs*] If George actually ended up directing it, what would have happened?

It is the peak and the end of directors' cinema, without a doubt. All that flush of it that was the '70s. That's an obvious thing to say and it's so true because *Star Wars* introduced producer cinema. That's a role that George obviously took upon himself.

I was about to say that *Apocalypse* is the opposite of product, but it's not; that's what's extraordinary about it. It is product and it's the opposite of product as well, because it is unclassifiable. It is about delivering certain feelings to the audience just as certainly as George was delivering them in *Star Wars*. And yet, it's also its antithesis as well. Jung says that, doesn't he? The two-face thing?

Duality is very much what this film is about. Much has been made about this. There was a whole documentary called *Hearts of Darkness* about the making of *Apocalypse Now*. . . .
BOYLE: My favorite moment in that is when Coppola just starts ranting about how terrible the thing is and how he doesn't know what he's doing. [*laughs*]

The subtitle of the documentary is *A Filmmaker's Apocalypse*. We alluded to it before, but let's talk about it now. It went way over its

shooting schedule; he mortgaged his house; Martin Sheen had a heart attack . . .

BOYLE: I heard about that in the run-up to the opening of the film because that was the baggage that accompanied the film. I think it made it more attractive to go and see rather than buried it. Because normally, that kind of reputation would bury a film, but actually—ironically—it made it more attractive.

Well, it helped. *Apocalypse Now* **shared the Palme d'Or with** *The Tin Drum* **as well, so it did have acclaim. But it had a rough beginning. Originally, Steve McQueen was supposed to play Willard, which didn't work out. Then they filmed a couple weeks with Harvey Keitel in the lead role. Have you ever dealt with miscasting?**

BOYLE: I don't think I've ever been through that. Certainly not in a way I've ever done anything about it. I sacked somebody once, but basically for misbehavior. I think this is the opposite. I think Coppola wanted to hire people who would misbehave.

Speaking of which, Dennis Hopper was high the whole time. He kept forgetting his lines.

BOYLE: I think sometimes with a film, its persona announces itself. Obviously because he was a megalomaniac and also a genius, that persona began to emerge in the film and he just embraced it. So he would not try to stabilize the film—you can see that—he would just go with the madness of it.

So he would sack Harvey Keitel and get someone else. And if Martin Sheen does have a heart attack, he does drag him back to work again, rather than quit. In a tiny, tiny way you can feel where the persona of a film declares itself, "This is a film and this how you're going to behave in it." This is just the maddest, craziest example of it, I guess.

How much was this film on your mind when you were making your own jungle picture, *The Beach***?**

BOYLE: [*laughs*] Yeah. We had an excerpt from it. I was hoping to find, in the way that we made the film, I was hoping to find connections with the film, but we never did. And, I think in a funny way, I was happy that we didn't keep trying to. There's a sequence of *Apocalypse Now* in the beginning, but apart from that it doesn't really stand up in any kind of comparison. I'm modest enough to admit that.

Well, there is an homage to *Apocalypse Now*, when Leonardo DiCaprio becomes one with the jungle.
BOYLE: Yeah, there's a bit of that in it. But in terms of comparisons to the original, it will not stand up. It will not stand up.

My interest is in not so much comparing the two. But while you were in the jungle making this movie and facing the various difficulties you had, was the ghost of *Apocalypse Now* in the back of your mind?
BOYLE: I was never able to use it in a way that would have been useful, really useful. I think also the danger is that you try and deliberately repeat it in some way. You know, not just copy it, but you do try and reinvoke it.

What I meant about the persona of the film—something natural occurs in the film. Something organic and natural that emerges as the personality of the film that says, "This is what it's gonna be, guys. It doesn't matter what you do technically; this is what it's gonna be."

Its source of light wiggles about, and it emerges and it's a very weird phenomena. Once you're shooting, you can't do much about it in a way, other than try and obey it. You can try and contradict it, but it's pretty pointless—and I think what he did was go with the flow, because he clearly just went with it, even though it was driving him insane.

His sets were being blown away. He would just rebuild them. The helicopters would disappear to fight a war or to fight rebels. He would just wait to get more of them.

Here's the other thing. Whenever I talk about this film with other directors, it's often in passing, and it's always become symbolic for the vanity product that goes horribly awry. It's your baby that you've put your life and family and livelihood and career and ego and everything into. Can you ever foresee a project for which you do that?
BOYLE: I think because it's become more of a producer's art form now; I don't think they'll let you get into that position anymore. It's much more difficult to get yourself into that position I think.

And, as a filmmaker, is that a safety net? That you're not able to go mad in the jungle?

BOYLE: I don't think you are anymore. I think they've learned to protect themselves from that. Some people would evoke certain other films that spiraled hideously out of control in a way. But none more appropriately than this, really, none with a context more appropriate than this.

You always dream of doing something like this but I think, when we were making *The Beach*, I certainly felt foolishly self-conscious because of trying to reinvoke it in some way. This is not some kind of ironic experience, repeating it, when this kind of thing happens. You can't control it. You can't actually force things to happen. It will just happen. So being ironic or trying to re-create bits of this is just ridiculous. It's infantile.

Well, and you probably know a bit of the history—Orson Welles tried to make *Heart of Darkness* for years and there were another couple of attempts by other filmmakers. But in your estimation, how was Coppola able to succeed where so many others had failed?

BOYLE: I think, principally, because he's a genius. He clearly was. He was supremely talented and not particularly a modernist in style terms, like Scorsese. He's actually a classical filmmaker, but a classical filmmaker who had all the adrenaline of a modernist because he was so at his peak of his powers as a classicist. Because there is an argument that a classicist cannot use what a modernist uses to create. A classicist at the absolute peak of his powers can do it effortlessly. Certainly when you watch *Apocalypse Now*, you are not aware of technique. You think you're just observing what's happening in front of you, not being manipulated with whip pans or crash zooms or all the techniques.

So he was at the absolute height of his powers and also at the peak of his arrogance, understandably, considering he decided to take on the system and had just won the Oscar for the second time with *The Godfather II*, which everyone thought was superior to the first one. You get the impression, again in the Biskind book, that he slightly disapproves of the first *Godfather*, doesn't he?

Well, it's because he fought for creative control.

BOYLE: [*As Coppola*] "I'll do it again, and I'll have all the creative control and do it even better!" No wonder he felt he could do anything.

Let's switch gears a bit and talk about performances. There's Brando, Sheen, Dennis Hopper. And if you look really closely, there's a cameo of post–*Star Wars* Harrison Ford. And if you look really, really close, his nametag says "G. Lucas."
BOYLE: Does it really?

As you'd expect, they're all fantastic. I don't think Martin Sheen has ever been better. The big one, of course, is Brando—with Brando's presence at the end. I do remember very vividly experiencing that the first time I saw the film. And when you read later on what a mess it was, that does teach you a lot about how you can pull something out of mistakes or just total errors—the way the film allows you to make something great of out something which is a catastrophe. The power of the film leads to him. It's breathtaking, really. I just felt . . . kind of breathless. You don't feel like you can take it in.

As you said, the momentum of the film leads to Brando. He's like Orson Welles and *The Third Man*. He's the boogieman in the background, and when you finally get to him, he can cash in on it with just a glance.
BOYLE: Some people say it's a hit-or-miss film. *Apocalypse Now and Then*, they call it, don't they? That it's great and awful. I love that entire sequence with Brando, personally, with Sheen hunting him down.

Mark Caro, a writer at the *Chicago Tribune*, told me how this film made him believe that a movie can still have huge flaws and still be a four-star film.
BOYLE: Yeah, that's the whole point of it, why it defies categorization, because it is deeply, deeply flawed and that's its nature. They've gone on to perfect films since then. There are perfect films, but I wouldn't nominate them as my favorite film of all time. This would be it for me.

How is it flawed then, even if we love it for those flaws?
BOYLE: Well, people say it's deeply dissatisfying—the conclusion of the film is deeply dissatisfying, that this hocus-pocus philosophy at the end is

nonsense. But, it seems to me they do hit nerves. Even nowadays, when Brando talks about how they chop off the arms of children who've been inoculated, there are moments where you get a glimpse of Pol Pot and you get a glimpse of that.

Some people call it popcorn intellectualism, but I found and I still find that it stretches my mind, really. It's an experience.

And one of the things that people point to as influential in the film is the use of music. The Doors' music begins and ends the film.
BOYLE: You don't think of it in the way Scorsese uses music. Music had always been invisible. Scorsese really championed music so it wasn't hidden, so that you were aware of it. It wasn't working on you in a hidden way. But again, you don't think of Coppola like that, because even though the two hits in the film—"The Ride of the Valkyries" and the Doors song "The End"—are incredible visible bits of music, very deliberately placed on there as pop culture moments. But you still think of them in a classical sense because he just isn't a stylist, he's a classicist. But as we all know, it's the most perfect placing of a psychedelic war, really, which is through the Doors and through the experience of the young men there.

And what do you make of the end? What happens afterward? Does he go back and explain all this to Kurtz's son?
BOYLE: I guess so, I don't know, really. When you watch films properly, they're moments. That's what you take away. And the film ends for me with the chopping down of Brando, with the killing of Brando and the bull. That, for me, is the end of the film. I don't think there are other bits that come after it. It's very difficult to explain, isn't it?

I think it's true. If you're honest about what you remember from a film, unless you have to study the whole film for a conversation like this . . . For the vast majority of people, a film remains three or four moments.

What do you think of the recut and extended version, *Apocalypse Now Redux*?
BOYLE: I was expecting to be deeply taken by it, to be really interested by it, and I wasn't particularly. I watched it and it didn't do particularly much

for me. And I think that's because my attachment to the film is clearly set in stone. I didn't find the changes in it—the extensions—I didn't find they really did anything for me. I sort of feel the film is perfect, despite what other people say about it and I wouldn't change it for anything.

When I watched it a couple weeks ago, I didn't watch the *Redux* version. I watched my original version, which I have on LaserDisc. I bought it on LaserDisc. [*laughs*]

[*laughs*] And, you know, that's part of my fear, is that the original will go away.
BOYLE: Oh, I don't think it will. I think the *Redux* will go away.

I hope so, but the marketing forces usually accept the newer version of the film.
BOYLE: Well, for something like this, this has its apostles everywhere.

My response was that the additions don't seem to add anything. You end up with three female characters, all of whom end up topless and babbling, and Coppola tries to shoehorn in a love scene in an existential war movie.
BOYLE: The whole point of the experience of this film is that you trust the madness that Coppola was in while editing it. And supposedly, he was literally holding editors ransom at the end, forcing them to try things. And from a cool, rational perspective, you would think, "Surely it's a good idea to let Francis have a relook at a film and think how he might want to change things." But no, the whole point about it, when you see it, when you see it at the end of—what was it?—a three- to four-year journey to make it, that's what you see. What you don't want to see is a reexamination of it from a more leisurely perspective. The fact that it's edited from inside the storm, that's where you want to see it edited from. You don't want to see it edited in a proper, rational, professional way. You want to see it edited by someone who is insane or going insane.

Do you identify at all with that temptation as a filmmaker? To maybe some day go back and recut and enhance a film in some way?

BOYLE: Oh yeah, it's very tempting to think, "Oh, um, we could do that, we could do that." And I think you can make a case that certain things would be better. But I think the overall thing would be less true and less faithful. For a lot of films, this doesn't apply because a lot of films aren't the kind of journey *Apocalypse Now* was. But when you have a journey like that, a huge mad vision, you've got to stay true to that.

The closest thing I've had to it, I guess, was *Trainspotting*—which is having a vision of something and trying to do it. I mean, we shot for thirty-five days. People didn't really understand, you know, so you just forced them to do it. And that's what it must have been like, to a zillion degrees, on *Apocalypse*.

Well, since the title of this book is *The Film That Changed My Life*, how palpably did this film change your life?

BOYLE: It just fueled my obsession with experiences in the cinema, really, of trying to create. There are risks attached to it. You're trying to stretch things, but you are also fundamentally committed to getting as many people to see it is as possible. And it's that battle, those two horses that he rode, and I don't think anybody ever rode it quite like he rode it. I think Scorsese did it as well in a different way, but nobody rode it like Coppola rode it, which is to drive those two chariots: your European art movie and a kind of tentpole, huge American opener.

As you've gotten older, and you've seen the film through the years, how has your perception of it changed?

BOYLE: I haven't cooled. I haven't cooled. I must watch it once every two to three years. So it may well be that the critics of it are right. That it's an indulgent mess, and really it doesn't grow. It doesn't change like a work of art changes. Works of art do change, I think, sometimes. As you get different ages, you read books in different ways when you go back to them. That's not what this is like for me. It feels fixed to me and my relationship with it, as well.

4

Bill Condon
Bonnie and Clyde

The links between Arthur Penn's *Bonnie and Clyde* and the films of Bill Condon aren't apparent at first. But a deeper reading reveals that both deal with outsiders doing what comes naturally to them, thereby testing the limits of society.

Condon points out that the themes of sexuality running through the film greatly affected him at his own moment of self-discovery. "There was something about *Bonnie and Clyde* that I think I connected to at a very, very basic level," he said. "There's a whole sexual tension there that I think was speaking to me in some way that I didn't even understand."

Bill Condon, selected filmography:
Gods and Monsters (1998)
Kinsey (2004)
Dreamgirls (2006)
The Twilight Saga: Breaking Dawn, Part 1 (2011)
The Twilight Saga: Breaking Dawn, Part 2 (2012)

Bonnie and Clyde
1967
Directed by Arthur Penn
Starring Warren Beatty, Faye Dunaway, Gene Hackman, Estelle Parsons, Michael J. Pollard, and Gene Wilder

How would you describe *Bonnie and Clyde* to someone who has never seen it?

CONDON: It is a film that, if you buy into the idea that there was a sort of golden age of American filmmaking in the late '60s and early '70s, for me, it seems at least that this is the film that began it. This is a film that was the first kind of French New Wave movie made in America. That influence just changed movies radically in a very short time.

It's about Clyde Barrow and Bonnie Parker and the Barrow gang, and Bonnie and Clyde were young bank robbers in the early '30s in the Depression who became legendary. They went on a robbing and killing spree across the Southwest.

Can you tell me about when and how you saw the film?

CONDON: I grew up in Queens in an Irish Catholic neighborhood with a father who was kind of skittish about all things sexual. But my mother was the opposite. My mother would get her friends together and go see *Who's Afraid of Virginia Woolf?* because my father wouldn't go, and she loved going to the theater, and she was very progressive. I always liked movies, but *Bonnie and Clyde*, I remember, was the first movie my older sisters got me into for the first time when it played at our local theater.

I probably had just turned twelve. Part of the movie is that it's sexual. And this was the first indelible, overwhelming experience I had where I felt myself drawn back over and over again. I saw it easily six, maybe eight times. When it's all so new to you, everything about the experience becomes powerful.

For example, the way that *Bonnie and Clyde* starts. It starts with these photographs coming up and just the very simple sound of a click of a camera, and then interspersed with titles, white titles, white letters, that fill with red, fill with blood. And just that, the sensual pleasure of that was something that I would always look forward to when seeing the movie again. There's something mysterious about how you're in touch with a film without being in touch with a hundred other kids, but you know what's interesting and new and what isn't.

I didn't understand on first viewing how revolutionary *Bonnie and Clyde* was. But one of the things that happened is that because it was so controversial and there was so much written about it, it also became my way into reading about movies, which became such a huge part of loving movies. The thing that made me more interested in movies and making movies was the fact that there were some great people writing about them. The first movie that was debated on that scale was *Bonnie and Clyde*.

It came out the same year as *The Graduate* and was followed two years later by *Easy Rider*. The film historian and critic Glenn Man says those were the three films that "exploded or questioned dominant myths." And if that rings true for you, what myths or cinematic structures was *Bonnie and Clyde* challenging?

CONDON: I don't think I knew enough to know what they were. I think he's right about those three seminal movies. Take that sort of shocking way that it opens, with Faye Dunaway clearly naked. And obviously that was something I had never seen before. There was something very blatant about the way it was shot. It seemed as if there was no way she couldn't have been naked and that's the beginning of the movie. I think all great movies are kind of contradictory in some way. And here's a movie that, in the spirit of the New Wave, was shot in Texas and had the sense of reality to it and that whole kind of Depression Era photography, but the thing that made it so powerful was that Faye Dunaway and Warren Beatty in that first scene are just such incredibly glamorous figures.

So if that's something that made it American, that made it so sensuous. The sexual ambiguity of Clyde Barrow and the fact that here's this beautiful woman who's coming on to him. And he doesn't/can't respond and yet she bugs him anyway. Obviously, as a very young gay guy, there was something about *Bonnie and Clyde* that I think I connected to at a very, very basic level.

You wonder if there's a ménage à trois going on with the Michael Pollard character. And there's one point in which Bonnie is so upset because Estelle Parsons and Gene Hackman are all over each other and the four of them are playing a game of checkers. Warren Beatty is sort of draped over Michael Pollard, and she's out in the cold. There's a whole sexual tension there that I think was speaking to me in some way that I didn't even understand.

A ménage à trois was in fact cut from the script. We talked about some of the subtext hitting you, but when were you fully aware of it?

CONDON: Oh, I think later on, like favorite movies you come back to. They change for you over time, and I do think probably when I was in college and saw it again and gave in, then you start to see other things that are there that in real life that was part of the appeal. It didn't happen in the first run, certainly.

Everything good has some sort of bad. The fact that candor and openness came next. We now live in a society that deals openly with homosexuality, but in movies we have lost all of the coded imagery. And I don't think I'd ever make that trade back. But you do look at a movie like *Bonnie and Clyde* now and you see him redoing her hair—he doesn't like the way her curl is and he redoes it. It's a little bit of Hitchcock—she's the Hitchcock blonde in a way—but also it's a little bit of simply being a hairdresser.

Sometimes that can be more powerful than making it explicit because, especially when it comes to gay things, especially at a young age, you are alone in the world. You are there with your parents, you don't understand how it happened, they don't know anything about it, and you don't think there are any other people like you, necessarily. So it's all about sort of pretending in a way and reading situations and reading clues and getting instinctual feelings. I wonder if the same movie twenty years later would have had the same powerful effect on me. That's the great thing about movies—they are of their time.

Just a little bit of background: Both Jean-Luc Godard and François Truffaut passed on the script. After it was made, it was panned by *Time* and *Newsweek* and the *New York Times* and then pulled from distribution. There's even a great story about how the Warner Bros. distributor said, "It's a piece of shit." But it was only a cry from the auteurist camp that saved it. And many people point to Pauline Kael's essay praising the film as the turning point of her career. Did you encounter that essay at the time?

CONDON: I believe I did, and if it wasn't then it was shortly after.

In the essay, she writes: "Our experience as we watch it has some connection with the way we reacted to movies in childhood: with how we came to love them and to feel they were ours—not an art that we

learned over the years to appreciate but simply and immediately ours."
How does *Bonnie and Clyde* achieve that?

CONDON: First of all, I feel lucky that that was my moment of discovering movies. It's a great moment to be discovering these things. In *Bonnie and Clyde*, there's a sense that each step that each character takes, they realize that they've just kind of signed their own death sentence. They've become these outlaws; they've crossed the line. There's that great scene toward the end where Clyde says, "At this point we ain't headin' to nowhere, we just runnin' from."

That's so played into as well as those other movies you mentioned, literally hundreds of others, but played into the feeling of being an adolescent in the late 1960s, when there was just such a sense of an absolute rejection of all your parents' values. Where did these kinds of communal ideas come from when you're not exposed to them?

And it is interesting now if you look at the movies that kids get turned on by, everything has a happy ending, and it has for twenty years.

Even though this is set in the Depression of the 1930s, it's really about the 1960s. And so what other things signal to you that it was about the time you were growing up in?

CONDON: I had a chance to look at it recently, and I do think the things that make it about the '60s are the least interesting things in it. There's something about being specific to a time and a place and a vision that paradoxically becomes universal, but when you're trying to connect to your own time and trying to make an explicit connection I think those things then become trite.

For example, every favorite movie—especially a movie you see over and over and over again—has its moments where if you watch it enough, you give yourself over to it. For me, for example, it's that scene with Gene Wilder and Evans Evans where they're kidnapped. It has a great punch line where he turns out to be an undertaker and Bonnie gets him thrown out of the car. But until then it seems to me like a classic '60s movie. Hippies and renegades making fun of preppies, of people who were straight, and the establishment. It was like a thousand other scenes that you came to see in those movies. It's something *Bonnie and Clyde* does so brilliantly. So brilliantly conceived and written that they would never let it be about just one thing, and it does have that great ending. It was just that idea of Bonnie starting to become more and more obsessed with issues of mortality.

This movie pretty much ended critic Bosley Crowther's run at the *New York Times*. He attacked it three times in print and then they replaced him with a twenty-six-year-old. Both *Time* and *Newsweek* reversed their reviews. So were you aware of that and did it have any effect on you?

CONDON: Part of the pleasure of it was a completely instinctual thing that drew me into the world of writing about movies. Suddenly it became all of your senses—your mind was engaged by it. The most pleasurable thing was that you felt as if you were part of the movement and part of that fun.

With historical fidelity in mind, did you have a sort of a guiding philosophy, either with *Gods and Monsters* or with *Kinsey*, about representing history and how much license you could take?

CONDON: I do think if there's one big idea that viewing *Bonnie and Clyde* got into my bones, it was that of the ability of a movie to shift tones, have radical shifts of tones, and still remain as a piece. And I do think that informs both *Gods and Monsters* and *Kinsey*—where there's the level at which they play at social comedy and also the play of ideas. Every movie is different, and *Bonnie and Clyde* was probably less of a bio picture than the ones that I've made.

Do you have a guiding philosophy when you're dealing with somebody's life on film?

CONDON: There are obviously conventions all over the place in both of those movies, but you hope that that gets to some kind of essential truth about that person. Because that's why you wanted to make a movie about them in the first place because there's something fascinating about them, something kind of illuminating about their story.

We talked briefly about this before, but the violence of the film, it was shocking to a great number of people. As a twelve-year-old, how did that affect you?

CONDON: I remember the first time I saw a character take a bullet in the eye, it was so unbelievably shocking. That's the thing about *Bonnie and Clyde*.

Obviously those things are harder to recapture in later years, but it was always thrilling. It was an exciting movie to watch. I know so much has been written about what kind of violence it is and whether it's real. It just explodes out of real moments, and I think that's true. But I also think it was an introduction for me into the beauty of violence in an abstract way, which I think is still a disturbing idea.

For years, cowriter David Newman caught hell for it. And his response was always, "It's not gratuitous; if you choose to make your living as an outlaw you'd better know that pain and blood and horror come with that territory."

CONDON: But the movie is so clever. One thing is it builds and builds and builds, but I think you're well over an hour into the movie before Faye Dunaway gets shot in that river and Beatty gets shot in the arm, and it is a shock. It's so cleverly built because we've seen their victims.

How did your perception of the film change through subsequent viewings?

CONDON: I think there was a time when it first came out on video in the '80s and suddenly you're aware of all the things that are dated about it. And you reject things that meant so much to you. But then I got it again when it came out on DVD and looked at it, and I was just struck by the kind of brilliance of the writing.

Was there a moment in the film when you first saw it that galvanized your feelings toward it?

CONDON: I can't honestly remember that, but I have to say that looking at it again, I remember the reaction to certain scenes. Like the shock of Warren Beatty, when Faye Dunaway was trying to go down on him, of him turning over so he just basically smothers her and this look on her face of rage and of betrayal and frustration. It's unbelievable, and as you're entering puberty and worried about that, to see that kind of thing. I still think it is powerful filmmaking that you don't much see in movies. You never think of these things consciously, but looking at it the other day, it is interesting—Warren Beatty and his reputation as a ladies' man and then playing this person.

And then there's a little of that with Liam Neeson in *Kinsey*. Liam Neeson, who famously knows his way with the ladies, having this disastrous first sexual encounter. And so it's weird how certain things and little moments work their way in and you're not even aware of it.

It's filled with moments that I love. I love that Michael J. Pollard's father, Dub Taylor, the actor, keeps hitting him because of the tattoos. That's a very '60s thing, but that's a '60s idea that is grounded in the reality of the time, too. That's when it's done well. I would say probably the scenes that I keep coming back to are the scenes between Bonnie and Clyde. There's great fun with everything else, and Gene Hackman is amazing and Estelle Parsons does great stuff. But every time that they're in that bedroom together and trying to figure out this weird family that they've created, those seem to be the best. Maybe it is that scene where we're finally so deep into the movie and he's comforting her and it finally looks like they're gonna get it on and he still can't do it. That seems, I don't know, "favorite" seems like an odd word for that, but it is one of the most powerful.

Have you ever met anybody connected with the film?
CONDON: Actually, I was at the SAG Awards the other day with Laura Linney, and I met Warren Beatty and we talked about *Shampoo* because we were talking about *Kinsey*. We didn't talk about *Bonnie and Clyde*. The latter part of *Kinsey* is about this sexual experiment where Kinsey tries to create these open marriages and sort of environment where people can have sex without consequence, and there's the sense that *Shampoo* deals with similar ideas.

Did you ever think about how your life might have been different if you hadn't seen the film when you saw it? Would you still be a director?
CONDON: That's a good question. It's hard to know, but I think the way I've probably described this before is that *Bonnie and Clyde* led to two things—a love of movies at a fortunate moment when movies were really interesting, and also a love of writing about movies, because *Bonnie and Clyde* was written about so much. And that's what kind of ultimately pointed me in the direction of making movies as opposed to theater.

5

Richard Kelly
Brazil

Richard Kelly's transition into film in college came as a result of seeing Terry Gilliam's *Brazil*. The hyperbolic yet relevant societal messages encoded in the film inspired Kelly to pursue similar aims in cinema.

Though preferring to keep the influence of others' styles and methods inconspicuous in his films, Kelly admits that Gilliam's meticulous scene-setting led him to do much the same. Says Kelly, "I think the greatest thing I learned from Terry is that every frame is worthy of attention to detail. Every frame is worthy of being frozen in time and then thrown on a wall like an oil painting, and if you work hard on every frame, the meaning of your film becomes deeper, more enhanced."

Richard Kelly, selected filmography:
Donnie Darko (2001)
Southland Tales (2006)
The Box (2009)

Brazil
1985
Directed by Terry Gilliam
Starring Jonathan Pryce, Kim Greist, Katherine Helmond, Ian Holm, Jim Broadbent, Michael Palin, Bob Hoskins, and Robert De Niro

Terry Gilliam called this film "Walter Mitty meets Franz Kafka." How would you describe it?

KELLY: I would best describe *Brazil* as a portrait of bureaucracy run amok, or capitalism run amok. It's probably the most visionary example of an alternate universe portrayed with such incredible logic. It's incredibly absurd, but it's incredibly accurate to the system that exists in our world.

I would call it one of the most profound social satires that has ever been filmed. It is unlike any film that has ever been made before or after. It is also incredibly difficult to describe to someone who has never seen it. You just have to say to someone, "This is a film you must see, and you must experience it without any preconceived notions of what you're going to be watching." I wouldn't even know how to explain it to someone or sell it to someone. That's what's so great about it.

Brazil is about this character who is part of this corporate, Big Brother institution known as the Ministry of Information, and he works in information retrieval and he's offered a promotion. His boss, played by Ian Holm, doesn't want to lose him because he is such a valuable employee. This entire circumstance is thrown out of whack because a dead beetle has fallen into a typewriter and mistakenly replaced the letter *T* in Tuttle with *B* in the last name Buttle. And in a case of misidentification, the Big Brother government has tortured and killed the wrong man. These circumstances are set in motion by something as arbitrary and absurd as a dead beetle.

***Brazil* had several different edits and cuts, including a completely different American television version . . .**

KELLY: . . . the "Love Conquers All" version, which was pretty hilarious.

So which one did you see when you first saw it?

KELLY: It was *Brazil* on LaserDisc at the University of Southern California Film School in my freshman year of college, in the cinema library. It really changed my life. It blew my mind. When it was over, I found myself affected emotionally by what I experienced. The world that Gilliam created didn't even completely make sense on a logical level but somehow hit me on an emotional level. I then immediately went back and watched the film two or three more times, and started putting the pieces together and putting the worlds together, and really getting the meaning of the film. I believe the version that I saw was the American version that was shown to the Los Angeles film critics in 1985 and then was subsequently released mostly because of their enthusiasm for the film.

I've since seen Terry's longer assembled cut that appeared on the Criterion Collection three-disc edition, and I've also seen the wretched Sid Sheinberg love-conquers-all version, which is truly hilarious. I love Gilliam for the fact that he included that on a separate disc on his three-disc Criterion set.

How did you first hear about the film?

KELLY: I grew up as a huge fan of *Time Bandits*. *Time Bandits* had always affected me as a kid, and I had memories of that from when I was very small, and it frightened me. I remembered when the dwarves came into the little kid's bedroom and started pushing his bedroom wall and it opened up to this abyssal tunnel, and the image of them falling from this light grid in the sky captured my imagination as a really young child. Those images stayed with me—they burned themselves into the back of my head. I started reading about Terry's other films, having seen *The Fisher King* prior to that. I was aware of *The Adventures of Baron Munchausen* but I had never seen *Brazil*. I grew up in Midlothian, Virginia, where you'd be lucky to find *Brazil* in a Blockbuster Video. It wasn't a film that was jumping off the shelves and available to someone in a town like Midlothian, Virginia. When I arrived in film school, I suddenly found myself with this gigantic library of LaserDiscs, and *Brazil* was one of the first ones I checked out at the library.

Most people, when they say "the film that changed my life," they mean the film that made them want to be a director, propelled them to film school. But you saw the film when you were already in film school. How did it change your life?

KELLY: In my freshman year of college, I was in the school of fine arts and hadn't yet been accepted into the film program. I had gotten an art scholarship for a lot of illustrations and drawings and paintings that I had done in junior high and high school. I immediately started dropping art classes and started taking the general film courses my freshman year and got guest

access passes to the film library, so I knew I was trying to get into the film
school, but I wasn't there yet. I was more in that transitional period, where I
was trying to gain confidence and put together my vision and my voice as an
artist and a filmmaker. Having discovered Terry's work and seeing that he
followed a similar course, beginning in the visual arts as a cartoonist working with Monty Python, I felt a kinship to him and felt like he was someone I
wanted to emulate in my career. The visual design in *Brazil* is so astonishing,
my head almost exploded.

You have to give Terry, Tom Stoppard, and Charles McKeown credit for
explaining what was wrong with the world in very elegant strokes that are
alien to us because the world is not our own, but it is incredibly familiar
because it is absolutely our own.

**Gilliam has said *Brazil* was a documentary. He said he made none of
it up.**

KELLY: It is a documentary film with the brushstrokes of a profoundly mad
genius who can create a fantasy world, but he created a fantasy world literally within—he re-created our world in a different visual language. I had
never seen that done in any other film. Fritz Lang's *Metropolis* is maybe the
closest approximation, but I think that *Brazil* certainly said many things that
Metropolis couldn't, maybe because Lang didn't have the benefit of sound.

Gilliam has an artist's eye. He is someone who sees every frame as an oil
painting. He meticulously assembles every frame with so much detail as to
make that image worth watching dozens and dozens of times. You end up
with a film that is timeless. It becomes this essential viewing experience that
seems to ultimately get better with age because as one matures, the meaning
of the film matures. That meticulous attention to detail is something that
only the greatest directors are capable of.

I remember images of a bunch of nuns buying rifles. I remember a wealthy
dowager with a little dog with masking tape over its ass so it wouldn't def-
ecate on the sidewalk. I remember Mrs. Ida Lowry (Katherine Helmond)
and her friends putting acid on their faces in plastic surgery. And the sight
gags you literally need to watch three or four times to catch all the jokes
hidden in every frame. They're not just crass, empty, cheap laughs; there's
profound irony invested in every frame, just an extraordinary amount of

social criticism invested in each one of the gags. It's incredibly valid: technology that's not working, the Big Brother corporate mentality, big business, personal vanity—I could go on and on. I don't think there's a scene that's not examined in some way.

I think the moment that got me was when Lowry was running through the shopping promenade, and Robert De Niro's character is suddenly overcome with hundreds and hundreds of sheets of paper blowing in the wind, and they start affixing themselves to his body. He's just standing, and there's nothing but paper blowing in the wind in every direction. That's when the film got me, and I finally understood what it was about. The whole film was about that scene. On one level, it was about how the system—bureaucracy or capitalism or whatever you want to call it, whether you want to get into a Marxist critique on modern life—how our means and methods of production and the Ministry of Information retrieval, how all these institutions can ultimately suffocate our humanity. And that's exactly what happened to Robert De Niro's character in that scene. He ceased to exist, and there was nothing left but a bunch of paper. It was just a profound image and, to me, one of the more emotional images in the film. With the terrorist bombings and the plastic surgery gone bad, we are living in *Brazil* right now. We get closer to *Brazil* with each passing week.

How did you interpret the title?
KELLY: There was a question mark lingering over the film, perhaps because of the title. You think of *Brazil* and you think of the country Brazil, which has nothing to do with what the film is about. I think it was ultimately named after the lines of the song because the song captured a tone or an ironic longing. Putting the song against such outlandish yet funny nightmarish images captured the sense of irony that the film has.

Gilliam first toyed with calling the film *The Ministry* or, more popularly, *1984½*, which was a tip both to George Orwell and to Federico Fellini for *8½*. One critic called it "*1984* with laughs," but Gilliam's totalitarian society is one that is absent of Big Brother. The system itself is the antagonist; there's no physical villain. How does that change the viewing experience?

KELLY: It makes it more demanding for the viewer. There are plenty of villains in history, but what you don't realize is that behind that villain lays an infrastructure, and it is the infrastructure that empowers that villain. And I think Terry and his collaborators were being very ahead of their time and looking less at a figurehead and more at an infrastructure that can be manipulated to create a figurehead, like . . . I don't want to mention any names here.

The great thing about the Monty Python experience is that it allowed him to hone his skills and really develop his voice as a filmmaker. I think those sketches and those short films and those pieces that they all put together gave Terry the vision to make something like *Brazil*, to go and apply his skills as a comedian and a satirist to a really bold and innovative narrative story that lasts well over two hours. The ability to get an honest, worthy laugh out of your audience is something that is incredibly difficult to do, and very few people know how to do it properly and very few people have earned the right to do it. I think that's something Terry developed early in life, and thank God that he did, because there are a lot of filmmakers out there who lack a sense of humor and others who think they have a sense of humor, and it is really forced, or it's cheap, or it's pandering to the lowest common denominator. Thank God Terry has such a great sense of humor because that's where his voices come from, ultimately. Aside from his humanity or his sense of moral anarchy or his visionary visual imagination, it is his sense of humor that ultimately keeps him alive.

Brazil is also famous for Gilliam's fight with producer Sidney Sheinberg, when he delivered a movie seventeen minutes longer than was contracted, so he took the film away from him and it was a yearlong battle before they released it here. Were you aware of this when you saw it?

KELLY: No, I wasn't and that's why, in subsequent years, I have become so obsessed with the film, because having to observe those battles on my first film and seeing and reading the history—there's a great book called *The Battle of Brazil*—and reading about the fight he put up gave me a lot of confidence. I never had to go to the lengths with *Donnie Darko* that he had to, but I had to fight like hell and I didn't win every battle. They gave me a director's cut later, so that was an indication that if you know you've done a good job, and you know that you have a voice and you're confident, it may get you in trouble in the short term, but in the long term all that matters is the film that is released. It isn't the fight, the memos, or the words that are exchanged—it's your art, it's what you are going to be judged for when you are dead and buried, and it's worth fighting for. Thank God that Terry fought for *Brazil*. Had "love conquered all," we would have been denied a real masterpiece.

The Los Angeles Film Critics Association forced Universal's hand; they named *Brazil* Best Picture of the year and Gilliam Best Director. It's the one documented case in which critics banded together to save a film, and that's a pretty complex relationship. What is the role of the critic? Is it to critique art or to influence it?

KELLY: Their perfunctory role is to critique art, but in every critic's heart is a desire to better the art form, in their dialogue, in their criticism, in the critical literature they are creating. They want to promote good films and suppress the bad films, and hopefully make the process better—contribute and support bold, risky, innovative filmmaking. It should be the duty of any film critic. I think that if you ask any film critic if he or she has an agenda to support those films, that critic will say "absolutely."

It really can make all the difference. You see it all the time, like with Patty Jenkins's film *Monster*, when Roger Ebert was one of the first critics out there to herald not only Charlize Theron's performance but also the film itself. An important film critic like Roger Ebert can certainly rescue a film from oblivion, and I think that has to warm any critic's heart to have the power to do something like that.

Gilliam told the *New York Times* in 1986 that "you can't talk about artistic values or social values or philosophical values; economic values are the only ones that count." Has Hollywood changed?

KELLY: I think economic values have only been foregrounded in the vertical integration of studios. We're now seeing gigantic corporations merging with one another. There's talk of synergy and vertical integration. Karl Marx is chuckling in his grave somewhere because it all comes down to one word: money. It costs a lot of money to create these works of art, and ultimately they are not seen as works of art anymore by the people who are writing the checks. The fight has become that much more difficult, and you have to be that much more savvy and manipulative in order to work your way into the system and somehow emerge as a piece of art, not a piece of commerce.

Can you point to any specific ways that *Brazil* influenced your work?
KELLY: If I'm taking inspiration, or if I'm going to blatantly rip off my favorite artists, I try not to make it quite so blatant; I try to bury it in the DNA of the text of my film. But I think the greatest thing I learned from Terry is that every frame is worthy of attention to detail. Every frame is worthy of being frozen in time and then thrown on a wall like an oil painting, and if you work hard on every frame, the meaning of your film becomes deeper, more enhanced. New meaning emerges in your story because of your attention to detail. It is also developing a visual style that is your own, that is hopefully unlike anything that has been done before. I think Terry has one of the most pronounced, specific visual styles of any filmmaker. He gave me something to aspire to as a visual artist but also as a storyteller, as one who aspires to be a social satirist. I have a long way to go, but I aspire to do some of the things that Terry has done, and to do them as well as Terry has done. It's about being thorough, and having a great sense of humor and being able to laugh at the end.

I look at the film now, and it's more timely than ever. It makes more sense now than it did in 1985. That's a testament to ourselves, a testament to how much of a documentary it really is.

There are two kinds of satire. There's Juvenalian satire and there's Horatian satire. One of them says the world is a shitty place but in the end we'll all be taken care of, and the other says the world is a shitty place and in the end we're all fucked. One sees the glass as half-empty and the other sees the glass as half-full. Some may accuse Terry of seeing the glass as half-empty, but I think, really, in his heart, he sees it as half-full.

I think even as a little kid, I was the kind of person to bite off more than I could chew as an artist. My eyes are often bigger than my stomach. In this film, what Terry was doing—the level of detail, the complexity, the overwhelmingness of it all—I guess it challenged me. I guess that's how I've always been. Maybe I just saw part of myself there.

6

Peter Bogdanovich
Citizen Kane

It's tough to unravel one from the other: Orson Welles, the unappreciated master, and Peter Bogdanovich, the journalist-turned-auteur. But Welles and Bogdanovich were more than writer and subject, teacher and student—they were friends and collaborators.

Bogdanovich argues that not only were Welles and his films ahead of their time, but that *Citizen Kane* specifically *is* Welles—that it mirrors his youthful, revolutionary disposition.

Of *Citizen Kane*, Bogdanovich says, "For the first time you felt that somebody had directed it, because you could see the director. . . . It was absolutely extraordinary, the impact of that movie at the time. It galvanized me . . . more people were galvanized to be in movies by *Citizen Kane* I think than any other picture since *The Birth of a Nation.*"

Peter Bogdanovich, selected filmography:

Targets (1968)

The Last Picture Show (1971)

What's Up, Doc? (1972)

Paper Moon (1973)

Daisy Miller (1974)

At Long Last Love (1975)

Nickelodeon (1976)

Saint Jack (1979)

They All Laughed (1981)

Mask (1985)

Illegally Yours (1988)

Texasville (1990)
Noises Off . . . (1992)
The Thing Called Love (1993)
The Cat's Meow (2001)

Citizen Kane
1941
Directed by Orson Welles
Starring Orson Welles, Joseph Cotten, Dorothy Comingore,
Agnes Moorehead, and more

How would you describe *Citizen Kane* to someone who has never seen it?

BOGDANOVICH: The story, the life of a very rich and powerful man, how he got to be that way and what it did to him, told from the point of view of a number of people who knew him.

It's just not like any other movie you know. It's the first modern film: fragmented, not told straight ahead, jumping around. It anticipates everything that's being done now, and which is thought to be so modern. It's all become really decadent now, but it was certainly fresh then.

When did you first see it?

BOGDANOVICH: I first saw it when I was about fifteen. It was a revival of the picture in New York. It hadn't played in New York in fifteen years or something, hadn't been seen since its initial release, and some theater brought it back for a week or two. So they made sort of a big deal about it, and the press didn't write much about it, but I remember seeing an ad and went to see it. And it fucking flipped me out.

[*laughs*] Why specifically did it flip you out?

BOGDANOVICH: 'Cause, I mean, it was like no other movie. It still isn't—what movie is like it? Oh my God, and also, for the first time, I had a realization—somehow it was the first time, and I figured it out later why, it's obvious—but for the first time you felt that somebody had directed it, because you could see the director. There he was, he was acting in it, too. And yes, we have that with Chaplin and other people, obviously. But this director wasn't like most people. So it didn't look like any other movie.

It was absolutely extraordinary, the impact of that movie at the time. It galvanized me; I think it galvanized a lot of people; more people were galvanized to be in movies by *Citizen Kane* I think than any other picture since *The Birth of a Nation*.

Well, and François Truffaut said, more than any other director, you know in the first three minutes of a film that it's an Orson Welles film. And what in the opening of *Citizen Kane* tells us it's Welles?

BOGDANOVICH: Everything. [*both laugh*]

The whole beginning, the first five minutes is very unusual. It begins with that "No Trespassing" sign, and the camera moves up and then you see this mansion, and you keep moving closer and closer to this strange mansion, and then a light goes off and a light goes on and you see a face, and somebody, and this guy's obviously dying, and he says, "Rosebud" and drops something, and a nurse covers him, and then you go to a newsreel. Fucking newsreel, it's unbelievable. One of the great newsreels of all time. Well, that's not like any opening. [*laughs*]

In your book *This Is Orson Welles* you actually tell Welles that the film started production the same month you were conceived. So you seem to have a very strong link with this film.

BOGDANOVICH: Yeah, and he said to me, "Oh, shut up!" [*laughs*]

I just think a lot of people have a strong link to it; I think it's just an amazing film. It's an extraordinary combination of pessimism and optimism. It's probably the most pessimistic, downbeat film about America ever made, because no one wins anything, everything's sad, there's no happy ending. On any level. [*laughs*]

And it's just bleak. And yet the technique through which this bleak story is told is so dynamic and exciting that it actually makes you feel the opposite of what you would feel if you just go by the story. And that's the interesting tension in that movie.

How did it change your life? Can you palpably say: This is how it made me see things differently?
BOGDANOVICH: Well, it showed the extraordinary possibilities of the medium in such a galvanizing way that did not happen through any other film.

Every time I see it I'm still blown away by how young he is—he was twenty-six years old.
BOGDANOVICH: I think he was twenty-five. The performance alone is extraordinary. That's what a lot of people don't even talk about, the performance. To do that range of character, range of age, at that age. People don't even bother to talk about that; they're so busy talking about the directing and the writing. Or arguing about who wrote it. What a stupid argument.

Thematically, there's this sense of loss of innocence and then the corruption of power. Those are the central themes. But what do you think was the most thematically interesting to Welles?
BOGDANOVICH: I think Orson was very much interested in power, in what power does to people, what money does to people, what lack of love does to people. I think he was interested in all that.

And what's most compelling to you in the film?
BOGDANOVICH: Orson was also interested in age and aging. There's a lot of that in his movies—and what that does to people. Interested in loss, not just of innocence. There's a sense of elegy in the movie that appeals to me. That's one of the reasons Welles loved John Ford, because Ford had that sense of elegy.

And how do you think that manifests itself in the film?
BOGDANOVICH: The whole thing.

[laughs] Just a large statement of elegy?
BOGDANOVICH: It is an elegy, to this man. And power in America.

The original New York Times review took an advocate's position with it. The Times wrote that suppression of this film would be a crime, and

of course *Citizen Kane* had problems opening because it was perceived to be based on press king William Randolph Hearst. But do you think that embattled history enhanced its place in cinema history? Or was it hindered by it?

BOGDANOVICH: Hindered.

How so?

BOGDANOVICH: Because it didn't have the popular success that it should have. It was hampered by not having theaters to play in. You can't have a hit if you can't get into theaters. People didn't play it. It would have had a greater place in history if it had been more popular commercially. Look at all the crappy movies that are still famous and that were popular, and when you see them today you can't believe anyone could sit through them.

And *Citizen Kane* did not become a classic at least until the mid-1950s.

BOGDANOVICH: I would say it didn't really get fully established until the '60s.

But it still shows up as number one on almost all the film lists.

BOGDANOVICH: Now it does. It didn't used to. It took about twenty, twenty-five years. Well, look what happened to *The Rules of the Game*—that wasn't even shown. It was bought, burned, so to speak. They ruined that. Initially that picture was just hated, destroyed; then twenty years later they brought it back.

Now I'm guessing you're not one of those people who voted for *The Godfather* over *Citizen Kane* on a recent best films poll.

BOGDANOVICH: Oh, God. I don't know who votes in those polls.

How did your impression of the film change once you got to know Welles more?

BOGDANOVICH: I certainly didn't doubt who made it or who wrote it. The movie is very much like Orson. You know, seeing things from many different points of view, unusual way of telling stories, bored by cliche, innovative, excited by innovation, born storyteller. Exciting, you know, youthful—even in old age he was youthful. When you get to know somebody, of course everything they had ever done becomes more intimate. I mean I recognized Orson in it very strongly 'cause it was him; the performance reminds me of him at times.

Where specifically in the film?
BOGDANOVICH: That moment about his mother is still the most touching moment in the picture, when he talks about her to Susan Alexander. She says, "You know what mothers are like," and it just cut to him, and he says, "Yes." Good moment.

Now do you think the film takes on different dimensions when it's given its perceived parallel to Welles's own life?
BOGDANOVICH: I don't think it has that much of a parallel to Welles's own life. I never saw that.

What about the parallel of the "boy wonder" who has this success early and then loses it all. Hell, people have written the same thing about you.
BOGDANOVICH: Well, they say it about a lot of people. Kane wasn't really like that; Kane didn't have early success and then have it taken away from him. He had power until he died. Different story. I don't think there's any parallel between Kane and Orson. Kane is not an artist; Kane is a plutocrat. He's not misunderstood or a genius.

Almost the entire cast was brought over from Welles's Mercury Theatre. How do you think that's reflected in the film, in the performances?
BOGDANOVICH: It has cohesion and a kind of unity from an ensemble that's worked together in theater and radio. He was able to get that subtleness, the way the actors played with each other, the overlapping, all of that. A lot of them were familiar to each other.

One of the other things I like about this is just the pace of the writing, and it was, as you said, the first modern film. Welles shared the Oscar for Best Original Screenplay with Herman J. Mankiewicz. Do you think that was vindication for him or—

BOGDANOVICH: Considered a consolation prize. It was considered a consolation prize.

By him or by the industry?
BOGDANOVICH: Both.

Did he tell you anything about that night later in life?
BOGDANOVICH: He wasn't there. He was irritated. I think he felt it should have gotten more. And he's right.

Now, there was an HBO film, *RKO 281*, about the making of *Citizen Kane*. What did you think of it?
BOGDANOVICH: Completely inaccurate from beginning to end.

And in what ways? If we're setting the record straight, how do we do it?
BOGDANOVICH: Well, we haven't got the time. But let's just start with one basic premise. In *RKO 281* the sort of galvanizing moment is when Orson Welles is at a dinner party at Hearst's mansion, and they have some exchange of words. Am I correct?

Yes, I believe so.
BOGDANOVICH: At a dinner table at San Simeon. Okay, Orson Welles was never at San Simeon and never met Hearst until after the film was long made. George Schaefer never got into a fight with Orson. He loved him. The head of the studio loved him—right there is a dead giveaway that they were not interested in telling the story of what happened. There was not a vendetta against Hearst.

When we last talked, you said one of the biggest misconceptions was that it was based on Hearst. But what do you think are the other misconceptions that are constantly tacked to the movie?
BOGDANOVICH: That it was very expensive, that Orson didn't write it, that it was a flop because nobody liked it, that it didn't get good reviews. Any of that stuff—I've heard all that—it's all wrong.

And you were pointing out to me that Col. Robert McCormick, owner of the *Chicago Tribune*, was actually part of the inspiration for *Kane*, as well.

BOGDANOVICH: Big time. Robert McCormick had a girlfriend who was a singer for whom he built the Chicago Opera House. Well, I mean, hello? Is that a rather large part of the plot of *Citizen Kane*? He wasn't doing Hearst and Marion, 'cause he doesn't make her into a movie star. He doesn't build a studio around her. She's in opera; that's McCormick.

You were directed by Welles in *The Other Side of the Wind*, which at press time still has yet to be released. What was he like to work with as a director?

BOGDANOVICH: Oh, he was incredible. Directing is really creating an atmosphere, a particular kind of atmosphere and usually one that is very peculiar to the director. It doesn't necessarily have to be. Some directors have no personality and it shows. But one way or another, what the actors are doing or the crews are doing, they're trying to please the director.

And Orson, I can't say what he was like on *Kane*, but he always said he liked "to give the actors a good time" is the way he put it. And he did, he did. He always made it a lot of fun. He was funny; he was teasing; he was warm; he was encouraging; he was spontaneous. He loved anything that you did—he was effusive if he liked it, kidded around if he didn't, never made you feel anything except that you probably were gonna be better than you'd ever been in your life.

Was his directing style more like a theater director? Was it an ensemble feel, or did he—

BOGDANOVICH: Ensemble, yes. Very "We're all doing this together. It's all a kind of conspiracy that we've got here, and we're gonna put it over on somebody."

How did he influence your work? Where can you see it in your oeuvre?

BOGDANOVICH: Oh, I don't know. We're so different. Certainly I like his use of overlapping dialogue, but he does it differently than I do, and he does it differently than Howard Hawks did. But I sort of borrowed the idea from both of them, and I like to use overlapping dialogue. Hawks used it before Orson, but Orson did it on the radio, too. It's a great device. I look for it whenever I can do it; you have to have good actors.

What does it add to the film?
BOGDANOVICH: Sense of reality, the unrehearsed.

Welles famously told you, "God, how they'll love me when I'm dead." And so is the esteem this film is held in any vindication?
BOGDANOVICH: Well, it's not just *Citizen Kane*. Since he's died, *Touch of Evil* has become a classic. *Othello* has been acclaimed; it was originally dismissed in the United States. *Touch of Evil* was thrown away in the United States. *The Trial* is being constantly revived. *The Lady from Shanghai* is out on DVD and is highly thought of. I think he's become a legend rather quickly.

What kept him from that before, do you think?
BOGDANOVICH: People were threatened by him; he was too much when he was alive. Too much for people to handle, too intimidating, and too much of a rebuke to mediocrity.

7

John Dahl
A Clockwork Orange

John Dahl's life changed at a drive-in movie theater. How many of us can say that? Dahl discovered Stanley Kubrick's apocalyptic morality tale *A Clockwork Orange* on a date, at a drive-in theater in Montana.

He remembers being struck by "the desire for society to find some quick solution to violence and crime, to find treatment that would curb or stop that. If we could just sit somebody in a chair and weld their eyes open, and then all of a sudden they would be a model citizen. That's a pretty powerful concept for a movie. I think it still is."

John Dahl, selected filmography:
Red Rock West (1993)
The Last Seduction (1994)
Unforgettable (1996)
Rounders (1998)
Joy Ride (2001)
The Great Raid (2005)
You Kill Me (2007)

A Clockwork Orange
1971
Directed by Stanley Kubrick
Starring Malcolm McDowell, Patrick Magee, Michael Bates,
Warren Clarke, and Adrienne Corri

How would you describe *A Clockwork Orange* to someone who has never seen it?
DAHL: It stars Malcolm McDowell as Alex, and it's set in the near future. He's a violent gang member who is arrested for murder, sentenced to jail, and gets the opportunity to be rehabilitated through the Ludovico technique to be cured of his violent tendencies, though it doesn't work out so well. You can describe it as an amoral world.

You saw this first at a drive-in movie. Would you tell me that story?
DAHL: I was seventeen. I saw it at the Motor View drive-in in Billings, Montana. I took a date to this movie—I had no idea what it was; it just looked kind of cool. I liked it so much that I went back the next night and watched it by myself. What I liked about it is that it combined music and art. It was the first time I paid attention to the sets and the way the film was made.

Was there a particular scene that compelled you?
DAHL: There was a style to the movie. I was really interested in art and rock 'n' roll at that point, so I really liked the way the art worked, the modern clean spaces, and the use of Beethoven. I thought that was unique at that time. The other thing he had done with the music, was some of it was very classical and some of it had been done with a synthesizer. When I saw this movie it was a completely different—I don't even know what else came out that year, but there was nothing else like it. It was a very avant-garde movie at the time. And then there's the *Crime and Punishment* elements. Can you rehabilitate somebody? And if you do, do you take away their free will?

The film is in this mix of English and—I think it's called Nadsat—which is Anthony Burgess's language of made-up Russian root words. Did you have trouble making sense of that? What was your reaction to it?
DAHL: Not at all. It engaged me because they were speaking English, but they were using foreign words—and it was fun that you still understood what they were talking about. In a strange way, I don't know really what that has to do with the movie other than just making it feel like it's from another time. Now it looks very dated to the '70s, but I think he was trying to push the edge, extend it into the future a little bit. So it was a futuristic glimpse.

For example, I would say, even with the movies that I've done, like *Round-ers*, it never bothered me that everybody spoke in poker terms and that I had no idea what they were. I watch it now and it makes complete sense to me, but when I made the film I had never heard half these terms; at least I recognize that that's the way people speak and that the audience will figure it out.

When this came out it was a contemporary of *Straw Dogs*, the Sam Peckinpah film with Dustin Hoffman. Critics were up in arms about the violence of *Straw Dogs*. How were you affected by the violence in *A Clockwork Orange*?

DAHL: I just thought it was awesome. It was violence for the sake of vio-lence. I've never been in a fight in my life. It's completely foreign to me, but it just seemed like stuff of literature; something of another world and exotic in that respect. It seemed like good material for stories. There's a scene where they leave the milk bar and they run into those guys who are dressed in another gang costume. They're about to rape this girl, and there's this gang fight with Beethoven blaring away in the background. It's just one shot of random violence: guys getting their heads bashed with windows, landing on tables. It's not even in a sequence. It's just jumped-together shots of people being bashed over the head with Beethoven going.

There's another scene I remember really getting my attention: while walking in slow motion, Alex beats two guys and throws them in the water. I had never seen slow motion like that before.

One of the reasons it was controversial was that it really divided critics. Vincent Canby championed the film. Pauline Kael of *The New Yorker* at the time accused it as "sucking up to the thugs in the audience." Roger Ebert was particularly disgusted by it, calling it "an ideological mess, a paranoid right-wing fantasy masquerading as an Orwellian warning." Is any of that stuff fair, or are they just missing something?

DAHL: I don't know. I saw it when I was seventeen, so I had a completely different reaction to it than watching it this week almost thirty years later. I guess what struck me, and I would hope that I would have seen it even back then, is the desire for society to find some quick solution to violence and crime, to find treatment that would curb or stop that. If we could just sit somebody in a chair and weld their eyes open, and then all of a sudden they would be a model citizen.

That's a pretty powerful concept for a movie. I think it still is. There's the quaint '70s style of it all, but I think it's a powerful movie about rehabilitating criminals. Can you? And if you could, would you?

There's also this friction between the quick-fix totalitarian state and the desire for order, which is what Burgess was reacting against. He was living among the mods in London. There was a bunch of fiery rhetoric around the violence. Was it responsible to release this? Kubrick himself pulled the movie from distribution in London, fearful of copycat crimes and whatnot. Is there any kind of violence in films that you might regard as socially dangerous?
DAHL: Well, my point of view about it is this: I hardly ever blame the artist for making the artwork or the desire to make the film. I have a bigger issue with the companies that put it out there to make a profit. I think they have to take more responsibility for the public's reaction to artwork, because they're the filter. An artist is going to do what an artist is going to do. Before, a painter made a painting and stuck it into a gallery, or somebody wrote a book. Now, when you're talking about mass media as a conduit to millions of people, I think the people running the companies have to be the final filter on what people see and what they don't see.

That is what this film is addressing: Do you want heads of corporations or politicians deciding what we see or don't see?
DAHL: Well they do anyway, don't they? Of course they do. Whatever the company, corporation, or government—they are final arbitrator of what people see. I suppose you can point to the artist and say, "Why did you make that?" But I think with artists, I don't even know if they really know what they're making sometimes. Ultimately, I think the responsibility to society is from the companies that pay for the film, put it out there, and profit from it.

You're echoing something that Kubrick said about artists and what the different causes of violence are. He says, "To try to fasten any responsibility on art as the cause of life seems to me to put the case the wrong

way around. Art consists of reshaping life but it does not create life, nor cause life." Of course life is, in his view in the film, violent and morally complex.

DAHL: Right. For example, I saw this movie at a very young age and it had a huge impact on me. I liked the clothing. I liked the fashion. I liked the artwork. I liked the music. Forever, I was trying to figure out how to make a movie like Stanley Kubrick, but I also clearly knew that violence is wrong. I also recognized the fact that, in young men, there is a glee and joy in violence. Violence is part of life. You can't ignore it. You can't walk away from it. I think the one thing about this film is that it revels in that youthful abandon. I can only imagine people's reactions. Alex is sitting there in the prison reading the Bible, and then they cut to him whipping Christ as he's carrying the cross. That's just so nasty. But what Kubrick's trying to do is show the warped mind of someone who is a sociopath.

How did this change your life?

DAHL: Again, I was growing up in Montana. I didn't really know anybody who made movies. Making movies wasn't even something that even was remotely possible. When I was in high school I did some animation because I was in an art class and some friends of mine had a 16mm camera. We shot a couple of home movies, but the idea of actually moving to Hollywood and becoming a filmmaker never really entered my mind. This film captured my imagination so much. It was the first film that I saw that made me realize that somebody has to make this stuff. Somebody has to build those sets. Somebody has to paint those paintings. All of a sudden it became accessible. The movie was so compelling and interesting to me on so many levels. The one thing that struck me was that somebody made a movie, and that it was something that maybe, possibly, I could do.

You had talked about this film's profound influence in your own canon and that it kept creeping up in your own movies. Can you articulate that for me? What have its direct influences been? Have there been any homages?

DAHL: It had a profound impact on films I did as a student. I made movies with three guys walking around in uniforms beating the crap out of people.

The idea of the juxtaposition with music in a way: taking extremely modern situations and putting classical music to it. Particularly, with homages, one of the things that I finally realized as I was finishing up film school at the American Film Institute is that there really was only one Stanley Kubrick: there really wasn't a way to imitate his movies.

When I realized that you could actually go to film school, Stanley Kubrick's films had a huge impact on me. The symmetry that he uses in his compositions, the sort of stylized, over-the-top acting in *A Clockwork Orange.*

I saw how you can combine art and music and make a movie. I really came at it from that approach. As I became more of a student of filmmaking and storytelling, I realized that's kind of a bad thing.

I started out doing music videos, and as a director, you don't want to stop everything and show people a picture. You need to move the story along. Kubrick does that. You'll see these really wide-angle 18mm lenses where he establishes the scene. Then he goes into more traditional over-the-shoulder coverage and you get sucked into the story. Very few people can actually do that and pull it off in a way that's engaging to an audience. Even watching the movie now, I think it's a fantastic movie, but parts of it are almost—I wouldn't say amateur—but it really goes back to the '60s and '70s. Filmmaking is so much more sophisticated now.

Is that to say Kubrick's film was unsophisticated?
DAHL: I think unsophisticated is a bad word choice. I think he was less exploratory and more focused—if there is a word for that. If the movie were being made now there would have been much greater pressure to move the story along. Would you really sit there and watch the English officer go through the signing of three forms? Or walking through the record store and there's a copy of *2001*, the album of music from his own movie in there. There are great details that a director at that time, like Stanley Kubrick, could put into his movie. Parts of it feel like the fun of a student film, because he's discovering things, in a way.

In your own work as a filmmaker, how difficult is it to please the author or to please the screenwriter? What are the dangers of too much fidelity to material and, again, making an enemy of the author's voice?

DAHL: It's interesting. I've actually never done a movie from a novel. I've done *The Great Raid* from books of history, and that was very complicated because you're trying to balance history with filmmaking. That's really difficult. I chose to honor the history and the people involved because they're still alive. I didn't feel that I could shortchange their experience for a more gratifying movie. I didn't feel like I had the license to do that.

The films that I've directed from other people's material—I've always had a good relationship with those authors. For the most part—and you'd have to ask them—I think they've been pleased with the movies. To me, I think that's the thing that's most challenging. You've probably heard this expression, but you make a movie three times: once when you write it, once when you shoot it, and once when you edit it. The reason why it's so important to take that approach is that you have to do your best job to get it right on paper, and at some point it goes from being on paper to being all these different personalities, and that's the job of the director: to manage all these different personalities.

When you're shooting, it is a completely different thing. Then, you invariably have to leave that experience, take it into an editing room, and completely change it all over again. You have to be willing to basically throw the script out and to throw out all that experience—all the hardships you've just endured. All of a sudden it just becomes this pliable material that you push around until you can find the best way to make it work. I think that some people get into this trap: "Well, it worked in the script like this. If we just put it in like that it will be fine." You have to be willing to let the material take you there as long as you're not getting off track.

What did you make of the title when you first saw it?
DAHL: I had no idea what it meant. I still don't know what it means. It's almost like nonsense.

Do you want to know the author's take?
DAHL: Sure.

It was based on Burgess's obsession with a Cockney phrase for something as barmy or stupid as "a clockwork orange." It was, basically, a

commentary on the fact that this procedure was taking something that was organic and full of life and color and making it clockwork, making it mechanical. Alex is the clockwork orange—or they attempt to make him such. Does that fit?

DAHL: Sure. I guess what I thought was clever about it was that I recognized that one politician was trying to manipulate the situation to make himself look good and solve a criminal problem. Then the writer in the movie was in opposition to whatever that party represented.

Does Alex win at the end? I don't know how Anthony Burgess felt about it, but I feel like a terrible compromise has been made. This man's going to go out and commit more crimes, and I'm in no way gleeful about it. That's a very powerful juxtaposition with the use of an incredibly happy song, you know, "Singin' in the Rain." You have this incredibly chipper, bright song leading you to this dark, terrible moment. There's the music, and the press is there, and he goes back into his zone. In that very last image, he's in snow with these Victorians surrounding him. And then you're out. I don't know what Anthony Burgess's politics are, or what he was so greatly offended about. If the idea was that there are no quick fixes to the ills of the world, yes, his book is always going to be more pure in his mind. To bring that idea to the cinema and have millions and millions of people see it and continue to watch it . . . I can understand where he's coming from. I think the movie accomplished what he was hoping to accomplish.

The only thing that I thought was a wrong turn was the murder scene because, in the book, he's much younger. But how are you going to get a child to do that level of acting? That's a necessary fix. In the book, the woman whom he murders is, in fact, an elderly woman, and he smashes her head in with a statue of Ludwig van Beethoven. I thought they lost a lot of symbolism there. The instrument of his destruction is what he loves most, but he has to give that up—he's repulsed by Beethoven after his "treatment." Instead, what is his murder weapon? A giant ceramic penis. His libido.

DAHL: I would argue that it's his libido and his lust that gets him into trouble. It's ironic that it's Beethoven that ultimately gets him caught in the book.

My only other criticism is that Burgess made a futuristic universe, but Kubrick had set it squarely in the '70s with the giant ceramic penis.
DAHL: Even that scene with "William Tell Overture," where he's having sex with the girls from the record shop. That was pretty bold for that time.

There's a great Kubrick quote: "When you think of the greatest moments of film, I think you're almost always involved with images rather than scenes, and certainly never dialogue." When you think of A Clockwork Orange, what does that become in your head?
DAHL: Certainly that scene where he's been confronted by Georgie Boy, and they're walking along the huge slope, and some Beethoven music is coming out of the window. He slugs one guy, and he cuts his friend's hand. I guess that scene was pretty powerful.

What I was struck with watching it this time—and I've always liked this about the film—is that every now and then there's a close-up where the sky is very bright behind somebody and there's a close-up of a person. There's just sort of surrealism to the film in a way.

In your career, have you ever run across or met anyone associated with the film?
DAHL: No. I never have because Kubrick's world is pretty small. I have met actors that have worked on other movies with him, and I'm always trying to collect Kubrick stories. Matthew Modine, who starred in *Full Metal Jacket*—I've met him. When I was in college at the AFI, the man who did the score for *Barry Lyndon* came and spoke. Everybody wanted to hear his Kubrick stories.

He told the story about a piece of music that they recorded ninety-nine times. It's rare when you actually have the orchestra go through the piece three times. These people are so good. Many times it's one, maybe two takes. If it's three or four takes there's clearly something missing. So he keeps doing it over and over again because it's Stanley Kubrick, and then finally he just says, "Why am I doing this ninety-nine times? What is wrong? You've got to tell me." This would have taken probably six hours. It would have been a huge expense. These are professionals who do this every day. Kubrick was sitting there with a stopwatch and he wanted it to end at an exact spot on the watch that you could filter out with reverb. There are a number of ways to solve that problem. People tell those kinds of stories about Kubrick.

One of the most famous examples is *Eyes Wide Shut*. The production for that went so long that they had to recast Harvey Keitel's role. Sydney Pollack had to come in and do it. This film, *A Clockwork Orange*, was scheduled for ten weeks and he shot it over eight months. He was a real obsessive guy, something that would not be tolerated in modern Hollywood.

DAHL: That's the unique thing about him. He had this reputation and this ability to make films exactly the way he wanted, which is very rare.

How did your perception of the film change over time with subsequent viewings?

DAHL: This is a movie I probably watched ten times. The first few times I saw this, I had to see it on film. It wasn't until the early '80s that videotape decks came in and you could actually rent any movie you wanted. It struck me when I was watching it this week how powerful some of it is and, at the same time, some of it feels a little amateurish. Let me take that back. You can see a guy having fun making this movie, almost like a student film, in a way. Maybe it's because I related to it as a student filmmaker, and I so tried to imitate this movie in my student films. Certainly every movie I made has something from *A Clockwork Orange* in it. I guess I find it still incredibly entertaining and still relevant. I guess it moved along with me and I still find it to be a compelling film.

8

Henry Jaglom
8½

Henry Jaglom champions one of the most fought-over films in the book. Numerous directors, from Terry Gilliam to Kimberly Peirce, have pointed to Federico Fellini's self-referential masterwork as the film that turned them on to directing. For this book, Jaglom just got there first—with an insightful, fun conversation and tangential stories too numerous to include.

Of 8½, Jaglom says, "I was set on that path by Fellini. Film can be either autobiographical or emotionally autobiographical, if not literally autobiographical."

Henry Jaglom, selected filmography:
A Safe Place (1971)
Someone to Love (1987)
Venice/Venice (1992)
Déjà Vu (1997)
Festival in Cannes (2001)
Going Shopping (2005)
Hollywood Dreams (2006)
Irene in Time (2009)
Queen of the Lot (2010)

8½
1963
Directed by Federico Fellini
Starring Marcello Mastroianni, Claudia Cardinale, Anouk Aimée, Sandra Milo, Rossella Falk, and Barbara Steele

How would you describe 8½ to someone who has never seen it?

JAGLOM: It's the ultimate film about a movie director, because it's about a movie director who doesn't know what movie to make next. It becomes a metaphor for any individual at a turning point in their life, who is asked to make a certain kind of move that seems inevitable to the people around them. They do not know what move to make or what move they want to make, or what the exact goal of their life is or the purpose of their life is. Of course, because the protagonist is a filmmaker, somebody like myself seeing it suddenly realized that that's what I was. I thought I was an actor until I saw that film. It's about a man having to decide what to do next in his life.

This is also one of the first metafilms. It comments on the film being made, which is the film itself. The film 8½ is about the making of 8½.

JAGLOM: I can't think of another film that does that. It's possibly the first self-referential film.

I saw it at the Festival Theater on 57th Street in New York, near 5th Avenue. What I remember most vividly was, it was dark. When I walked in, it was light. When I walked out, it was dark. And I'm a New Yorker and yet I had no idea where I was or which way to go—which way was east, north, south, or west. I was in another universe. I had a hard time understanding where I was; it had that big of an impact on me.

Can you talk about that transition, from actor to director?

JAGLOM: Well, yes. Going into that theater, I was extremely excited because I loved Marcello Mastroianni. I was young. In '63, I was twenty years old. I thought this was a terrific acting model for me. He had an essence, a quality I had seen in other films, which captivated me. I went in looking for, as an actor, that confirmation for that part of myself. He played, of course, Fellini, the director. I had always been interested in filmmaking, but I had always thought I was essentially an actor.

The film changed my identity. I realized that what I wanted to do was make films. Not only that, but I realized what I wanted to make films about: my own life, to some extent. I've gone both ways on that, but I suddenly have been criticized for doing that a lot, and you can blame Fellini. Don't blame me, blame Fellini. I saw a film that truly investigated what the filmmaker was going through. It was the most autobiographical film ever made, yet it was universal because he was telling about issues that all people deal with. I recognized that, even at the age of twenty.

Was there a particular scene or line?
JAGLOM: From the moment it began. I wear a hat. And people always comment on the fact: Why do you wear a hat? I know that somewhere deep inside, all I can tell you is it has something to do with Mastroianni wearing that hat, which he only wore because Fellini wore a hat. I remember thinking, when I came home, "Oh, I need a hat." I mean, it was that superficial at that level, because I was twenty and trying to find a sense of myself. It also defined me because the issues he was looking at, how to take his life and turn it into a film, and feeling the impossibility of that task.

I was always amazed at Mastroianni, and that one gesture of looking over his glasses defined that whole character. It's almost like he's genuflecting.

That's a great image. For me, the ultimate image is: He's that young boy in a white band uniform, leading all the characters in his life on this circular parade. He's got in the background, this meaningless space station thing that he's never going to make. The young boy is just leading all the characters in his life. He's just showing us who he is, and how it happened. As I saw it over the years, it became a deeper and more profound film for me, as I started to live my life and had events to deal with. I'm rather amazed now when I see it, that I felt that at twenty, because it's a very grown-up film in a lot of ways.

Can you articulate that? Anything specifically that you realized upon subsequent viewings?
JAGLOM: At twenty, I did not understand anything about the relationship to women in that film, or the need to be the center of attention and finding the person who's going to solve the problems. I didn't understand anything about the moviemaking process. I had never been on a movie set, let alone directed a movie. The fact of everybody coming at you with their idea of what you should do, and telling you who you should be, and you're completely overwhelmed by it. The whole essence of the film was something that just . . . I was stunned that I understood it at twenty. It's

something that, as you live your life, and as you become a filmmaker, it becomes more and more meaningful on every viewing. I just saw it again four months ago, and it's much more powerful now, in a way. It's no less powerful and much more meaningful.

Do you think that's one of the hallmarks of great art? That you can come back to it and find greater depth?
JAGLOM: Yes, absolutely. If not greater depth, each time you can find different things that you didn't see before. You're never bored by it, even though it's not about the story because you know what is going to happen next. It just has a kind of shape and dynamic to it; it is the never-ending story. It just appeals to you on so many different levels that interest can't possibly run out. When somebody tells me that they want to become a filmmaker— when I meet kids or talk to students, film classes—I tell them that the first thing they should do is see that film and make sure they really want to be a filmmaker.

There's a great introduction on the Criterion DVD with Terry Gilliam talking about the hotel lobby scene, where Mastroianni dances among members of his crew, all of whom have problems that need answers. He says that's exactly what it's like directing a film. Having directed many films yourself, is that a fair assessment?
JAGLOM: Oh yeah, it is. It's the ultimate dance between people and not knowing what you're doing, and acting as if you know what you're doing. It's a very strange universe in which you are both the ruler and your own victim. You seem to be in charge of everybody and everything, and you have to have answers for everybody and everything. More often than not, you don't have an answer, but you have to give an answer. It's a kind of universe that you make up as you go along.

Why do you think so many films about films, about Hollywood, spin out of control? The narratives spin out of control? The director, Guido, just loses control?
JAGLOM: I've never thought of that, but probably because the filmmaking process is a completely chaotic one and a terrifying one. Like life, it can spin

out of control. A good filmmaker probably realizes that that's a dramatic storyline. I've never thought of that; that's a very interesting question. If done incorrectly, it's a very narcissistic subject; it does not have a universal application. It has to be about something much bigger than that: *8½* is about a man's life, the women in his life, and about the act of creativity.

Did you see my version of *8½*, *Venice/Venice*? I try to address myself to that exact issue. I think the process is uncontrollable, so if you're making an authentic film about it you're going to show that. Being a movie director is like being an absolute dictator who can suddenly say, "I want the police to move all those people from here over to there. I want a thousand elephants right here." Then there will be some people hired to do that, and yet there is no control. It's an illusion. Spinning out of control reflects the fear every filmmaker has.

What is the allure then, of making films about films? Or in your case, films about film festivals?

JAGLOM: It's that old writers' thing about writing what you know. Everybody, every filmmaker eventually wants to make a film about what they know best. I distinguish very strongly between directors who are hired to do other people's scripts and filmmakers who don't necessarily write it but are involved from the inception and every aspect, like Fellini. Although he had a writer, it is certainly his film. Like *Sunset Blvd.* is Billy Wilder's film.

A filmmaker, as opposed to a hired film director, is somebody who is dealing with this enormous and strange illusion of having a universe that he can create. Then, of course, it comes to the end. There you are, you are alone.

We talked about the allure, but what is the danger of doing films about Hollywood?

JAGLOM: The danger is that you do it too narrowly, that your view of it is too rarified. That the audience is not going to be interested. I don't think there's an inherent danger. If it's something so close to you, so rarified that you don't connect with people, then it is dangerous. I think that's also its great potential. I've always had a different view of what filmmaking is all about. For me, it is about using your own life as much as possible. Telling the truth and trying to capture that on the screen, and hoping that you're not so isolated that it'll be too rarified for the audience. You hope that they can take a bigger understanding of a narrow subject. And I think that's what Fellini does so brilliantly. I don't think you have to know anything about filmmaking to be totally entranced with that movie.

Can you talk about how 8½ has informed your body of work?
JAGLOM: It taught me that it was OK to do the very thing that I'm criticized for, which is to use my own life as the subject, such as my emotions or those of the people very close to me. It's something that nobody questions in the other arts, but since movies are the so-called popular medium, people do question whether that is too narcissistic. I talk about this subject a lot in my character in *Venice/Venice*. People try to tell you that it's wrong because movies are a popular medium, and therefore you should find a popular common denominator. If you have the temerity to think of movies as art, then I don't think that should apply.

You were already a Mastroianni fan going into 8½, but did the film itself open you up to other genres?
JAGLOM: It was a whole new understanding of what filmmaking could be.

Are there any specific homages you pay to 8½ in any of your films?
JAGLOM: Well, the star of my film *Festival in Cannes* was Anouk Aimée. To me, she's the ultimate. I feel one degree of separation from Fellini, which is enormously gratifying. I tried very hard to use the mythology of her characters, not just in 8½ but in the movies.

I don't believe in homage very much. I make comments on other movies that I've seen, certainly, and steal things without realizing that they have influenced me. Anouk was also in *A Man and a Woman*, and I did a whole circular camera thing at the end of this last movie because of that.

I was set on that path by Fellini. Film can be either autobiographical or emotionally autobiographical, if not literally autobiographical. Orson Welles said to me that my films were not cinema verité, but cinema of emotional verité. For me, 8½ is the great film of emotional verité. It's not the truth. It's not a documentary, certainly, and it's not really what Fellini's life was really like, but it's what his feelings were really like.

Over the years, I'm guessing you've showed it to other friends and directors.
JAGLOM: It's blown people away. I just showed it to this young girl, Tanna Frederick, who is starring in a play I had written. She's going to be a huge star. She said looking at the film was like entering another kind of universe. It wasn't like any other film she's ever seen. And I realized that's what happened to me when I saw it; I stepped into another universe. It was the universe I wanted to live in, to inhabit somehow.

Its original title was *The Beautiful Confusion*.

But did you know that 8½ was a reference to Fellini's previously completed eight and a half films?
JAGLOM: Yeah, it was sort of publicized. It didn't mean much to me then. I thought of calling *Venice/Venice* "11." That would have been the ultimate homage in filmmaking. I was just going to give it a number. Actually, it would have been called *11½*, because I did a half a movie I never talk about because I was so embarrassed by the results.

Which one was that, out of curiosity?
JAGLOM: *National Lampoon Goes to the Movies*. I did half of it; then somebody took it and recut it. It's the one thing I never talk about.

But that's right, I was going to call it *11½*. On the set, thank God somebody prevailed, I think it was my producer, convinced me that calling it *11½* wasn't a very good idea, because then people would say, "Well, it's no *8½*."

What I've been amazed by is the number of things influenced by it—there's the Broadway production and movie adaptation of that production called *Nine*, Peter Greenaway directed *8½ Women*, and then there's *8 Femmes*. There's not a filmmaker alive who wasn't influenced by that film. I used to argue with Orson about it a lot. He had a different idea about filmmaking. He recognized Fellini's great genius, he said, but he didn't like the films. He just didn't like them.

He told Peter Bogdanovich in *This is Orson Welles* that Fellini was just a boy who had not come to Rome yet—
JAGLOM: —which Fellini would be the first person to say. It's how he shows himself. Of course Orson gave a good answer to that.

I was thinking about the one time I saw Fellini on an airplane. I was in business class, and he was sitting up in first class. I walked by him five times wanting to talk to him, but I was too shy to do it. It's not something I'm known for, shyness or reticence. I told people, and they couldn't believe it. It was the only time in my life that I wanted to talk to someone and was not capable of doing it. I had just made a film called *Always* about the end of my first marriage, and in 1983 I was cutting *Always*. It was a few years before he died, and he was on the plane with Giulietta Masina. And I just wanted so much to go up to him. I thought, "He's not going to know my movies; what am I going to say to him?" I remember thinking, this movie, I already had a deal for it, and I knew it was going to play in Rome. I was already fantasizing about him seeing this movie and telling me, "Yes, good." It was a really strange, strong regret I had when he died.

When I finished *Venice/Venice* I thought to myself, "This is going to be a really hard movie to get an audience for because it messes around with time and things, which I know audiences don't like." I also thought, "I really would be completely proud to show this to Fellini." I remember thinking that. I was completely right; it was the hardest movie I had to get an audience for. It's my favorite of my movies. It most specifically captures my sense of life—which I'm sure *8½* captured for Fellini, his sense of life. Just like Bob Fosse in *All That Jazz* captured what his life was like.

What's the proper way to see this film?
JAGLOM: On the big screen. In your house, if you have a big screen.

With friends?
JAGLOM: No, you should see this alone. This is going to sound pretentious, especially in print, and I realize this, but there is a difference between movies and films for me. This is a film. It can also be a movie, but a movie is popular entertainment, which is fun to see with others or in an audience. A film is something more like a painting—something you can absorb most effectively by yourself in a dark room where light is pinpointed on it.

9

Brian Herzlinger
E.T.: The Extra-Terrestrial

Herzlinger has no reservations about declaring admiration for *E.T.: The Extra-Terrestrial*. Once you hear about the impact the film had on him, it comes as no surprise that his own breakout film centers on *E.T.*'s starlet, Drew Barrymore.

Says Herzlinger, "I think it is the best movie ever made, because it works on every level, every demographic. It really is that universal appeal/theme/approach that anybody—whatever your age is—can grasp and enjoy it to the utmost."

Brian Herzlinger, selected filmography:
My Date with Drew (2004)
Baby on Board (2009)

E.T.: The Extra-Terrestrial
1982
Directed by Steven Spielberg
Starring Henry Thomas, Drew Barrymore, Robert MacNaughton, Dee Wallace, Peter Coyote, and C. Thomas Howell

How would you describe *E.T.* to somebody who has never seen it?
HERZLINGER: *E.T.* is a story about friendship that knows no bounds. A little alien is left behind by his spaceship and his friends, and winds up being saved by a young boy who is in need of a friend. And it's a friendship that forms that knows no limits to the universe. And then they have to get him back to the ship.

Tell me the story of when you saw the film.

HERZLINGER: *E.T.: The Extra-Terrestrial* was released in 1982 in the theater, and I grew up in New Jersey, and I remember my parents took me and my little sister to go see it at the Eric 5 Theatre in Pennsauken, New Jersey.

I was six years old. I just remember being so excited. Keep in mind, I'd only been going to the movies since 1980. The first movie I saw at the theater was *The Empire Strikes Back*. And I just couldn't get over what I was looking at, and at the time I didn't understand how important marketing campaigns were or what a marketing campaign even was, but everywhere I looked, there was *E.T.* There were trading cards, there was bubble gum, there were action figures, dolls. I went out and got all of them.

Did you actually own the trading cards before you saw the film?

HERZLINGER: Of course, and even then I realized, when I saw the movie I was disappointed, because there were images on the trading cards that weren't in the movie. I didn't know anything about deleted scenes. I can explain the design of these trading cards; I had the whole set. The blue background with the stars all about it, and the picture was a shot of Elliott, played by Henry Thomas—one of the best performances by any actor, let alone a child actor—being levitated in a chair. And what I found out years later as I grew up was that it was a deleted scene: he went to the principal's office, and the principal was played by none other than Harrison Ford.

Your parents took you . . .

HERZLINGER: . . . and my sister Stacey, who is two years younger than I am. So we all went to see it, and I remember just being in awe of the fact that I was afraid. And remember, at six years old, I'm recognizing that this is something being projected on the screen, but it's so much more than that.

Every time I've watched the beginning of the movie since then, I always hoped that E.T. would catch up with the ship and not get stranded. That movie is so visceral, it's so organic an experience. I was so into the movie when Elliott saved E.T. and brought him into the house with the Reese's Pieces, I became addicted to Reese's Pieces because of that.

And then I do remember something that has never happened since then in my entire moviegoing experience. The film burnt out. The film burnt out during the scene where Elliott gets drunk and E.T. gets drunk. They were able to patch it together so that the movie picked up five minutes later. But here's the amazing thing: I had no idea that scene existed until the rerelease in like '85.

I had to special-order *E.T.* on Betamax. I remember just bawling my eyes out when E.T. got sick. I couldn't get over it; it was just detrimental to my development as a child. I couldn't even look at the screen when he's all ash-white and reaching out for Elliott to help him, and Elliott's mother, played by Dee Wallace, is just doing her job as a mom to keep her kid safe, and all Elliott's doing is reaching back to E.T.

E.T., much like he was in the very beginning of the movie, is alone. And when he dies . . . at that point, I don't think I'd ever experienced death in my family. And it was crushing, absolutely crushing. But as crushing as that moment was—the moment when his heart comes alive and he says, "E.T. phone home," and the perfect John Williams score kicks in—the devastation was matched and exceeded by elation of that moment.

How did this film specifically change your life?
HERZLINGER: Well, what *Empire Strikes Back* did for me was open up the world of movies and the movie theater. What *E.T.* did for me was open up the world of what movies can do to you as a viewer.

You hear all filmmakers like Steven Spielberg and George Lucas and Francis Ford Coppola talking about the movies that inspired them as a child, and they're talking about Michelangelo Antonioni, they're talking about John Ford, John Huston. Those are the movies growing up. And the first movie that Spielberg saw in the theater was *The Greatest Show on Earth*, the Cecil B. DeMille movie. His father told him he was taking him to a circus. And it blew him away. For me, *E.T.* is my *Greatest Show on Earth*. Those were the movies that were coming out at the time that were aimed at my age group. *E.T.* is the exception because it transcended children. It has universal themes, universal appeal. Adults and children alike were sobbing when he died and rejoicing when he lived. Again, having the lump in their throats during the entire act three, culminating when he says, "I'll be right here," hugs Elliott, and says good-bye. I get choked up talking about it!

The original concept for the movie was going to be something akin to *Close Encounters of the Third Kind*.

HERZLINGER: And you know what's amazing, something I've learned as a filmmaker is how organic the process is. Every time you make a movie you make three different movies. You make the movie that's on the page, you make the movie that you're shooting on the day, and then you make the movie that you're editing in post. And they're three different beasts entirely.

In the first stage, you can have *The Wizard of Oz*; by the second stage you've got *Basic Instinct*; and by the third stage you've got *Silence of the Lambs*. They are three separate entities, and that's one of the things I love as a filmmaker and as a film fan, is how organic the process and the experience is.

Getting back to *E.T.*, when I left that theater, I just wanted to go in again. I've never done any drugs in my life, but I think that is what an addiction feels like.

E.T. also has the biggest emotional range of any film I can think of.

HERZLINGER: You experience every emotion and every fraction of any emotion we're capable of feeling in that movie.

It's one of two movies where, culturally, it's OK for men to cry. There's *E.T.*, and there's *Old Yeller*.

HERZLINGER: You're absolutely right. I've seen my dad cry twice in my lifetime. One is when we had to put my dog to sleep. The other is when he was watching *E.T.*

I didn't understand what I was feeling when I watched it the first time, but through the years as you grow up, you understand. These are images of light, color, light, and sound that are being projected on a flat screen that are making you feel emotions that maybe you haven't felt in years. Or, if you're at a Spielberg film, and you have the great fantasies that made me want to make movies in the first place.

It allows you to escape from your life for two hours and go on a ride, go on a journey that you can't otherwise experience. Sure, you can read a book and escape and go into that world of a book. You're creating that world in your own imagination. It's wonderful, it's great. For me, the idea of seeing that world brought to life in a way that I didn't have access to, in a way that was tangible, something I could literally touch—it blew me away.

Tell me about your favorite scene.

HERZLINGER: God, there's so many of them. I'd say there are two moments for me in *E.T.* where it all came together. The first one is not necessarily the one that most people will talk about, but it's the one that I really got a kick out of as a six-year-old and as a thirty-six-year-old. When Elliott has his first kiss with the young Erika Eleniak in the scene in the school when he's letting all the frogs go free because E.T.'s connected to them through his brain while watching *The Quiet Man.*

Elliott frees the frogs and lets them go, and then you see the kiss on the screen that E.T. is watching—and Elliott does the exact same thing. And it's basically match for match, move for move, to what E.T. is seeing. Two moments within that scene that get me are, Elliott's too short to kiss her. And you have a kid who is crawling on the floor because he's afraid of all the frogs, and Elliott steps on the kid's back to reach up to her to kiss her. At that moment, which I think is crucial in any movie that's gonna affect anybody, John Williams's music just blossoms in. He takes the score from the quiet and blossoms it into that moment, and it's a moment where everything comes together. Elliott in essence becomes a man; he has his first kiss. Right? This whole journey, I mean we're talking about a kid who's alone and doesn't have a father figure in his life. E.T. has given him this moment, and they are more connected than they ever are.

Tell me about the second moment.

HERZLINGER: The second moment is when E.T. leaves. It's all setup and pay-off—he recalls the "ouch" moment, from when Elliott cut his finger on the little saw. He associates the hurt that Elliott felt and the pain that he's feeling in his heart for having to say good-bye. And just when he says "Ouch" and Elliott repeats it, they've grown enough together to know that when E.T. says, "I'll be right here."

"I'll be right here" is what Elliott says to E.T. to make him feel comfortable in the house. This is the second setup and payoff within a minute; you can't get away with that in another movie, but you get away with that here because you know what he means. After he recalls that moment, he gets up and leaves Elliott a total 180 degrees from what Elliott was in the beginning of the movie. Elliott is a man.

It's just a perfect movie. And it's a perfect journey. And it is so broad and big in its themes and what it tackles, and yet so intimate.

Spielberg says it's his most personal film, about his parents' divorce, at a time when divorce rates were climbing. How resonant was that for you?
HERZLINGER: Well, here's the thing, for me, it wasn't resonant at all, because my parents are still happily married.

In the film, the scientist played by Peter Coyote tells Elliott, essentially: "I've been looking for this creature, E.T., all my life. He visited me as a child." Do you believe him?
HERZLINGER: Do I think that another alien visited Peter Coyote as a child? No. Do I believe that in his imagination and in his heart of hearts it's true? Yes. The beautiful part about the Peter Coyote character is this: he is an absolute good guy. And look at his scenario. He's a guy who's in touch with his inner child. He's a guy who's in touch with what this means overall. He's not there to dissect the thing. He's surrounded by the people who are more concerned about defense and more concerned about protecting the secret and the security of the nation. But he's the guy who is Elliott grown up. I think he's Elliott as an adult.

Tell me about the cultural impact of this film, what it was like to grow up when this film came out.
HERZLINGER: Yeah, you know, I cannot imagine being a six-year-old kid and not having this movie out there. I think what's important about it is it validates you as a child to believe in what's out there, or to believe in anything that you know otherwise would seem ridiculous to believe in. When you are sitting in a theater filled with people who are all experiencing this and believing, you believe that in this alien—this is a character with personality, with heart—this is a being.

I think it gave us permission to believe, and I'll tell you right now, one of my biggest things as a person, as a filmmaker, is being able to believe. If I didn't have that and didn't have that ability, I would have failed at this business.

You met Spielberg as a kid. Can you tell me that story?

HERZLINGER: I was a senior at Cherokee High School in Marlton, New Jersey, and everybody knew, among the students and the faculty, that I loved Spielberg and I loved *E.T.*

So my teacher, Mrs. Underwood—her son was a cadet at the U.S. Naval Academy in Annapolis, Maryland, and even he knew how much I loved Spielberg. So he called his mother and told her to tell me that Spielberg was getting an award for *Schindler's List* at the U.S. Naval Academy, which is a three-hour drive from where I lived in New Jersey. So she told me that. My dad took off work, I took off school, and we drove down to Annapolis, Maryland, with an 8x10 picture in hand of Steven and no real way of getting to the academy because the son wasn't gonna get us in.

So we drove down and, basically, we went on the campus and were told by numerous people that it was sold out and you couldn't get into the presentation and even if you did, there was no way you were gonna meet him. My dad was so great to stick this out for me, and he talked to everybody, and we wound up talking with a lieutenant named Scott Alan, and I showed him the picture, "I'm a big fan, and I'd just love to meet him." And he said, Spielberg is in the mess hall getting something to eat. And he goes, "You want to come into the mess hall?"

Now, meanwhile, my dad is videotaping everything. He's got my Hi8 video camera and we go into the mess hall and it looks like a matte painting of ten thousand Navy midshipmen, just all in white, all around the auditorium, and the middle was the podium and the chaplain—who, by the way, had told us that the chances of me meeting Steven were nil—and here they are introducing the guest of honor, Steven Spielberg.

And now I'm in there, and I see Spielberg take his hat off as he comes down to the podium and I see this hand with a hat coming toward me and I can't see over anybody in front of me. And in this sea of people, I see this red hat, and I'm like, "Oh my God, he's coming toward me," and then it makes a sharp right, to the table right near me, and he sits down and everybody around, all ten thousand people, wait for him to sit down.

As he sits, the lieutenant goes over to him, tells him about me and waves for me to come over, and I come over, and the lieutenant begins to tell him the story of how he's my favorite director and how I had organized a trip for the senior class to see *Schindler's List* that year, and he was getting the story all wrong, so I jumped in, and I said, "Hi, Steven, I took 381 kids to go see *Schindler's List*, and God, that is a flawless film and congratulations on winning your Oscar. I firmly believe that you should have won an Oscar for *E.T.* and *Raiders* . . ."

And he smiled and he goes, "Yeah, I do too, I do too." And I gotta tell you, he couldn't have been nicer, and in a room filled with ten thousand Navy midshipmen, who were waiting for Spielberg to start eating before they ate, he talked to me for ten minutes, just he and I.

I told him, "I'm from South Jersey." And he said, "I'm from South Jersey." He grew up in Haddonfield [or, according to other sources, nearby Haddon Heights —ed.], and I grew up five minutes away from there. And I said, "My goal is to come to Hollywood and work at Amblin. I'm going to film school this fall, at Ithaca College, and I'm gonna make it out there." And he goes, "Well, I'll see you at Amblin. I believe you will." And then he signed my picture, "To Brian, Make it—Steven Spielberg."

Where is that picture now?

HERZLINGER: It's actually in my bedroom, framed. And here's the best part: Three years later, I got my internship at Amblin, and it took me a year of phone calls from my dorm room in New York once a month to talk with Pat from Human Resources to secure that internship. Got the internship, ran into Spielberg in the hall—and when you get the internship, they say, "Listen, don't talk to Steven, don't look him in the eye unless he talks to you first."

And I'm like, "Come on, he's a guy! He puts his pants on one leg at a time." And I was making a photocopy of this script and walking out of the Xerox room and Spielberg was walking out of his office. And now he and I are walking in the same direction, down the same hallway, side by side, just the two of us. And I looked at him and I say, "How's it going, Mr. Spielberg?"

And then he pats me on the shoulder, and he says, "Good, good. How are you doing?" And I said, "I'm good. This is gonna sound really weird, you're not gonna remember this, but I met you three years ago at the U.S. Naval Academy in Annapolis."

And he says, "Oh, were you a cadet?" and I said, "No, no. Look at me, I'm not a cadet. I'm a scrawny Jew and not a cadet. I met you there, and I told you I was gonna work at Amblin, and here I am."

And he stops in the hallway and he looks me up and down and he says, "I remember you." And I'm thinking, he's just being nice, and he says, "Your father was videotaping it, right?" and I said, "Oh my God, you remember."

And I don't even know what I said after that. I just started gushing. And the last thing he said to me was he was proud of me. And he said he looked forward to good things, and he went on his way. And I went back to the Xerox room, collapsed, and called my parents.

Have you had any contact with him since you've been a director?
HERZLINGER: Not since. Basically what happened was *My Date with Drew* was my first feature film, and that wound up on his desk. He looked at the DVD cover design and said, "Oh, that looks cute," and that was the last I heard.

But the beauty part is that I have an open door at DreamWorks now because of my internship in '97 and because the same people who were creative executives back then are now running the studio. On the opening day of *My Date with Drew*, I got a handwritten letter from one of the executives at DreamWorks, saying he couldn't have been prouder of me, everybody there was rooting for my success, and I have an open door to pitch to them.

So, you know, everything happens for a reason, and that was definitely one of those life-changing moments—meeting Spielberg. Especially when you have someone so built-up in your head and he's basically responsible for your life's passion. To have him not only meet but exceed your expectations when you meet him is something you really can't describe. That happened twice in my life, with Spielberg and with Drew Barrymore.

***E.T.* was directly responsible for your first film, *My Date with Drew*, correct?**
HERZLINGER: Yes, I was a proud member of the Drew Barrymore fan club growing up in New Jersey. When I saw *E.T.*, I saw her for the first time, as did the majority of the world, and thought, "Wow, she's really pretty, and I'm six years old and she's six years old . . ." I didn't know what pretty meant, but I knew that she was that.

She was the girl on the poster in my room growing up; everybody had that. She represented the impossible. I lived my life and got turned down by various girls and continued on.

In 2003 in Los Angeles, I basically had hit my bottom. I'd hit my wall and was like, "This is a roadless industry. How do you create a road for yourself to be a director in a roadless industry?" And for me, I'd worked my way up as an intern, I'd worked my way up being a production assistant, worked my way up to being an executive producer's assistant, and then worked my way up to being unemployed. All the while, shooting my own short films and building up my director's reel and couldn't get that break.

I ended up taking a job at the graveyard shift at a postproduction company, which was just a really crushing, demoralizing job. I was handing out editing supplies to editors who were cutting and editing trailers. I met some very nice people there, but it just wasn't what I moved out there to do; it wasn't my dream. And it left my days free, which left me time to audition for a game show that a friend of mine told me about. That game show was a pilot game show, and there was not much winnings to be had, but I won the grand prize of eleven hundred dollars. That in itself is just jaw-dropping, right? But what's really cool is that the winning answer was "Drew Barrymore."

And you used that money to make a film about getting a date with Barrymore. But let's not ruin the ending of your documentary. Back to E.T., has the film aged well?
HERZLINGER: *E.T.* absolutely has aged perfectly. This is one of those movies that will stand the test of time just purely thematically. There is nothing that dates that movie other than the products and the *Star Wars* toys, but I hate to tell you this *Star Wars* is gonna be around for the rest of our lives. You know, if you look at *Raiders of the Lost Ark*, for example, this is a movie that takes place in the '30s that came out in the '80s that is timeless, even though it takes place in a certain time. *E.T.* is that way.

Why did its twentieth anniversary release fail to capture fans from a younger audience?
HERZLINGER: I think it's hard to get anybody to go see a movie in the theater if they already own it. It worked for *Star Wars* when it was released in '97

in theaters because it promoted the hell out of the new special effects, these new scenes that no one had ever seen but had heard rumors they existed. For example, Jabba the Hutt and Han Solo in a room together, that's worth my ten dollars. For *E.T.*, yes, it was modified with the visual effects, which I don't think it should have been. I think that the scenes that were cut out of the movie should have stayed out.

The biggest changes: The word *terrorist* was traded out for *hippie*. Most famously, the agents' guns were replaced by walkie-talkies—leading some people to say the film hasn't aged well because it was not allowed to age.
HERZLINGER: But Spielberg gives you the option. When it came out on DVD, you could own the new version or the original version. And I will always respect him immensely for that. I also respect him as a filmmaker for wanting to make the touch-ups.

I went to the premiere of it, which was amazing just for one reason only: to see *E.T.* on the big screen again and being accompanied by a live orchestra which John Williams was conducting. One of the best experiences I've ever had. I will never watch the new version again; I've seen it. The original was always the best—it's the same reason why Spielberg said he would never make a sequel of *E.T.*

How has your experience with the film changed over time?
HERZLINGER: I can watch *E.T.* and feel and get emotionally as involved as I did as a six-year-old. Is there a little more to the movie now that I see it as an adult? Absolutely. When I watched it as a teenager I could identify with his older brother. As a thirty-two-year-old guy in a relationship, I can identify with how hurt the mother is and how hard it must be to be a single mother and support three kids and a mortgage, and her kids are harboring an alien.

Now I can understand why she is pulling Elliott away from E.T. at the end—she's scared for her child's safety. Does that change the way the movie works for me? Absolutely not, because I think it is the best movie ever made, because it works on every level, every demographic. It really is that universal appeal/theme/approach that anybody—whatever your age is—can grasp and enjoy it to the utmost.

And how many times have you seen that in a movie? *The Wizard of Oz* does it. You know, I heard a story that before they started shooting *E.T.*, Spielberg made them watch *It's a Wonderful Life* and said, "This is the movie we're trying to make."

I read *Peter Pan* as a kid, I have that *Jaws* toy, I have the *Star Wars* figures, I have the desire to be a part of something extraordinary, and no filmmaker, domestic or foreign, accomplishes that better than Steven Spielberg.

10

Alex Gibney
The Exterminating Angel

When I asked Oscar-winning documentarian Alex Gibney to choose a film for this book, I expected him to choose, naturally, a documentary. I couldn't have been more wrong.

Instead, he chose a difficult film from a surrealist master, then eloquently explained why the choice made sense. "One of the things that I like about [Luis] Buñuel is that he seems to embrace the contradictions of everyday life, even though he's mounting them in a fictional way," Gibney says. "He did do a documentary once; it was called *Las Hurdes*, which was interesting. It was very brutal and bitter, and doesn't lend itself well to simple, liberal solutions to the way life works. He chronicles it almost as an anthropologist. There can be sort of a surreal quality to everyday life, which I like to embrace."

Alex Gibney, selected filmography:
Enron: The Smartest Guys in the Room (2005)
Taxi to the Dark Side (2007)
Gonzo: The Life and Work of Dr. Hunter S. Thompson (2008)
Casino Jack and the United States of Money (2010)
Freakonomics (2010)
Magic Bus (2011)

The Exterminating Angel
1962
Directed by Luis Buñuel
Starring Silvia Pinal, Enrique Rambal, Claudio Brook, José Baviera, Augusto Benedico, Antonio Bravo, Jacqueline Andere,

César del Campo, Rosa Elena Durgel, Lucy Gallardo, Enrique
García Álvarez, and more

How would you describe *The Exterminating Angel* to someone who has never seen it?

GIBNEY: *The Exterminating Angel* is a film about a group of people who go to a dinner party and suddenly realize that they can't leave the room. The movie is about what happens when they realize that and how the veneer of all of their civilized conventions breaks down. It's dark, but it's also wickedly funny and mysterious in ways that can't be reduced to a simple, analytical explanation. I always thought that's what's great about movies sometimes— the best movies have to be experienced; they can't just be written about.

When did you first see it?

GIBNEY: I saw it in college. When I went to Yale, there were a tremendous number of film societies. And every night there would be another movie to go see at a film society. I had heard about *Andalusian Dog—Un chien andalou—* but I never really knew much about the films of Luis Buñuel. Somebody said, "You should check this one out." So, one night—I think it was at a Berkeley Film Society—I went to see *Exterminating Angel*. And it rocked my world.

How so? You left the theater thinking . . . what?

GIBNEY: Well, it was such an interesting use of cinema. Suddenly there was a film outside of plot points. It was a film in which things happen that are so mysterious and embrace the contradictions of everyday life. You didn't know whether to laugh or cry or get really angry. There was a tremendous sense of irony and mystery, and also the sense of a mischievous filmmaker behind all of this. So, it wasn't just the story unfolding—you got this sense that there was an artist trying to tell you something.

That was very interesting for me. But particularly, the surrealist mode had a way of embracing the contradictions of everyday life, so that there was a multilayered experience. The idea that you didn't know whether to laugh or cry, at times. That was really something.

The humor was so pointed and political. So many political films have a kind of hand-wringing, whining, or propagandistic quality to them. This one was political in a more profound sense, in that it challenged the very basis of conventions of everyday society and did so in a way that showed just how cruel and vicious those conventions can be. And indeed, how they sometimes mask cruelty and viciousness. All of that was done in a way that was very deft and funny, even while sometimes being very dark and angry.

It was a sense of humor that appealed to me, even within this world that was very harshly critical of these seemingly civilized people, who are in fact, in some ways, no better than animals. And animals are always appearing in the film. These sheep actually come into the room that these people can't get out of, for some mysterious reason. The doors are all open. Suddenly these sheep wander in, and they slaughter them. And then there's a bear, running loose in the mansion. Wild animals just keep appearing more frequently as the wild, animalistic nature of the people is making itself manifest.

Sure. I was thinking about how to describe this to other people. And the best thing I could come up with was *Hotel California* meets *Lord of the Flies*.
GIBNEY: [*laughs*] Yeah. That's pretty good.

[*laughs*] The film was originally called *The Castaways of Providence Street*. So what do you make of the symbolism? And what does the title "*Exterminating Angel*" mean to you?
GIBNEY: I'm not sure what it means. I'm told that Buñuel liked the title or that he felt it might be commercial in some way. It implies that God is not so merciful, and certainly Buñuel had a very cynical view of the Catholic Church, which is evident in this film. But there is this sense of some other force—that's outside of the control of these people—that is cruel and not at all benign. So, that's what it means to me.

Castaways of Providence Street—I forgot that that was the original title. He always seemed to be interested in castaways. He did a version of *Robinson Crusoe*. And *Providence Street*, I think the mansion is on Providence Street. But the idea of *providence* is deeply ironic: That they're going to be delivered somehow to providence. Well, they're not delivered to providence at all. Providence Street turns out to be just the opposite.

It turns out to be purgatory.
GIBNEY: Yeah.

You're right. The title is not from him, it's from his co-collaborator on the project, Jose Bergamin. Buñuel told him, "You know, if I saw *The Exterminating Angel* on a marquee, I'd go in and see it on the spot."
GIBNEY: Sometimes that's the way it works, and *Exterminating Angel* certainly does have a catchy vibe to it. It does seem to resonate. It's always tempting with Buñuel films to get overly analytical.

I wrote him a letter once, asking him to let me do a documentary about him, which he kindly refused. But I also sent him an essay I had written about *The Discreet Charm of the Bourgeoisie*. He wrote back and said he thought it was great in terms of the Sherlock Holmes aspect of trying to figure out what his movie was about, but I think these were things he didn't give too much thought to. He put them in the movie because he liked them, not because he had some kind of carefully constructed scaffolding of themes and ideas. He goes where he wants to.

I don't know whether he was being gentle or whether he was being sincere.

Did you have any other contact with him?
GIBNEY: No, just that one letter. I think it was like '81 or '82. I wrote him a letter, and then I got a very nice letter back, which I have mounted on my wall at my office. He basically said, "I love your essay. It was like Sherlock Holmes and I love Sherlock Holmes. As for your proposal, forget about it." [*laughs*]

He said, "Jean-Claude Carrière did a film about me that was at the Cannes Film Festival. I didn't like it at all, and I retired from all moviemaking activities. But if you ever come to Mexico City, look me up." Unfortunately, by the time I got there, he was gone. He died in 1983.

Whenever you think about the film, what's the one scene that haunts you?
GIBNEY: It's not the darker stuff toward the end of the film. It's really the opening of the film, the early scenes of the film that really, to me, are so masterful. Because you have a series of sequences where the servants are mysteriously all asking to be excused, or they're all slipping out the back.

There's one scene where two maids are about to go out the front door, and then they see all the guests arriving, and they quickly skitter back. They hide until the guests arrive and then they move quickly out the front door, exactly like rats leaving a sinking ship.

So there's a wonderful and delicious irony, and he plays it so straight in those scenes. When the mistress of the house finds out they're doing this, she gets all huffy. "Haven't you liked working here?" "Yes, ma'am, of course I have, but I'm afraid I must leave."

You're giving up a job you've had for five years for mysterious reasons you can't really understand? There's something wonderfully comical and mysterious about it. In the meantime, everybody's trying to sort of keep their poise in a completely ridiculous situation. So in a funny way, those early scenes were very transformative for me, because they have so many layers, and they were so mysterious and disturbing.

There is another scene early on in the film, as I watched it recently, that I didn't get the first time, though. One of the few remaining servants comes in and trips and falls with a huge tray full of food, and everybody at the table laughs hysterically. They compliment the host for putting together such a wonderful prank and trick for their amusement. You can see the servant embarrassed, dirty, feeling very small, and kind of slinking out of the room. It's a very dark and telling moment. That's where the laugh catches you in the throat.

In the first half of the film, there are two very obvious repeated scenes, but Buñuel says there are at least twenty throughout the film. How did you react to the first of those repeated scenes?
GIBNEY: Is one of them where the guy is giving the speech, giving the toast?

Yes. The guests enter the house twice, and then a man gives a toast twice. Those are the two most obvious.
GIBNEY: I was amused by it. Again, it's one of those things that are very disturbing. You think, "What's going on here?" There's a method to his madness, but you're kind of astonished. You're learning to be astonished as the film goes on, to expect the unexpected.

And I think—without getting too pointy-headed and analytical about Buñuel, who sometimes just throws in this stuff for fun—there's a kind of repetitious mindlessness. Repetitiousness in the rituals of the bourgeoisie that underlines this kind of repetition, where they keep going through these rituals over and over and over again, in a slavish way. And it has that impact. Also, in the midst of a film, with no particular warning, it really knocks you for a loop.

One of the interviewers in the booklet that comes with the Criterion DVD points out that this film seems to be a better-dressed version of *The Discreet Charm of the Bourgeoisie*. What do you think of that?
GIBNEY: Well, I think there are certain themes that come up with Buñuel over and over again. In *The Discreet Charm of the Bourgeoisie* he had evolved a little bit more. He takes this theme and works it out a little bit more playfully.

But I do think they're very similar. They all revolve around eating. He did another film that I didn't think was quite so successful in which he kind of set that ritual: People excuse themselves to go to the eating room, and meanwhile the dining table is actually the defecating table, where everybody's shitting together. And then he has them excuse themselves to go and actually grab something to eat in what looks like a bathroom but has become the eating room, as a way of showing how arbitrary these rituals are.

That wasn't so successful for me, but *The Discreet Charm of the Bourgeoisie*, which I think is a brilliant film, does take off on the same idea of *The Exterminating Angel*—these rituals that never really seem to lead anywhere. In the case of *The Exterminating Angel*, it's a roach motel. They can check in but they can't check out. In *The Discreet Charm of the Bourgeoisie*, they never get to eat. They always show up for these dinners, or even tea, and the restaurant is mysteriously closed. So they always try to eat and they never get to. It's always interrupted. In *Exterminating Angel*, they can't leave. It's similar.

Buñuel had a very particular way of dealing with his actors. There's a famous story about how he smeared them with bits of honey and dirt to make them uncomfortable. I'm wondering what, as a filmmaker,

you've had to do to deal with difficult sources or what you do to set the stage.

GIBNEY: It's a difficult thing because it's a little bit different in a documentary. The only thing that I take from Buñuel in that mode is when I'm back in the cutting room; I'm always looking for moments when I see these contradictions. There's a moment when somebody seems to be saying one thing but revealing something else in how they're looking. You look for those moments and enjoy them, rather than worry about whether or not they're consistent with your theme. Because, in the end, they make everything much richer.

When I interview people, I have more of a Columbo-like technique, which is to be so bumbling and utterly incompetent that people feel sorry for me and actually open up. But in the cutting room, hopefully I've been vulnerable enough, which allows them to reveal something of themselves. And then in the cutting room you make certain choices that, hopefully, like Buñuel, find those moments where the formality of the interview nevertheless reveals a certain underlying piece of character, in part because of the formality of the interview.

What's great about the way Buñuel treats his actors is he puts them in these ridiculous situations and then always asks them to act as if they don't think the situations are ridiculous at all. He shoots them from a medium distance, rarely shooting them in close-up, which has a tense, but sometimes partly comic effect. You know, you never shoot comedy in close-up. So, in that way, there may be something that relates to the documentarian in me. There's a sense that he puts people in extreme situations and watches what happens with them. As a director he instructs them to behave as if they don't know that those situations are extreme. But we, the audience, realize that they are.

You're a documentary filmmaker. Why this film, then? Why didn't this film spur you to become a dramatic fiction filmmaker?

GIBNEY: Well, that's an interesting and tough question, which gets into: "How does your personal history roll itself out?" Sometimes things just happen that you don't expect. The fact is I actually started out as a fiction film editor and was pursuing that path for some while until I got frustrated with the films that I was cutting, and then I got high on my own shingle and started to make documentaries, in part because the process of getting money for them wasn't so horrifyingly difficult.

When I was in college, I was always interested in both. The next night after Buñuel, I probably would've gone to see the Maysles brothers' *Gimme Shelter*, or something like that. I think that back in the late '70s, when I was going to college—and to some extent, it happens today—there was a sense that either you make a documentary or you make a fiction film, and they're both movies. There weren't these hard-and-fast distinctions, and I see that in the kind of documentaries that I make. I feel like I use a lot of fiction film techniques, and I remain interested in fiction films. It just hasn't worked out for me to direct one yet. So I don't see the distinctions as quite as hard and fast as some might.

But it seems like a contradiction that you'd choose this film as the one that changed your life. Buñuel is surrealistic and all about the imagination, telling lies to get to the bigger truth. Documentary films seem to be all about truth and what happened, and getting to the inner truth. Does that make sense?

GIBNEY: I think so, but I think it may be two paths to the same end zone. Because, like I say, one of the things that I like about Buñuel is that he seems to embrace the contradictions of everyday life, even though he's mounting them in a fictional way. He did do a documentary once; it was called *Las Hurdes*, which was interesting. It was very brutal and bitter, and doesn't lend itself well to simple, liberal solutions to the way life works. He chronicles it almost as an anthropologist. There can be sort of a surreal quality to every-day life, which I like to embrace.

I think of the sequence in *Enron* when you have Enron's electricity trad-ers howling with laughter as they take down the California grids for fun and profit, even as people are being hurt and possibly dying because of the electricity going off. Well, the way I put that scene together—one could have done it in a rather different way, which is to put in some really sad music and emphasize at greater length the plight of the victims. But I wanted to put people in the lap of these traders, and there's a very ramped-up, high octane, heavy bass-line music there saying, "OK, you're in the frat house now, enjoy the party"—even as you realize the kind of damage that this party is causing.

I would say that there's a sequence that comes in a kind of roundabout way to me from Buñuel. But *The Exterminating Angel* certainly got me interested in pursuing movies as a career.

So how might this film translate for modern audiences?
GIBNEY: I think the first thirty minutes of the film hold up very well. I think the back half of the film, when it gets darker, there are moments that are very interesting. But oddly enough, the terror and the horror of this brutality that these people are exhibiting toward each other doesn't come across as well as it might. He runs out of surprises after awhile, and that ends up being a little disappointing.

So, in terms of it holding up, it's really important to me because it turned me on to Buñuel. But it's not my absolute favorite Buñuel film. The opening thirty minutes I think are masterful. After that there are moments of greatness but also moments that are somewhat mundane.

Please, finish your thought. It's not your favorite Buñuel film. Then what is, and why?
GIBNEY: I guess my favorite is the one he won the Academy Award for, *The Discreet Charm of the Bourgeoisie*. I have a lot of favorites for different reasons: I love *Viridiana*, I love *That Obscure Object of Desire*, and I also love *Los olvidados*, which is a very tough film.

But *The Discreet Charm of the Bourgeoisie* found a tone that, on the one hand, he does a kind of masterful job of making these people very amusing and witty, and he also filmed it in a way that almost becomes an enjoyable bourgeois French film. But what's going on inside it is so [*laughs*] so wildly funny and so subversive, that I think he mastered a style where he made it glossily commercial and utterly subversive at the same time. And that is really something.

And also, in terms of the way he did the dream sequences, there was none of this sort of "dissolving." They were dreams within dreams within dreams, and it was all kind of artfully constructed in the scenario, but directed in such a way that, visually, there didn't seem to be any particular distinction between the dream world and the world of everyday life. So I think it's a masterful film.

And then he finds certain odd things that he just throws in there that, in a peculiar way, just work, and that's a sort of a documentary quality to it, too. The shots of these people walking on a road: they're all dressed up with nowhere to go, and they're just walking on a road, for no purpose. And he just throws that shot in from time to time in between these sequences, and it takes your breath away. It's like finding some random shot as a documentarian, and throwing it in there because it has some kind of power you can't quite identify.

11

Kimberly Peirce
The Godfather

Peirce originally wanted to talk about Federico Fellini's *8½* as the film that changed her life, but since that masterpiece was already taken (and fought for) by other directors in the book, she had no problem picking Francis Ford Coppola's *The Godfather*, which she calls "a quintessential American movie."

She says, "I always love how the Italians are racist against the blacks, the Wasps are racist against the Italians. It's always wanting to be accepted, right? And Michael thinks if he earns enough money and if he gives money to the right people, he won't be a wop. . . . That's just something I love over and over and over—the outsiders trying to become the insiders."

Kimberly Peirce, selected filmography:
Boys Don't Cry (1999)
Stop-Loss (2008)

The Godfather
1972
Directed by Francis Ford Coppola
Starring Al Pacino, Marlon Brando, James Caan, Robert Duvall, Diane Keaton, Talia Shire, Sterling Hayden, and more

How would you describe *The Godfather* to someone who has never seen it?
PEIRCE: It's probably the most entertaining movie experience you're ever going to have. It's probably the definitive gangster family movie, with humor and passion, that we've had. I think it really is the godfather of gangster movies.

More directly, it's about a war hero [Al Pacino] who is drawn into his Mafia family's business. On the surface, at least. Tell me about when you first saw *The Godfather*.

PEIRCE: My first encounter was pretty young, I don't remember exactly what age, but I was just enthralled with it.

I'm Jewish and Italian, so in my family there's a lot of talking, there's a lot of eating, there's a lot of fighting, there's a lot of loud voices—it was one of those wonderful experiences also, like when I saw Federico Fellini for the first time, it was like, "Oh my God!—you can put this on-screen? These people talk and act the way my family does!" So it was familiar and I loved it.

I was a huge fan of like the '30s gangster films: *The Public Enemy*, *Angels with Dirty Faces*, and then *Bonnie and Clyde*. I loved *Scarface*—the original obviously being more relevant—and its greediness. What was nice about seeing *The Godfather*—it truly did answer the dialogue that had been started by all those filmmakers, but took it to another level. So it really hit me on an emotional level as a kid, and then it really re-hit me as a filmmaker as being truly the most entertaining movie I probably have ever seen.

Did *The Godfather* make you see cinema differently? How did it change your life?

PEIRCE: It showed me that I can take that love of the gangster movie and I can screen it through a family drama. In both my movies family is really important, violence is really important. I'm really interested in the psychological and the authentic portrayal of violence—particularly violence that comes out of emotions. Before *The Godfather*, I don't know that you could have such a violent psychological film that was that broadly entertaining.

Tell me about the most compelling act of violence in the film, for you.

PEIRCE: I so much love the transformation of Michael [Pacino]. Michael really is just a character I've loved for most of my life, the idea of him. In the beginning, he says, "That's my family; that's not me." He's this innocent who doesn't foresee being dragged into the family business. But as time goes by and his father is incapacitated, his two older brothers are not up to the cause. When he goes to the hospital, I love that scene. He sees that there's no security on his father. He's gathered the guy who brought flowers, and he gets him to act like he has a gun. They both go out there; they fend off the guys who come barreling by in the car. He's started to transform into this consummate gangster. But even then we're not to the violent scene, right?

Then there's the scene before he kills Sollozzo in the restaurant. I actually took a class at Columbia University with the guy who designed the sound for *The Godfather*, and he let us hear the sound of the leather. It was so important because Michael doesn't say much in the beginning of that scene, and it's how he sits down, and you hear the power of the leather seat. But when he finally says, "I can kill Sollozzo, I'm the best one to do it . . ."

You have so much to build up to—I love that. They don't think he can do it because he's the kid brother—but he does it perfectly, blows him away. That probably would have to be my favorite moment simply because of such good drama leading up to it.

And it is the hero, or antihero, who fulfills his destiny.
PEIRCE: *Yeah.* He's like a magnet sucked into this position. It's his calling. He's the smartest, he's the shrewdest—the one they're going to trust the most because of his innocence. And yet it's in that moment that he surrenders that innocence. He takes on the role of the head of the family even though he's not really yet.

What I love about the movie, compared to contemporary movies, is that I feel strongly that the amount of violence that we have in movies is making it less fun to watch them. It's making them less tense. I mean, forget about any sort of moral reaction, because I'm mostly just interested in what's going to engage me. I could just rewatch that *Godfather* scene a hundred times because of the build-up. The violence is just gruesome, but Coppola just understood when to expand it so that you were hit the hardest. And it was always tracking the development of this character. And I love the Apollonia scene.

Which one? You're talking, of course, about the woman he meets in Italy while in hiding over the murders.
PEIRCE: I just love when he sees her for the first time, and it's like the thunderbolt. That can so easily fall short in movies. That, to me, is great direct-

ing. The way he filmed it was simple enough that the audience got the thunderbolt the way Michael did. I'd even go back and look at the coverage if I were to do a scene that reflected that.

And then that day the car bomb goes off. You see his driver, his bodyguard runs, and then, boom! It's really a testament to Coppola's awareness of how people watch movies to say: "OK, I can get away with showing that one movement. I don't have long before the audience is going to get it and then be bored, but I got to give it away just as it's happening so that you're in Michael's point of view." And then the way it hardens him is extraordinary.

He realized that people can get to him and he still can get hurt this way.
PEIRCE: Do you mean it's the end of Michael's innocence?

Finishing off whatever amount he had left, yes.
PEIRCE: Yeah, and then he comes back to America, and he's ready to clean house. I think that's the other reason; over time it's seeping into people's consciousness in a deeper way. There's an inherent sense of scope. He's the young military guy, then he's the gangster, then he goes all the way to Rome, and he has a possibility of another life, and then he comes back. We don't have that many movies that have that kind of scope. What can you compare to *The Godfather*?

I'm curious what the draw for women would be to *The Godfather*, because this film is largely about men in a man's world and, from Kay's [Diane Keaton's] point of view, about the futility of women in this world.
PEIRCE: Well, I'm unusual, compared to most women. Both my movies deal with masculinity and deal with relationships. In *Boys Don't Cry*, it was a woman who wanted to be a man among other men. In *Stop-Loss*, it's about these guys who go to war, and they feel what real love and meaning in life is when they're willing to die for something. So I think I'm different than most women in my basic outlook and my socialization.

I love worlds of men, but I also think that, as a New Yorker, the humor of the movie is incredibly satisfying. And the familial stuff—the eating and the love and the camaraderie and this sense of these little fights—I don't think it's a gender thing, but I think it'd appeal to all people.

Have you ever run into anybody associated with the film and talked about your passion for it?

PEIRCE: Oh sure, sure. I've spent time with Coppola. You always feel silly professing your absolute love for something like *The Godfather* to the person who made it, but you can't help yourself and it's a good thing you do. Very early on he was incredibly generous toward me, incredibly nice. I was beside myself with excitement that I was just getting to talk to my hero about a movie that really had changed my life.

Is this after *Boys Don't Cry*?

PEIRCE: Yeah. We were at some event, and Coppola came up to me and he told me he loved *Boys Don't Cry*. And, of course, I was overwhelmed and shocked and really humbled by it.

I had the chance to tell him how much I love *The Godfather* and how much, in many ways, Brandon [Hilary Swank's character in *Boys Don't Cry*] was the innocent version of Michael. And then I had looked at Michael and his relentless use of violence when I was trying to create the John character in *Boys*.

Coppola was great. I have the utmost respect and affection for him. He asked me if I wanted to run his studio, which I thought was really interesting. But I said no, I don't think I'd ever run a studio. But it was very interesting that it was on his mind, and now that I'm years into a career, I understand where that appetite and desire comes from. I think he's a man of huge appetites, but it makes sense that having been through what he's been through, he'd want to have some control of the means of production.

Coppola recently said *The Godfather* should have only been one movie, that it was a drama and should never have been a serial. What do you make of that?

PEIRCE: I loved them both, *The Godfather* and *The Godfather, Part II*. In many ways the second one is, I wouldn't say superior, because I loved both of them, but it does give you an outrageously ambitious structure that miraculously works.

You see *The Godfather* and you're just in love with these people, and you just wanted to go on and on. So you go to see *Part II* with this amazing appetite, and you don't even imagine it can ever live up to part one, and yet, in some ways it does, right?

I understand when he says there should've only been one movie, that it was complete. I think it's a miracle they made *Part II* work. Maybe he's more referring to the greed, what happened with *Part III*—we love those people so much, but in many ways it can't really go on and on and on because the story is complete.

It's like trying to do a follow-up to *Oedipus Rex* or *The Searchers*. I mean, there's a reason that they aren't serialized.

It's very interesting that it was so hard to make and so hard fought. Even years later Coppola talks about how it was just miserable. Even the death sequence with Brando—he had to talk people into shooting that sequence during a lunch break.

PEIRCE: It's total testament to his brilliance and his timeliness, particularly if he's not getting support, and he's fighting for these scenes. There's a simplicity and a brilliance to them, and you can tell by the way they're shot.

Let's take a minute to talk about the casting. The studio did not want Pacino . . .

PEIRCE: Having looked at the outtakes of *The Godfather*, it was just so clear no matter what you did, the people who he cast—the way he cast them—had to be done that way.

The studio wanted James Caan to play Michael. He's great, but there's no way, no way, no way. He's so perfect as Sonny, biting his hand when he's frustrated. That's the humor that I just fucking love. It's so great.

The only other thing that I really love, which I think does speak to it being a quintessential American movie: I always love how the Italians are racist against the blacks, the Wasps are racist against the Italians. It's always wanting to be accepted, right? And Michael thinks if he earns enough money and if he gives money to the right people, he won't be a wop.

There's something so lovely and deep and American about that, particularly because it's a culture that's such a melting pot. Coppola captured that so beautifully, but with humor. That's just something I love over and over and over—the outsiders trying to become the insiders.

12

Steve James
Harlan County U.S.A.

Steve James changed *my* life. Before I ever met him, his documentary *Stevie* spurred me to write my previous book, *Last Words of the Executed.* So it was a particular pleasure to meet him and ask him about the film that made him want to direct documentaries. His choice: Barbara Kopple's *Harlan County U.S.A.*

Like me, he got to meet the person who changed his life later in his career—but that's a story best told in the body of this interview. Of *Harlan County U.S.A.*, James says: "I just remember being really struck by it—being really struck by this gritty quality that it had. The raw honesty of it and the access that Barbara was able to achieve."

Steve James, selected filmography:
Higher Goals (1993)
Hoop Dreams (1994)
Prefontaine (1997)
Stevie (2002)
Reel Paradise (2005)
At the Death House Door (2008)
The Interrupters (2011)

Harlan County U.S.A.
1976
Directed by Barbara Kopple
Starring Norman Yarborough, Houston Elmore, Phil Sparks, and John Corcoran

How would you describe *Harlan County U.S.A.* to someone who has never seen it?
JAMES: It's a film about labor unrest in the '70s, a very pivotal time for labor's history. It focuses specifically on the mining community in Harlan County, Kentucky. In that particular mine, the workers were trying to unionize and met great resistance. Barbara Kopple went in there as a very young filmmaker; she followed this strike and got tremendous access to it. I guess I'm getting past the descriptive phase. I think what makes the film so memorable in so many ways is, number one, the access. It falls into that classic verité tradition.

Albert and David Maysles were at the center of the documentary world of the '60s and '70s, where filmmakers were able to get terrific access to people's lives and be there and really capture it as it unfolded. *Harlan County* certainly has a tremendous amount of that. It's not a piece of journalism. It's not a film that went in and said, "OK, let's look at what these striking miners are saying, and what management is saying, and really try to delve into presenting each side's positions and leave it up to the viewer to make judgments." The film is a piece of political activism.

Tell me about when you first saw the film.
JAMES: I first saw the film in graduate school at Southern Illinois University. The film came out in '76. I didn't see it when it came out, although I was just getting interested in film around that time. It was around '76 or '77 that I really was starting to get interested in film. But at that time, I was more focused on feature filmmaking, like a lot of filmmakers, including a lot of documentary filmmakers. Stanley Kubrick was a hero. Arthur Penn's *Bonnie and Clyde* and *Little Big Man* were films that I greatly admired. So I had it in mind that I was going to be a feature filmmaker. It wasn't until I got to graduate school at SIU and studied film that I became interested in *Harlan County*. The film was shown as part of the series there.

So I saw it a few years later; it was making the college circuit at that point. I just remember being really struck by it—being really struck by this gritty quality that it had. The raw honesty of it and the access that Barbara was able to achieve. You hear occasionally in the movie, her asking questions and prodding people. I've come to know Barbara since then, many years later. It's so true to her personality. She's the kind of person who as a person and as a filmmaker can talk anybody into doing an interview or sharing their opinion because she's so open in the way she approaches a subject and approaches people. She's very curious, and she doesn't approach people in a judgmental fashion. You see glimpses of that in the movie.

Tell me about your favorite moment.
JAMES: There's one moment in the film where this guy who's a union buster for the company drives up in a truck. It's the first time you see him in the film, his first encounter with Barbara and her film crew. He asks, "Who're you with?"

She has some bogus press credential thing that she's got, maybe not bogus. He says, "Well, let me see your card." Then she starts just talking to him, saying, "Who are you?" He says his name. She says, "What do you think of all this?"

He starts to answer, and then he's like, "I don't think I want to talk about this." He goes, "I need to see that press credential." She goes, "Well, could I see yours?" He goes, "I don't have it with me." She goes, "I don't think I have mine either." It's a very funny exchange, and you can see in the guy, he clearly perceives her right away as someone who's in league with the miners. There's this quality in that brief encounter; you see her ability to engage with people, even people who have every reason to be suspicious of her. She ends up getting access to him—not the kind of intimate access she has to the striking miners, but she does end up getting access to him.

That's a quality she has as a filmmaker and is known for, and you see it on display in this movie. It's her ability to look beneath the surface of the rhetoric and passions to understand some of the complexities of what's going on. In this case, in this movie, it's not about the two sides as much as it's about the fissures within the striking miners. You see some eruptions of anger within the group. You see some of the pressure that striking is putting on them. She shows all that. These folks, you see the pressure they're under and how they turn on each other sometimes. She's always had this focus on people at the center of these stories, not just the politics or the social commentary.

Just a little background for people: The miners even in the early 1970s had really bad living conditions. They lived in company towns, some

of them without running water. There's a very interesting scene where
somebody's getting a bath in a bowl.
JAMES: And black lung—all the issues with black lung.

**Yeah. It was very, very dire. The film won the 1976 Academy Award for
Best Documentary. Do you have another favorite moment?**
JAMES: What sticks in my head are moments right after this altercation
where this strike-buster guy talks about one of the strikers as being a "nigger." You hear this woman defend him with something like, "That nigger
is more of a man than you. Don't you call him that." Then there's a scene
among the union organizers and the miners, which is attended by men and
women. They talk about the need to be better organized, and the woman
talks about that incident. The black miner who was the focus is in the room,
and so they talk about it.

   Somebody says, "We need to get more of you guys out there, so you're not
the only black out there." You see people trying to grapple with their common purpose across lines of race at a very interesting moment in the film. The
woman even uses the N-word in her description of it. That's something that
today a white person would be very careful of. They'd say, "He called you the
N-word." It's a different time. You see people trying to grapple with class issues
that can get pushed into being race issues, and they're trying to maintain this
solidarity and not let themselves be divided along race lines. It's always been a
classic tactic to try and divide labor, and a very successful one in this country.

**You chose this film as the one that changed your life, not Kubrick, not
Arthur Penn. So why? How did it change your life?**
JAMES: There've been many documentaries over the years that have powerfully impacted me. I think this one came along at the time when I was more
interested in being a feature filmmaker than a documentary filmmaker. So it
came along at the beginning of a process of moving from an interest in feature
film to documentaries, and that's where my career has taken me. It came along
at the right time for me. It helped me see, "Ah, this is more what I want to do."
There's something very alive about this film. What it's about and the degree
to which the filmmaker courageously put herself into a situation that she was
not from. You don't have to have known her history to know that she was

an outsider. She had the courage to go into a situation, spend the time there, and really try to understand it. You feel that all through the movie. In many respects, she became a template for the kind of filmmaker I want to be.

You mentioned that you've gotten to know Barbara a little bit since then. Have you confessed to her that she derailed your first dream?
JAMES: I've certainly told her how much that film means to me. But she's made so many films. In some ways, this one stands as the perfect capstone, if you will. It's her first film. She's made so many important films over the years that impacted me, like *American Dream* and *Fallen Champ*.

You talked about what you take from *Harlan County*. Are there any other explicit lessons you take as a filmmaker, in terms of editing, approach, or dealing with subjects? Is there anything specifically that this film taught you?
JAMES: This is a film that's not pure verité at all. The Maysles brothers tended to be much more purist. Frederick Wiseman still is a purist. What Barbara did was to go into a classic verité situation, but then she really talked to people. The film is made up of many, many interviews. In fact, seeing it again after many years, I didn't remember that there were as many moments in the film where the subjects are just interacting with her as they are. My gut recollection was that it was more verité throughout.

For readers who don't know what verité means, let's put it in your words.
JAMES: "Cinema verité" or "direct cinema" is this concept of the observational filmmaker. Filmmakers go in and, in its purest essence, they capture unfolding reality and make no attempt at all to influence it in any way, including not interviewing; they would be a fly on the wall—they would be in the room observing but would have no impact. Now, of course, as a filmmaker, that's virtually impossible. I think even cinema verité filmmakers, the purists, know that. It's not like they're naive.

Right. I think with the Maysles brothers, that fabric quickly goes away. *Grey Gardens*—that exists, I'm convinced, because the daughter is in love with one of the Maysles brothers.

JAMES: Right. What Barbara did is a very distinctly original film to look at even today. I can't think of another film that weaves history, including even archival material from history, in with this very direct verité approach of being inside a situation like she is, and then scoring the film with music— the music of protest. It ends up being a very eclectic mix of things that you don't typically find in a film that, at its heart, is a verité film. Most verité filmmakers tend to eschew music unless it's happening in the scene. If they score, it's minimal, sparse and understated. It doesn't provide the kind of commentary that the songs do throughout this film. They are pushed front and center. The songs become very much a part of the storytelling. These are all qualities that make the film distinct and keep it fresh.

Kopple has said that she originally set out to cover an election.
JAMES: That makes sense because you see a lot of that material.

She originally set out to do this story about an election of officials and a longtime labor leader, but the film became something completely else. How many times in your experience as a filmmaker does that happen?
JAMES: I think it happens a lot, and usually that's a good thing. Usually, you start out with an idea that's very solid and may even be terrific. It's the act of going out and making the film that allows the film to take you where it wants to go. I used to read novelists saying they had no idea what their character was going to do because their character decided for themselves. I used to think, "Oh, that's a lot of bullshit, basically. You create the characters. You decide these things." On some level that's true, but I understand now more what they meant by that. In fiction or in documentary, if you try to be true to what it is you're trying to capture, then you have to give up some control in a way.

She's trying to cover an election, and you see strong remnants of that because it is important to the story. That election's aftermath is important, how this particular union reacts to the union head who is now having to navigate this contract. Their own beginning of fissures between membership in the union and the new leadership. All those things are part of the film and important parts, so it's good that she had that. It helps to broaden the story and make it a bigger story. But on the other hand, the heart of the film is not there. The heart of the film is what she discovered when she got out there, which was "I'm going to focus on this particular community of miners and family." And women! I think the other thing that the film . . . this is something I think, for Barbara, is important to her as a filmmaker. She's never been, in my view, a knee-jerk feminist filmmaker, but she's very attentive to the role that the wives of these miners played in this struggle.

Right. If there is a central character, it's the one female organizer, who in my favorite scene, pulls a revolver out of her bra.
JAMES: That's right. That's a great scene. She says, "I used to have a switch, and now I have a gun."

Part of what she did was also, quite literally, to put her life on the line and the lives of her crew. They were shot at. At one point, they were knocked down with the equipment. Have you ever encountered that while shooting?
JAMES: I've never been shot at, no. Thank God. Might happen on this current project [*The Interrupters*, a film with *There Are No Children Here* author Alex Kotlowitz], but I hope not. I've shot in neighborhoods where you have to be careful, but I've never had any real altercation like what she went through. But that's the thing about Barbara. She's a fearless person. She was very young when she made this movie. I'm sure that quality was in abundance then, just like it is now.

In the middle of the film, there's a death. In my mind, there's a series of documentaries where something happens in the middle that threatens to shut down the documentary. One that comes up is that Metallica doc, *Metallica: Some Kind of Monster*. [The band nearly broke up during the shoot.] *Gimme Shelter* is another one. In the middle of it, someone is stabbed to death. How do you navigate such drama, as a documentarian?
JAMES: Oftentimes, especially when you're telling a dramatic or desperate story over time where events can cause the subjects to sit back and ask: "Wait, what am I doing here? What am I consenting to be a part of? How is this going to look? How am I going to look?" I think that when it doesn't derail the film, it's usually because there's been a level of trust built between the filmmaker and the subjects. Sometimes those moments deepen the connection.

Can you give me an example? Was somebody in the middle of one of your films getting cold feet? How do you work through that?

JAMES: The example that springs to mind was when on *Hoop Dreams* Arthur was kicked out of Saint Joe's. That was a point in time where he felt very embarrassed that he was kicked out of school—that his family couldn't afford to pay their part of the tuition. That he'd been rejected by the school in a sense, and he was sent back to the public school in Chicago at Marshall. It wasn't that they at that point said, "I don't want you to film anymore," but there was this belief that we wouldn't be interested anymore once he was no longer at Saint Joe's—that he was a failure. And since he was a failure, why would we be interested? The fact that we remained interested and committed to the film, but also the story, meant something to them.

It happened again with that family, when Arthur's dad was out of the home, running the streets and getting in trouble. They went on welfare and got their power turned off. These were moments when I remember I talked to Sheila, Arthur's mother, at some length about what we were doing at that point—how I thought and hoped people would perceive them—and about allowing us to continue to film in the midst of that. There was a lot of embarrassment, a lot of feeling. She said on the phone and then later in the film, "I've never been on welfare before, so people are going to look at this and think that's the kind of person I am and think bad of us." It's at those moments where if you have a good foundation with your subjects, then it allows you to move on. I think with Barbara—perfect example—she had been in the trenches with those folks. She had put herself on the line with those folks. I'm sure that was in their thoughts, too, and trust allowed them to go on because they knew how committed she was to telling their story and to telling the real story. I'm sure it deepened her relationship to the subjects as a result. It's an unfortunate tragedy. You don't wish for anything like that to happen. But just like it can deepen relationships in real life, it can deepen relationships between filmmakers and subjects.

Some journalists have said that reporting a story is like a romance, but once the story is published, often the honeymoon is over. I get the sense from documentary filmmakers that this is not the case—that after the film is done, you become part of their lives.

JAMES: Sure. It was probably Janet Malcolm who said that in that essay she did for *The New Yorker*.

I think that by and large that has been true for me—that the making of the film has created a relationship between subjects and filmmakers that goes on after that is very satisfying and makes the whole project that you did together that much more rewarding. I really think of those films as partnerships between the filmmakers and the subjects in a way. We have all the editorial control, no question. It's our film and I'm not trying to soft-pedal that. In the best of circumstances, they really do feel a part of it beyond just being the subjects of the film, and you really care about what they think, which is one of the reasons why we show them the film before it's done—to really let them hear. Now, I've had experience, too, though, where the finished film has created friction and ended relationships. The most immediate example, but not the only one, would be Gene Pingatore in *Hoop Dreams*. We all did have a great relationship with him as a coach while we were making the film. And I like Gene Pingatore personally. I think there are a lot of good things that he has done. He has a lot of good intentions. But the fact that the film was critical of some of his actions essentially ended that relationship. But we still showed it to him before it was done and faced the music.

So when you show them the film, do you let them know that they have any power to alter the film or do you just say, "This is what it is; be prepared"?
JAMES: There are two philosophies among documentary filmmakers in how you deal with this. There are a lot of documentary filmmakers that operate with a journalistic model in which you can't let your subjects see the film until it's done because it's your film. It's your vision, it's your take on it, and you shouldn't have the subjects weigh in on that. That's a little different than saying, "So-and-so said something about you. Do you want to let us do an interview and you comment?" Most filmmakers would definitely do that because it makes the story more interesting.

It's different to say, "OK, I feel like this film is pretty much done. I'd like to show it to you and you tell me what you think." A lot of filmmakers resist that. The folks at Kartemquin and I, in general, feel like you owe it to the subjects to let them see it before it's done, especially in films where you've spent a considerable amount of time with the subjects. We don't show it to every person who's in the movie, but the key people that you've spent all this time with—those folks have trusted you enough to let you in. We feel like you need to let them see it with the understanding that they don't have editorial control, but that you're willing to listen. You're showing it to them because you really want to understand how they feel about it—what they think of it. Do they think it's accurate? If they don't, then tell us why.

For me, that has most always been a good experience, even though sometimes it's a difficult experience. I've not always had universal happiness with what they saw, and so it leads to a discussion. Oftentimes, though, it has made the film better because they may feel like I've got something wrong, and I will interview them. Usually, if the situation allows it, I will have a camera when I go to meet them so there's an opportunity for them to talk about something. If they say, "You really got that wrong," it's like, "OK, then tell me the way you think it is." Usually it has made the film better. One of the things I tell subjects going into these long-term projects is that they will have that opportunity, and I do think that makes a difference for them. I don't say they'll have editorial control. I'm very clear about that, but I tell them that they'll get a chance to look at it, to comment on it, and tell us what they think. We will take what they say very seriously. I think it makes a difference because it gives people more of a feeling that they can trust you in opening up.

It's interesting that you were talking about Barbara being able to talk people into an interview. I've talked to Fred Wiseman, and he refuses to do that. He's said, "I don't have time to talk anybody into anything." It's like: "This is what we're doing. Participate or not."
JAMES: He makes different kinds of films because he doesn't really interview people. He goes in primarily and shoots for a discrete amount of time—a lot, but over a very discrete amount of time, for a couple of months, a few months. And that's different than trying to build a relationship with a subject over a period of many months and even years. It's a different animal. This is not to say one is better than the other, but I can understand why he can take that position. If you're trying to make a film about somebody, where you're going to spend many, many months and even years with them, then you're going to build an actual relationship with that person. If it doesn't have some

give-and-take, then I don't know what you're going to get. He comes out of that pure verité tradition where he goes in and documents an institution or a situation and just films everything in sight for a period of months—whatever happens in front of him. He gets terrific things out of that. Wiseman's films are not character-driven. Individual people aren't at the center of those stories. When people are, then you've got to build a relationship about trust. It's not coming in and saying, "I'm filming—yea or nay?"

Is this kind of film even possible anymore, given the changes in culture and the presence of reality TV?
JAMES: I thought about that as I was watching it. I think that we live in a culture now in which there's so much media savvy or media awareness. I don't know that people are more savvy about media, but they're just much more aware, and aware of this whole notion of performance. As a result people are also more suspicious. It gets harder for people to be willing to let someone come in and just film in the way that *Harlan County U.S.A.* films. People want to know more these days, "What are you doing and why? What is this going to say?" They ask some of those harder questions. Many years ago with *Harlan County U.S.A.* and even when we were doing *Hoop Dreams*, there was more general acceptance that if you were interested enough to come and film, people would let you. If you seemed to be genuinely interested in what was going on and could convey that, people were more trusting. That's changed a lot. This is not deeply symbolic, but it is symbolic. When I go to the West Side of Chicago now to film, I can't just go there and film people on the streets without going up to those folks and explaining what I'm doing, why, and what I want it for. Oftentimes they'll be receptive; not always. But if you try to just stop and film those things, people get angry. They don't just accept that the media has this right to tell their story and take their picture. It's really kind of an interesting shift that I've seen. It's not necessarily a bad thing. I think subjects are being much more aware of the media and what the media can do and will often do.

Or even people just performing. They see that a camera's on and—
JAMES: It becomes a performance. I think it's one of the reasons why a lot of documentary filmmakers are shooting abroad. I'm sure a big part of it

is to want to tell compelling international stories. But I think abroad, it's a bit more like it was here twenty to thirty years ago, where people weren't so jaded and suspicious. People are more inclined to embrace you if you show an interest.

Tell me about your perception and experience with this film on subsequent viewings. You watched it as a younger man and now you watch it deep into your career. How has your perception of it changed?
JAMES: As I said earlier, I think my recollection of it before watching it again was that it was much more of a pure verité film. Seeing it now, I didn't even remember because it was so long ago that there were historical parts beyond just the credits at the beginning, which some films will typically do. She really puts that history in there. I think realizing what an eclectic documentary approach was, was something that I had not remembered.

In that, I could even find more of its influence on me, because I've always felt that it's important to interview subjects. And some of the best interviews are with subjects in the midst of a situation. Not sitting them down and saying, "OK, now we're going to have a formal interview." You see that all over this film, where people are standing out there right after a protest action or waiting for something to happen, and that's when Barbara's asking them questions about the moment. That was a way in which it influenced me.

How would your life or work be different if you hadn't seen the film when you saw it?
JAMES: Who knows? That's one of those impossible questions to answer. Maybe I might still be trying to make dramatic films. I like dramatic films, too, but the truth is that I think I would have found my way to documentary anyway. I think that documentary, or at least the kinds of documentary that I've tried to make, combined these two strong interests that I had. One was storytelling: to tell a story, not explore an issue, but tell a story. The other was journalism. Documentary just seemed like a perfect blend of that desire to want to tell a story that made me fall in love with Stanley Kubrick's work, Arthur Penn's work, but also to have it have the resonance that comes from good journalism. I think Barbara's film came along at just the right time. There were other films that influenced me, too. Certainly Michael Apted's

28 Up and *The Times of Harvey Milk* were two films I saw in that time period that also affected me.

And *The Times of Harvey Milk* is still amazing. It holds up incredibly well.
JAMES: It was such a moving film. It's funny; it's like you pick and choose certain things that really powerfully affect you. From Barbara's film, it was this kind of courageous commitment that she made as a filmmaker to tell that story whatever it took. To get inside that story whatever it took and win the trust of those people. They were very different from her. Those are all things that I feel like I try to apply in my own work. And then *Milk* was a film in which I realized just how powerfully moving a documentary can be. That really affected me. Apted's *28 Up* I'm sure planted the seed of, "What if you could tell a story literally over a large span of time and see how some- one changes?" He's doing it in a very different way than we did it in *Hoop Dreams* or a film like *Stevie*, but that notion of actually seeing people change in the course of a film really is a powerful thing. I would say those three films are . . .

The Holy Trinity?
JAMES: Those are probably the Holy Trinity in terms of my life at that time. They really impacted me and got me thinking, "God, this is what I want to do."

13

Austin Chick
Kings of the Road

The film that changed Austin Chick, as this book goes to press, is almost impossible to find in the United States. Though the film's director, Wim Wenders, is an acknowledged master, not all of his films have made it stateside, which is a shame.

Of *Kings of the Road*, Chick says, "It spoke to me in a way. I had a very personal experience with the film, partly because I was in this phase of my life where I was aimlessly wandering."

Austin Chick selected filmography:
XX/XY (2002)
August (2008)

Kings of the Road
1976
Directed by Wim Wenders
Starring Rüdiger Vogler, Hanns Zischler, Lisa Kreuzer, Rudolf Schündler, Marquard Bohm, and Hans Dieter Trayer

How would you describe *Kings of the Road* to someone who has never seen it?

CHICK: I haven't seen it in probably about fifteen years, but what I remember of it is that it was emotional. It's about two guys who meet—one of them seems to have walked away from his former life, and we don't really know a whole lot about what he was up to. He meets a man whose job it is to drive around fixing projectors in movie theaters, and the two of them embark on this aimless journey together.

Can you tell me about the first time you saw the film?

CHICK: The first time I saw the film was in the early '90s, about '91 or '92. I had dropped out of college, and I originally went to school—well, through high school I painted. I always thought I would do something in fine arts, and then after two years I had run out of money and decided I didn't want to be a painter.

I wasn't really sure what I wanted to do, so I dropped out of college. I had spent a year, maybe not quite a year yet, but I had spent a bunch of time wandering around the country. I had hitchhiked back and forth across the United States a few times, was in Hawaii, and I ended up sneaking onto a military base and living there. I kind of needed to be a private in the Army for a while. I had been wandering, inspired by this friend of mine, who had spent a lot of time hitchhiking.

I ran into him in Berkeley, and he was a big Wenders fan. *Kings of the Road* was playing there; there was a newly restored print, and the two of us went to see it together. I definitely had seen *Paris, Texas*—that may have been the only other Wenders film I had seen—*Paris, Texas* when it came out in '84. I was young. Probably more than anything else, it felt like it spoke to me, in a way. I had a very personal experience with the film, partly because I was in this phase of my life where I was aimlessly wandering.

So how exactly did it impact your life?

CHICK: Well, having come from New Hampshire, filmmaking was not something that I had ever really considered as a career. I never met a filmmaker. I never thought about filmmaking as a viable career option. I grew up in an artistic community, but none of the people were filmmakers. So it never really occurred to me that it was something that I could do. But when I left Sarah Lawrence I had become disillusioned by the New York art world. It had caused me to abandon my ideas, abandon painting or fine art as a career path.

It had a lot to do with the fact that at that point narrative and realism were out of style, and the art world was dominated by a lot of conceptual art, and it didn't interest me. I was very much interested in some sort of narrative structure. I felt like, when I was a painter, it was mostly realistic, and that was not something that people were doing at that point. I liked the idea. The other problem I found with the New York art world was that it was a very insular, elitist community, and I didn't really feel like I wanted to be making art for that community.

I wanted to be doing something that was a little bit more, I don't know, populist? More accessible. I felt like a narrative interested me, and it wasn't until I saw *Kings of the Road* that I realized that film was a place that might make sense for me.

The narrative structure is still peculiar for a couple of reasons. It begins by announcing it is film, then announces its aspect ratio, the date and locations of the shoot. And then you don't know anything about the main characters, even their names or professions, for almost thirty minutes into the film. As a viewer how did you experience that?
CHICK: I think one of the things that I found really exciting about it was its apparent lack of story or structure. Visually it's a stunning film, and for me there's something really liberating about seeing a movie where story or plot was not first and foremost driving the film. Remind me how it opened. The way I remember it opening is with the blond guy—what's his name?

Bruno Winter.
CHICK: Yeah, exactly. The blond guy is sitting in his truck waking up. And the other character drives the Volkswagen into the river. Is that the way the movie opened?

There's a little prologue before the opening credits, which is Bruno talking to an Asian movie theater owner about movie projectors.
CHICK: That's right.

And then the first scene after the credits is exactly what you just described. Is that the image that's burned into your head about the film?
CHICK: Yeah, that opening more than anything else is what I remember of the film. And then there are a number of other conversations they have. The conversation about how the Americans have colonized their subconscious.

Which is the most famous Wenders quote from the film.

CHICK: Yeah, I mean I remember that scene really clearly. And actually, you've seen it recently. What's the song that is stuck in his head? He tells the story about getting in a fight with his girlfriend. And the whole time there's a song stuck in his head. It's like "I've got a girl . . ."

The song is "I Got a Woman." But I wanted to come back to this other quote that you talked about. Because that quote, "The Yanks have colonized our subconscious," is mostly said about music. And it's not a line that's said with malice or regret. In the context of the film it's an open admission of American influence on Wenders himself.
CHICK: Yeah, definitely. They're sitting in the bunker, the U.S. bunker, and they pick up the phone, and they get an operator in the United States.

This is when East and West Germany were split, and critics had said that this was the "German *Easy Rider*." I thought after seeing it, "It's *Easy Rider* meets *Cinema Paradiso*." Are any of those descriptions fair? How would you describe it?
CHICK: *Easy Rider* to a certain degree is a fair comparison, but it feels like you know the Wenders version. I think in some ways it harkens back more to Walker Evans, and to me that imagery feels very Walker Evans. A lot of those shots of small towns—and didn't they stop at a gas station at one point? They're getting gas and there's this old man sitting there, and there's no dialogue exchange at all but the guy looks like he's a forgotten Walker character.

And there's almost no dialogue for nearly thirty minutes. As a filmgoer was that unusual or shocking or puzzling? Or were you willing to hang with it?
CHICK: It was probably the only art house theater in New Hampshire, and it was in the town that I lived in. It was called the Winton Town Hall Theater, and it showed a bunch of European films. So it wasn't like I had never been exposed to European films, films with that kind of pacing, but it was definitely a different experience. That movie is ridiculously slow paced, glacially paced, but to me, maybe it was because I had spent the last two months hitchhiking around, I was in a place where I was used to a long period of

silence, especially having spent a lot of time on the road. It somehow made sense to me, at the time.

Wenders has this very interesting take on the male body. For example, watch Bruno: The scene opens essentially with him naked getting out of a truck. He later catches a projectionist masturbating, and then famously he defecates on-screen. It's misleading because he says, "I have to go pee," and then Wenders shows him squatting. It's a slow-motion car wreck, and you can't look away.
CHICK: He takes down his overalls, kind of in foreground, and he takes a big black turd right onto the white sand, as I remember. I think the other guy vomits in the next scene. In a public rest stop or a restroom. I remember thinking like, "Wow, he just got every bodily function."

I don't remember seeing that in any film, and perhaps don't need to see it ever again. The character who does most of the duty is Rüdiger Vogler, who is a longtime Wenders actor. Wenders talked about how this role typecast Vogler as this isolationist. He has shown up in *The American Friend* and a couple others.
CHICK: He's the star of *Alice in the Cities*?

Yeah. He's also got a small part in *Until the End of the World* as well. The German name of this film was *In the Course of Time* but, of course, it was renamed *Kings of the Road* for American audiences. Let's talk about the music, though, because *Kings of the Road* is taken from the song of the same name. There's also a Johnny Cash song in there, and a Pink Floyd–esque operatic soundtrack.
CHICK: I remember there was a lot of what he's done more and more throughout his career: he throws in more and more of the rock 'n' roll that's influencing him at the time. It's got a lot of '60s rock in it, right? It's a big influence on the character, but it doesn't feel like it's a far stretch back to Wenders himself. The character's interest in the music seems like it's not very clearly separated from Wenders's own interest in that music.

Did this film have any direct influence on your films?

CHICK: The very first film I made in my first year in film school. Well, back-tracking a little bit: I saw that Wenders movie, and then it was later in that year that I suddenly realized that film was what I should try to do. It didn't imme-diately dawn on me. I knew there were two ways to become a filmmaker. You work on a film and you try to work your way up. And obviously a lot of people were going to film school. I didn't really know anything about film school, but I ended up figuring out where I should go and going to film school.

So the very first film that I made there was really just a straight-up Wenders rip-off. Films of that time, *Kings of the Road, Alice in the Cities,* films with an essential protagonist, two protagonists, sort of wandering aimlessly. With some bare bones to the story, but really just an excuse to sort of move the camera through a bunch of different locations and to create a feeling. Maybe explore some thematic issues but not really any real plot. So I did this short; it was ten minutes. It was the only short I've ever done.

What was it called?
CHICK: It was called *Arrive.* It opens in an airport, JFK. It's about a guy who returns to New York who had been traveling in India for a while, and he's come back without telling anyone he's come back. He is without any place to go. So he calls a friend, looking for a place to stay. He calls a number of people, and he's unable to reach anybody, including his friend upstate. He figures he'll just go up there and hope he's able to reach him. So he takes a train to upstate New York, gets there, still can't reach his friend, and ends up wandering around this unnamed upstate town. We actually shot it in Peaks Hill, and Ossining, and a couple of other places, so we combined the small towns within an hour of the city. He wanders around all day killing time, calling his friend. This is the early '90s before cell phones, so he keeps getting the guy's answering machine, and the outgoing message on the machine is "Blues for Sale." You know that song?

I think so, yeah.
CHICK: Great song. He keeps calling and leaving messages and ultimately never gets ahold of his friend. He wanders out of town and sleeps in the woods. That's the end of the film. I shot it in black and white, 16mm black and white. It was all shot without any sound, so all the sound was dubbed

in later. There's no on-screen dialogue, but you hear these messages from the guy who's wandering around, killing time, trying to figure out what to do with himself. He waits. It was a direct homage, but rip-off is probably more appropriate.

It sounds like you re-created exactly what Wenders did around this time. Wenders said he was just writing with the camera, letting the camera discover the story. Is that what you were doing, or did you have more structure?

CHICK: That's definitely what I was doing. I had some idea of what I wanted to get, but most of the way that film was shot, which I think is often the way *Kings of the Road* was shot, was me and the actor and one other person driving around in a car until we saw something that inspired some sort of visual idea. Like, "Let's do a shot of you walking through this part of town here," and then we'd shoot it. We did the entire thing without permits. We shot an entire afternoon in JFK with all this equipment without any permit. We went to JFK and we went from one terminal to the next trying to get past security, in times before 9/11. I had a big huge battery belt pack around my waist. I didn't get past security until we were in, I think it was the TWA terminal, and then we were able to go in, look around, figure out the most visually interesting part of the terminal—making it up as we went along.

I want to swing back around to some of the encounters in *Kings of the Road*, because again it's very episodic. Early on there's an exchange between Bruno and Robert in which Bruno says, "No need to tell me your stories," and Robert says, "Well, what do you want to hear?" Bruno says, "Who you are," and Robert says, "I am my stories." Is that the core of what we are? Are we just the sum of our stories?

CHICK: I think that's an interesting lifelong question because I've definitely felt that. Wenders also talks about—and I don't remember where I read this—that there are stories where plotting it is the first step toward death. Something like that. But I feel like Wenders is reluctant to apply a real classic story with a beginning, middle, and end. He's more interested in the inciting incident—in that sort of open-ended question—than creating a story with a clear conclusion.

But this does have a conclusion; he does get there. Tell me about some of the other conversations in the film that stuck with you.

CHICK: I'm trying to think of . . . is there an episode where they go to one guy's childhood summerhouse on an island, and they find something under the stairs?

They go back to his hometown and commandeer a motorcycle, and it's the only time the movie feels like *Easy Rider*. It feels like the cemetery scene in *Easy Rider*. Nobody's tripping, but there's still a bunch of angles and emotional anguish; it's the closest you get to Bruno in the film.

CHICK: That section of the film seems a little out of character somehow. The main thing that's interesting is that you always see the film through the looking glass of where you are in your life. You know, the reason why this film has such significance for me is because it directly reflects what was going on in my life. A lot of the films that were really influential early on, like Wenders's stuff—I don't know that I would respond to them at all if I would see them at this point in my life. The films that really inspired me to get involved in making movies were these incredibly ponderous, barely plotted films. And I guess that allowed me to think about film. At this point I have a lot less patience.

Well, you and the rest of America.

CHICK: Yeah, me and the rest of America. I don't know that America ever has that much patience. In general, I think the films that appeal to me now are more plotted, more structured.

What makes his films unique?

CHICK: The sense of visual design and pacing. The lack of rigorous narrative structure. To me, all those things are very much a specific type of filmmaking that clearly influenced a number of other people. I feel like *Paris, Texas* is sort of the culmination of that style for him.

And that's also his self-fulfilling prophecy. Because he says, "The Yanks have colonized our subconscious." Then, of course, like many directors, he immigrates to America and starts making films.

CHICK: Oh, you know what I just realized? I actually have an ex-girlfriend who worked with Wenders. Her name is Alexandra Auder. Her mother was Viva, of the Andy Warhol Factory days. And Viva was cast in *The State of Things*. I believe she played the wife of the director or something. And Alex, who was her daughter in real life, played her daughter in the movie. And the film is about a crew who are in some small town to shoot a film and they run out of money, and the producer runs off to try and get money so they can continue shooting. He goes to Hollywood where he ends up getting killed by gangsters.

A lot of the movie is the crew hanging around waiting to resume production, and it's the interpersonal stuff that happens as the crew is basically killing time in a small town. And Alex was nine, maybe ten, and there was another kid on the film, and she told me that she and this other kid would be playing during the day and that Wenders would come up and tell them, "Remember what you're doing right now, because tomorrow we're going to shoot it." He'd see them playing a game, and he would add it into the movie, incorporate it into the following day's shoot. He was always looking for the material of his film, even right there on the set of their shooting.

Is that a lesson you've incorporated into your own filmmaking?
CHICK: I think so. Making films in the United States, in the current environment, you can't be that open to everything. You have to have a script, and I don't have the luxury to be able to raise money to shoot a film without a script. Everything comes together around a script. I do feel like I have tried to as much as possible to be open to those things that can happen on a set, when you're in production. I think that those are the most interesting things and the most surprising. Whether it's working with actors in a way that allows them to feel like they are really in control of where the scene is going, that there's room for mistakes or surprises. The most interesting stuff happens when you have a plan, but you don't have blinders on, and you're able to sort of see what's different, recognize what's exciting about and different from the plan and incorporate that.

14

Guy Maddin
L'âge d'or

Guy Maddin thinks surrealism is the perfect mode in which to tell a love story.

"It has the shape of boy meets girl, gets girl, and loses girl, and then gets to go magma-headedly, mad love crazy," he says. "The real connection for me comes from the climax of the movie, when Gaston Modot has lost Lya to another, even older man. He's just completely molten-headed with jealousy and despair, and he starts throwing flaming pine trees out the window. He starts ripping apart pillows and walking around with handfuls of feathers. He's doing all the things that I felt I had just done just earlier that year when I had been dumped and walked around with a plow in my living room."

Here, Maddin describes his and his friends' first encounter with the film: "We had an analogous little gang, and just the excitement of a primitive movie made by people who weren't slick and didn't have any experience or training and yet still told this great mad love story with so much froth excited me because it made me realize I didn't need to go to film school."

Guy Maddin selected filmography:
Careful (1992)
The Heart of the World (2000)
Dracula: Pages from a Virgin's Diary (2002)
Cowards Bend the Knee or *The Blue Hands* (2003)
The Saddest Music in the World (2003)
Brand Upon the Brain! (2006)
My Winnipeg (2007)

L'âge d'or
1930
Directed by Luis Buñuel
Starring Gaston Modot, Lya Lys, Caridad de Laberdesque,
Max Ernst, Josep Llorens Artigas, Lionel Salem, and Germaine
Noizet

How would you describe *L'âge d'or* to someone who has never seen it?
MADDIN: It's Luis Buñuel and Salvador Dalí's follow-up to their first sur-realist masterpiece, *Un chien andalou*. I like this one more, for the reason that this one spoke directly to me. It's a series of unrelated gags that aren't funny for any fun reason. It's a movie presented in a number of sections, one section for each segment of a scorpion's tail and a stinger at the end. The longer section in the middle takes up most of the movie, and that's the one that really zings me. It's just a love story, every bit as surreal as a love story deserves to be. It's delirious and it's primitively put together as any movie ever has been, and it's acted out by Gaston Modot, the only actor with a lot of experience in the movie, and he carries the whole thing.

The woman whom he falls in love with is this quintessentially surreal *l'amour fou*, who is played by Luis Buñuel's mistress at the time, Lya Lys. The rest of the roles are filled out by famous and not-so-famous surrealist art-ists. The whole movie was shot on the Townsend Noir estate, so there are all these far left–leaning artists messing around with the bourgeois playthings, or films. They seem to be slashing and pasting scenes together, and you can tell they have no experience. They're not quite sure what they're doing, but the sheer energy and hubris of it all puts it over.

It had never really occurred to me to make a film until I saw *L'âge d'or* and looked around at some of my clever pals. We all loved each other, and each of us loved ourselves. We had an analogous little gang, and just the excite-ment of a primitive movie made by people who weren't slick and didn't have any experience or training and yet still told this great mad love story with so much froth excited me because it made me realize I didn't need to go to film school. I didn't need a lot of practice. I even seemed to be the same age that Buñuel was when he made the movie, and I just thought it was time to make a movie myself. My methods were sort of initially found by looking in the direction that Buñuel pointed me in with this picture.

How did you see the film?
Maddin: I stumbled across it up here in Canada. The Canadian Broadcasting Corporation, the French network, used to run silent movies on Sunday night. For some reason, I was in the habit of tuning into the French channel because they also ran a lot of nudity. It was something you kept trying to dial on your TV like a slot machine, just to see what kind of jackpot you could hit on the French channel. Every now and then, it was remarkable what you could come across. This is what I came across one night.

Atom Egoyan, who is also in this book, discovered *Persona* in exactly the same way, expressly because he was looking for nudity.
Maddin: Yeah, it literally is like a slot machine sitting in the corner of your living room, and when you were alone, you would just go over there and spin the channel selector and hope it comes up cherries or whatever. It was a tradition that I'd forgotten about until just now. So I did stumble across it, and then my muses and I played it over and over again. We wore out the tape. It was one of the first movies that I ever videotaped, actually, in a beautiful sepia-toned unsubtitled version. So when I became obsessed with the movie later, I bought one of the scripts. They're really necessary in the prevideotape days. They help you remember it. I was able to get the English translation and realized it made no more sense than the untranslated version. That was pretty delightful to me, too, and I bought into the Surrealist Manifesto that everyone else had been sick of for years. It was like 1930 all over again for me. It just hit me with the full force of its year.

What part of the Surrealist Manifesto particularly appealed to you?
Maddin: It seems so old a hat now, but the idea of using completely disparate or unconnected objects and combining them to create a subconscious product and to create an indecipherable effect. It worked every now and then. A lot of times it didn't, but you were willing to, like your favorite baseball player, settle for a .300 average, and then when it did work, it was really nifty.

It created the kind of tingles you got from a great dream. Then, in spite of the denials by Buñuel and Dalí, they were making a narrative that had clear narrative shape in the central section. It has the shape of boy meets girl, gets girl, and loses girl, and then gets to go magma-headedly, mad love crazy. The real connection for me comes from the climax of the movie, when Gaston Modot has lost Lya to another, even older man. He's just completely molten-headed with jealousy and despair, and he starts throwing flaming pine trees out the window. He starts ripping apart pillows and walking around with handfuls of feathers. He's doing all the things that I felt I had just done just earlier that year when I had been dumped and walked around with a plow in my living room and dropped a bust.

Also a lot of the things he did earlier in the movie, before the breakup when he was courting Lya, reminded me of the kinds of mad things that we all do. When he brings a dress to the party and throws it on a chair to make Lya jealous, just because it's an empty dress, then he abandons the dress on the chair and he starts working on her. I don't know, just everything had the same shape as a courtship that goes well for a while and then falls completely apart. The details are all different, but the shape and the flavors just reminded me of my own life. The program was actually working—the surrealistic program, which exhausted everyone by the year 1980.

Did you see it in 1980? Because that was the year after the new negative arose in 1979. It had been censored, actually, for more than forty years.
MADDIN: I heard it had been banned for a long time. The print was great. By the time I wore out the tape it looked terrible again, but I remember the beautiful print. It was really nice. I was twenty-four when I saw it.

And had you been aware of either of them separately, or *Un chien andalou*?
MADDIN: I was just starting to watch films as a grown-up. I had certainly heard of Dalí, but I don't think I'd heard of Buñuel yet. But then right away I started looking into it. I can't remember the exact order of things, but I probably tracked down *Chien andalou* right after. For some reason, I liked the breathing room the one-hour *L'âge d'or* had. I can really appreciate what *Chien andalou* has.

It has a great shape, and it's a great romance, as well, but for some reason all of us seemed to understand Gaston Modot. He seemed to be leading the way, with his flared nostrils and his agonized face and his wax toupee. He was all the male humiliation we'd been feeling for a number of years. He was lust incarnate. Lya Lys is so sexy, and I knew a woman that kind of looked like her. It just grabbed me by the balls.

The surrealist way about it really worked for me. Plus, it's a great feeling watching humiliation set pieces, and when Gaston agonizes, he agonizes. The completely uninhibited nature of feelings in surrealist pictures is really fun. Also, he is a real charismatic actor, but the fact that nifty-looking people were clearly not acting well, but were still producing a powerful effect, was really exhilarating to me. It was like discovering a few years earlier how much I loved punk bands that couldn't play. The real excitement lay in their fresh acquaintance with the instruments they were holding in their hands, and their inability to really do anything sophisticated with them. They still manage to unleash a power that astonished them and mesmerized their fans. I saw a quick analogy there with basement bands and L'âge d'or.

I watched your films _Cowards Bend the Knee_ and _The Saddest Music in the World_ again last night. The filmmaking styles of the 1930s are particularly pronounced in your own work. To what do you attribute that affection, stylistically, in your canon?
MADDIN: I don't know what it is. I remember making an analogy in my head: I loved the basement band music, the second British invasion, so it had already been sort of swelling my bosom with rock music thrills for five years. When I saw that film could do the same thing if it went underground at that moment, I just felt that maybe I could do the same thing. I knew I could never be a rock musician, but I thought I could be a filmmaker, and it just felt like only a matter of months, or minutes even, before everyone would be naturally watching and pogo-ing away to my films of this nature, as well. I couldn't believe that it seems to have taken the world almost two decades to start.

How might _L'âge d'or_ play to a modern audience?
MADDIN: It's really harsh. It's strange, the way in pop culture film always seems so much slower than music. I guess music can turn around more

quickly. The do-it-yourself aesthetic of music in 1977 took a long time to bleed through to film, that's for sure.

You've talked about Buñuel and Dalí as film novices, as primitives, and the kind of accidents you have when you're a klutzy novice filmmaker that lend themselves to surrealism. But has technology made breaking into film harder or easier?

MADDIN: I don't know. There were all sorts of other underground films that were pretty exciting that had already found their maximum audience. I later discovered them and then quickly started making my own pictures. I began to realize that it would never catch on in a big way.

It just seems like people who watch films expect more earthbound things from the medium than they do from any other art form, because a lot of people forget that it's art, and that it's even artificial. You hear people complaining all the time that movies aren't realistic, as if they have an obligation to be realistic, or if they're even trying to be realistic. I hate using the word *realistic*. You don't hear people complaining about music being unrealistic or paintings being unrealistic or photographs being unrealistic. "Hey, a photo only has two dimensions—what's with that?"

For some reason, even if you took the most hardcore mohawked punk rockers from 1979 and showed them an experimental film, half the time they'd walk out of it. They'd rather watch a big-budget Hollywood movie of the time. Now it's different. And I expected more when I watched art films or experimental films with dancers. You'd expect them to be more open-minded, but they would complain that the film was unrealistic. A lot of people have trouble with melodrama because they find the performances over-the-top. That's an expression you hear over and over again.

It just seems like primitive film—the same thing as melodrama. So, many people when they sit down to watch a movie, all of a sudden get . . . I guess they get sucked into the spell of film and actually start watching it for signs of surface implausibility, continuity errors, and all sorts of other odd things. Thank God jump cuts are starting to proliferate. In the past few years were those books, which logged all the continuity errors.

***Roman Soldiers Don't Wear Watches.* I remember that.**

MADDIN: Oh my God, it's just a continuity ellipsis. It's analogous to a brush-stroke in a painting. It'd be like people writing books listing all the different brush sizes used in the Louvre or something like that. I think I'm just express-ing memories of disappointment with the general viewing public.

I love the sounds of part-talkies, and the first part-talkie I saw was *L'âge d'or*. You know, it's partially silent. Every now and then they'd talk, and I love when you can hear the tape recorder or whatever they used, the big discs, when they started recording the sound. You can hear the stylus digging into the grooves and you could hear the silence ending, the records being changed in the soundtrack. I loved the feeling, the clunkiness. It's like look-ing at a painting and loving the paint and not what it's representing. I just have a feeling of what went into making the painting and the soundtrack of *L'âge d'or*. You could just feel the torn edges of the collage overlapping with each other and the way it was put together. You could just feel it, and it was like a big celebration of the way it was put together. It felt really good to me.

It's kind of half-silent, half-talkie. It's got a pre–World War I documen-tary about scorpions tacked onto the front of the film, but then it's also historical. It's a melodrama. It's a piece, according to Buñuel, about desire and the frustration that comes with that. What other genres do you think it straddles?
MADDIN: The frustration was really good, and he started in that movie right in the beginning, by hammering home the fact that people don't really want sexual gratification. There's that fantastic sequence in *L'âge d'or* where the two lovers, when they finally have a chance to be alone together in that gravel garden, intentionally sabotage any chance of consummation in one of those stillborn Jerry Lewis slapstick routines.

Gaston Modot picks up Lya Lys, who slides out of his arms. Then they're on the ground, they bonk heads, and just when they're about ready to kiss, he gets distracted by a statue. They just don't know what to do with each other, and all they really have to do is what comes naturally for so many people. They're just delaying what could only be anticlimactic. He's always got people delaying, and he does it with food, too. He never has people actu-ally putting food in their mouths. It's just such a simple look at desire, and yet there's just so much truth in it.

L'âge d'or **follows some of the fundamentals of surrealism, such as sex should be veiled, not pornographic or realistic. But even if you see Dalí a few years later, he's almost completely turned around from that.**
MADDIN: Yeah, he's getting horny again.

Even in the titles of his paintings . . .
MADDIN: Yeah, he perverted himself somehow, whereas Buñuel kept his hand on the pillar.

Do you think that's a product of his Jesuit education?
MADDIN: I think he just had a clearer idea. Dalí just got spoiled, and Buñuel certainly didn't get spoiled after *L'âge d'or*, because he didn't get to make another movie for a very long time. I think he just stayed more true to his beliefs, and I know at the end of his career he was able to say he never included a single shot against his will or took one out against his will. Most of his movies are really good, whereas Dalí seemed to incarnate corruption early on. He maybe even turned that into a shtick. It's not a very interesting shtick, really, whereas everything Buñuel does is just so true, cutting, cynical, and actually has taught me that I'm not alone in the way I've struggled to find love.

Other than that message, can you point to another specific impact Buñuel has had on your career or style?
MADDIN: There's just so much mischief in him, and it's sort of taught me that something's not quite done until it's got . . . an extra twist. It just seems like a film isn't quite right unless it's got just that Buñuelian twist, that little sense of mischief. Where it's just this soupçon of cynicism, but mostly kind of acrid truth. It's always funny, surprising, and it survives repeated viewings.

Some of the stuff in the movie is supposedly shocking. But since it's also a secret shameful truth that's about all of us, it actually gets better with each viewing, and the shock effects become inconsequential. I'm always trying to think along those lines. I would never even in a million years say I've done it, but I'm always trying to tell the truth about myself in my movies, but certainly not with any self-pity. I literally try to do it masochistically because it should hurt a little bit to put that stuff out. So when I'm writing my scripts or shooting things, I literally just get myself on a 180-degree nipple twist, and it's kind of like dialing in Buñuel. It's just uncomfortable and stinging down there in my chest. He was like movie experience number one for me, and the influence has never really gone away.

In their first film, Buñuel and Dalí said, they rejected "any image that might give us a rational explanation." But for me, symbolism seems to permeate those two films.
MADDIN: Yeah, they seem to be explicable.

Are we as viewers putting the symbolism there or is Buñuel just being clever and dodging the question?
MADDIN: I think he's lying most of the time in interviews. I think it just made for a nice flip explanation, but also, compared to what most of the world was used to, it did feel pretty irrational and almost insoluble for most viewers. They might feel smugly secure in the notion that not many people could have solved those things. They just have the conspicuous shape of relationships, both those movies, and fortunately most relationships defy rational explanation too.

Melodrama and surrealism were put on this earth to tell love stories, and that's what they do best. They don't make political arguments, although they can. I just think that the fervid irrationality of love at its best makes us all a little bit crazy, and it is the stuff of melodrama and surrealism.

Buñuel and Dalí fought fiercely over this film. Dalí later disowned it altogether, saying it "betrayed his original vision" or it "placed his own authentic sacrilege with a primary anticlericalism and over-explicit political message." Does that criticism hold any weight?
MADDIN: As much as I've watched the movie, the political message seemed generically antibourgeoisie, and that's fine with me. I didn't feel like I wanted to go eliminate the bourgeoisie, but it always felt like fair game for it to be open season on them all the time. That would be about as far as I'd go with it.

I'm excited by the fact that Buñuel used found footage in the early part, but I always kind of liked the fact that the scorpion sequence doesn't really work very well. I find it kind of boring, but it did turn me on to reading entomology books because I'd heard that Buñuel loved them. So not just Jean Henri Fabre but Maurice Maeterlinck's descriptions of insect behavior, which are every bit as surreal in the depiction of the way insects love and behave. It's like parallel universes to human behavior, and they're really cool.

But other than that, I don't know. Most of those sections have to be deliciously endured the way you have to wait through Christmas Eve to get to the presents in the morning. Especially that bandit sequence, which was pretty dull. When you finally get to Gaston and Lya, then things are great. So I always try to make myself watch the movie from start to finish, but many times I've cheated and just watched the Gaston and Lya sections.

One of the most controversial scenes is in the sixth section of the film: Christ comes out after murdering somebody whom he's presumably raped, and then there are scalps on the cross. What did you make of that, if anything, when you first saw it?
MADDIN: I'd always been pretty secular, and I kind of bought it. It always seemed like fair game to kind of scalp the church somehow. It just seemed kind of quaint that the savagery of Buñuel's attack always seemed kind of charmingly distanced for me because I'd already made quite a happy secular space for myself—that it felt a bit like looking at a picture book of World War I, or something. There was so much time and space between me and it that I just saw it as something that must have been pretty important to the artist.

It gave me a thrill, because clearly he was saving this up to the end and it really seemed to matter. It just seemed like a Winnipegger sitting pretty far upwind from the Bible Belt. That curious form of rebellion was like looking at something under glass, so it didn't lash me into excitement in any way.

For 1930, it was much more controversial. According to some scholars, it's his invocation of Marquis de Sade's *120 Days of Sodom*.
MADDIN: Well, I'm sure, you know, you couldn't see that type of scene in any American studio film then or now without controversy. It would still be pretty controversial for some people, but for some reason it is the movie that changed my life the most—made me make movies. It was his approach

to the way we love. The way he used such broad strokes but still seemed to get to details within my heart and endeared to my soul—that really changed my life the most.

Do you have any direct references or homages to *L'âge d'or* in any of your films?

MADDIN: A lot of the shots seemed accidental. I loved the way the little top-hatted guy, some sort of sculptor, starts the ceremony. When the movie is switching over from silent film to a talkie, he clears his throat first. We thought that there was maybe some technical reason for this, where the throat-clearing might help the transition, the clunking over from one reel to the next, but he clears his throat, and you can hear it all of a sudden. It's in sync, and then he starts talking. In my first movie ever, when someone speaks for the first time, I just have him clear his throat.

Shots of Gaston Modot's abdomen coming toward the camera, sort of ending up on a button, on his lowest button on his jacket or a button on his fly. Then it goes out of focus and switches to a reverse shot. I love that. That button just seemed so inexplicable somehow. I've tried sticking that in a few places.

Where specifically?

MADDIN: I'm trying to remember if I kept it in my pictures, but I know I loved that button. I think in *The Dead Father* once again, because I was really under its influence while making that movie. I haven't had the nerve to watch that movie for a long time because it's way too long. But it was made while in love—which is maybe not the right time to make something—in love with *L'âge d'or*.

Through the film's first screening, Dalí supported the film. It was only later that there was the big falling-out because he was among the people who had signed a petition against the film. He was supportive, yet two-faced, which never made sense to me.

MADDIN: I'll give Dalí credit—classic George Costanza/Daffy Duck figure, where there doesn't seem to be an equivalent in the sitcom world for Buñuel.

I wanted to talk briefly about style. The title of this book is *The Film That Changed My Life*, and, oddly, the film that changed Buñuel's life was Fritz Lang's *The Weary Death*.

MADDIN: Which I've never seen.

My question is, do you see a Lang influence either in this film or in Buñuel's canon?

MADDIN: You know, I wasn't aware of that. And yet, there is a meanness in Lang that's kind of a necessary meanness, a peeling back to get at the truth of things. My only complaint with Lang is with pacing; while as measured and delivered as Hitchcock, it doesn't reward as well. He's willing to be every bit as cruel as Hitchcock and Buñuel. And he's never bogus.

Speaking of other filmmakers, François Truffaut was a big Buñuel fan. He called him "At once a builder and a destroyer." Federico Fellini said, "Buñuel re-established film in its true expression. Non-narrative film in a literary sense. . . . He used film as an expression that is closer to dreams. This seems to me film in its truly heraldic expression. His film language is the language of dreams."

MADDIN: And so often directors are cited for being dreamlike. They're most dreamlike or whatever, so it starts to feel like maybe dreams are proliferating out there as products. He at least set out as his initial mandate to try to duplicate dreams through chance encounters with things. It's interesting, even when he goes with his more disciplined narratives, like *Wuthering Heights*, which is a pretty tight narrative, he still manages to get passions high enough to take people into that heater zone, where all the lines get happily blurred. I really like his *Wuthering Heights*, as well, even though it's classic literary storytelling, although I think he starts in the middle of the novel somehow. So he has this hilarious micromontage with really rapid voiceover that requires that you speed-read the subtitles to bring you up to pace. It's almost like Preston Sturges has directed the beginning, in the opening four minutes.

I've only seen the movie once, but it has a proper ending. It makes total sense that *Wuthering Heights* would be a Mexican movie somehow. I just see that the spicy, spice-induced temperatures must be running a lot higher in that *Wuthering Heights*, and it is pretty crazy. I guess, just by sticking to similar subject matter from picture to picture, he was able to work in the areas where a dreamlike rendering works best and the kind of delirium with which the bourgeois would operate, and certainly lovers. There are other types of delirium that he didn't touch on much, childhood recollection and things like that, but maybe he just would have been too cruel for that. Of course, he had *Los olvidados*. I watched that on Christmas Eve. It ends with Pedro being dumped in a garbage heap. Just before I opened my presents, that was un-fucking-believable. We had to watch *Los olvidados* first, before anyone could open presents.

How do you think your life or your work might have been different if you hadn't seen *L'âge d'or* at the age and the time that you did?
MADDIN: I don't even know if I would have even known how to begin making movies. He made moviemaking seem necessary to me. I guess a number of other directors could have told me the same thing, Joseph Cornell or George Cukor. People I loved just as much almost at the time could have told me the same thing. It was the urgency of what Buñuel's *L'âge d'or* was about, this passionate affair ending in disaster. That was all I could relate to at that point in my life.

It was all I really had, short-lived splendors crashing and burning just at the most ecstatic point. Seeing these precise feelings reproduced by rather primitively performed roles and clunkily sliced-together shots really galvanized me and made me realize I could start putting my own lurid confessions up for anyone who wanted to see on film. I stood a chance of having a style and speaking to people as powerfully as the basement bands did with their crudely put-together little outbursts and things. I don't even want to think about what would have happened if I hadn't encountered *L'âge d'or*, because I don't even think I ever would have picked up a camera.

15

Michel Gondry
Le voyage en ballon

Michel Gondry is French and his films are dreamlike, so it's only natural that he'd choose a film that's both dreamlike and French. Gondry, who went from directing commercials and videos to features such as *Eternal Sunshine of the Spotless Mind*, chose to talk about a director who shared a similar path: Albert Lamorisse, best known for his short *The Red Balloon*.

He says: "It's the first film I remember. It's the film I like to rewatch the best. When you're young, you're very receptive to all the stuff you see, the emotions. And then you try all the time to match up with those sensations. So in this sense it may have changed my life because I'm always trying to re-create this feeling of watching this movie."

Michel Gondry, selected filmography:
Human Nature (2001)
Eternal Sunshine of the Spotless Mind (2004)
Dave Chappelle's Block Party (2005)
The Science of Sleep (2006)
Be Kind Rewind (2008)
The Green Hornet (2011)

Le voyage en ballon/Stowaway in the Sky
1960
Directed by Albert Lamorisse
Starring Maurice Baquet, André Gille, and Pascal Lamorisse;
English version narrated by Jack Lemmon

How you would describe *Le voyage en ballon* to someone who has never seen it?

GONDRY: It's a story of a child and his grandfather—the guy is like an inventor—and they just travel about France. He invented a new system to travel in a hot-air balloon, and they just travel from the North of France to the South, going in zigzag, and covering all the area of France.

Tell me about the first time you saw this film.

GONDRY: I was probably eight or I would say even less—maybe five. It was on a Saturday afternoon, and I was in France at the time. Both my parents were working and there was a system where you would stay at school and do activities. That time of the year, we watched movies. They put a tent in the yard of the school and they screened 16mm prints.

That's a great way to see a movie.

GONDRY: Yeah, I know. In fact, it's one of my most vivid memories. And each time I saw it again, I was never disappointed. A lot of times when you see a movie you saw when you were a kid, you're kind of disappointed. But I never was.

How did it influence your life?

GONDRY: It's the first film I remember. It's the film I like to rewatch the best. When you're young, you're very receptive to all the stuff you see, the emotions. And then you try all the time to match up with those sensations. So in this sense it may have changed my life because I'm always trying to re-create this feeling of watching this movie.

The director, Albert Lamorisse, was a helicopter operator, and he had invented stuff to shoot from. In this one he had his son in a basket hanging under the real helicopter. It's not like studio stuff. It's really flying. It's under the helicopter; it's always super windy and they have to change the sound because when you travel in a balloon, you don't have wind because you move with the wind. So it's very quiet. They had to post-direct all the sound, but it's dubbed very roughly—that gives it a very dreamy quality.

One of the things that struck me was its dreamlike quality, something that I notice in your films as well.

GONDRY: It's not an intentional dreamlike quality—there's a little something and you can't really point to it. It's a combination of things. The way they shoot only in good weather. I think that when you shoot with a helicopter you can really move quickly, and even when it becomes cloudy you can really target the area that was sunny and go there. It's sort of like French movies in the '60s because they could afford to wait for the good weather. It's very rare that you have all sorts of weather in movies.

When I was watching it, it seemed to me very much like a Disney documentary from that time.
GONDRY: Yeah it's true, but did you enjoy it?

Yes, yes. Such amazing colors, as well.
GONDRY: It's a good point you're bringing up because they were the first ones to use 16mm, and they used 16mm Kodachrome and then printed after in Technicolor.

When you saw it, did you want to be that little kid?
GONDRY: Of course, and I was dreaming of building my own balloon. I remember in *Before Night Falls*, they build this balloon and it gets torn and it's really frustrating.

Charlie Kaufman wrote a script for *Confessions of a Dangerous Mind*, and in the script my favorite cut scene was: he wanted to escape over the Berlin Wall and he had this inflatable small plane and it was blue. That was my favorite moment in the script. Like a video I just finished for a band called Willowz, for a song called "I Wonder." In the video, a guy builds a car from trash. It's very dreamlike to build a machine that's not supposed to work, yet it works.

In the film, there's also a shot where they let the white shirt fall to the ground and it dances around. It really reminded me of the plastic bag in *American Beauty*.
GONDRY: Oh yeah, that's true. I know the director. I think very likely it's just a coincidence. You see those plastic bags flying in a mini-tornado. I don't think you need to have seen this movie to get this idea. I will ask him, but I doubt so. This movie has not been seen so much.

You're right. In fact, when it came to America it was renamed *Stowaway in the Sky* and narrated by Jack Lemmon. Who narrated the action in France?
GONDRY: The guy who was following on the ground with the car! His name was Maurice Baquet, and he was a figure from the '60s. He was a musician and kind of a mime. He was an artist and part of a guild, and he was appearing in movies like that, a little bit surreal.

He has some of the best shots. He's the mechanic, the guy who can't keep his car on the road. He keeps like letting go of the steering wheel. . . .
GONDRY: That's the very best of Buster Keaton.

There seem to be a lot of silent film moments—and accidents. There's a shot where a horse actually throws a rider and a farmer falls off his wagon, and then one of the balloons blows up. For you, what is the importance of incorporating accidents into filming?
GONDRY: It may be something that you talk about, but maybe the director didn't even think of it, maybe because he's watching a lot of things. To him, it's a very simple storyline so he needs to create accidents and impose meaning, literal and nonliteral. Or maybe because you observe a lot and you see these things happening. He actually died in a helicopter accident.

Yes, Lamorisse's last film was called *The Lovers' Wind*, and he died in a helicopter crash while filming it in Tehran in 1970.
GONDRY: He probably had that in the back of his head, flying all the time. The thing is: When you fly with the camera you don't have any sense of danger because you're focused on what you're doing. Like when I did a video for Björk in the Icelandic landscape, "Joga." We had small planes and a helicopter, and I was hanging out of the helicopter.

Ordinarily, I would never do that. I'm really scared when I fly, and I had just a safety rope with a little hook. If I forgot to put the hook on, I would just be dead, basically. When I was shooting, I was never afraid of anything. But when the film would start to run out, I would realize, "Whoa! What's happening here?" and panic. A lot of accidents occur like that because people are focused on what they have to do and they forgot about safety.

There was a really horrible story about this guy who forgot to put on his parachute, and because everything was ready and he was thinking of the camera, he jumped with only the camera, so he died. You kind of become fearless, and despite all the untrendiness of fear, it's here for a reason: to keep us here, to keep us alive.

I talk to directors and writers, and sometimes the question comes up of how they want to die. Writers say, "I want to die at my computer" or "I want to die in front of my typewriter with my boots on." You often hear that from directors, as well: "Oh, I want to die on set." Does that ever even occur to you?

GONDRY: I want to die as late as possible. I want the biggest drop of life I could have.

But would you prefer it to be on set or off set? While you were working?

GONDRY: I would say on set. I would feel safer. There would be a lot of people trying to save my life. If I'm alone in my house and I'm dying, I would feel very lonely.

I want to back up just a little bit. This director, Albert Lamorisse, was well-known for *White Mane* in 1953, and his most famous film was a short, *The Red Balloon*.

GONDRY: *White Mane*—it's really dark, and really it's very sad. Those stories are so sad. It's amazing they were made for children because they basically tell that there is only happiness in death.

One parallel between you and Lamorisse is that you both seem to have this passion for physical effects or in-camera effects.

GONDRY: Yes, obviously. He had no choice because of the era. But, for me, it's more than the physical effect I like. I would say it's more like a twist in the way you see the effect. The perspective—it's like a different logic, basically. What you find while dreaming is that there is a logic, but it's a different type.

I think they have a different sense in their own world in their own way. I think it's interesting to work like that.

Lamorisse attempted to make the jump from short films to feature films, but it didn't work out and he had to go back to short films. From your perspective, you're one of the few directors who made that jump successfully, from commercials and videos to features.
GONDRY: Oh, well, I could still fail. It's a very interesting point you're bringing up because I like a lot of directors like George Pal. He did one of my favorite movies, *The Time Machine*. He's really a technician and an immigrant from Hungary. He invented this technique of taking shapes and just replacing them when they animate. When they go into the future you see all those models with all the time-lapse effects with the flower growing at full speed. It's just really charming.

The Time Machine included this very poetic view of the world by this kind of humble technician. This kind of thing, I really like. There's a movie done by Saul Bass, who designed a lot of Hitchcock's credit sequences. He did this movie called *Phase IV*, which is like a horror movie with ants. It's brilliant, sort of halfway between commentary and fiction. These are the things I like.

Back to my question: historically, why do so many short filmmakers have a hard time following up with longer forms?
GONDRY: It takes a lot of guts. It's scary and you're not necessarily bound to survive it. But I don't know about this question; it's hard for me to tell. Obviously the form is different, too, but the form is defined, so you have to match it and cope with all the difficulties.

It takes a lot more. It takes stubbornness to have any kind of success, I guess. You have to be blindly stubborn, basically because that way you'd just give up after the first preview. In fact, if you're stubborn, you learn a lot from failure—much more from failure than from success.

Seeing this as a young man, did it influence the way you thought about cinema?
GONDRY: It's more like, "Oh that's exciting! That's interesting! That makes me want to try something else with this adventurous thinking." It's more

like that. What's important, especially for children, you want to have that curiosity elevated as high as possible. Then their reactions are aware and they become imaginative and they find their own perspective.

What was it like, seeing it again recently?
GONDRY: It made me reconnect to the time I saw it first, which is rare because a lot of times you just see how naive you were. I've been dreaming of flying. When I watch this movie, I dream I'm flying and then I do stories where people are flying. I think it's directly influencing.

16

Michael Polish
Once Upon a Time in America

Director Michael Polish is so enamored with Sergio Leone's *Once Upon a Time in America*, and in particular James Woods's performance in it, that Polish cast Woods in his own surreal epic, *Northfork*.

Below, Polish talks about Leone's fractured masterpiece, which was released in a condensed version in 1984, but then given new life with a restored version. He says of Leone, "If any film was going to kill him, it was *Once Upon a Time in America*. You can't make a film like that, for that many years, and have it released at an hour and forty-five minutes and expect to have any reason to live after that."

Michael Polish, selected filmography:
Twin Falls Idaho (1999)
Jackpot (2001)
Northfork (2003)
The Astronaut Farmer (2006)
The Smell of Success (2009)

Once Upon a Time in America
1984
Directed by Sergio Leone
Starring Robert De Niro, James Woods, Elizabeth McGovern, Joe Pesci, Burt Young, Tuesday Weld, Treat Williams, Danny Aiello, and more

How would you describe *Once Upon a Time in America* to someone who has never seen it?

POLISH: It's an epic tale of a group of Jewish gangsters in New York from childhood through their glory during Prohibition and their meeting thirty-five years later, but that still doesn't do it justice because there are so many interpretations, whether it was a dream of ether or heroin? Or was it a real, chronological tale of these gangsters growing older and becoming politicians?

I don't like to say I know everything about this movie, but just internally it speaks to me, as just a human, a person alone. I can watch this movie alone and be a fan. Whether a filmmaker or not, I can be a fan because it has so many symbols and situations that reflect life itself, growing up. Even growing up in the suburbs, you still have friendships the same way these kids have friendships.

Your dad introduced you to it?

POLISH: Yes. It was a longer version, at the Tower Theatre in Sacramento. I remember it having an intermission. It was the first movie I saw to have an intermission. He would take me to all kinds of movies which I wasn't ready for, like *Dog Day Afternoon*. When it came out I was too young. *Once Upon a Time in America* was a rerelease when I saw it, the restored version.

We also rented it a year or two later. It was in two tapes, and it was the longer version my dad brought home on video. I remember watching it several times, not quite sure why I liked something like that at all. When I was sixteen or seventeen I watched it again and put the story together and really felt the ambience of it all.

Leone wants to create mood with style, and that's because he allows time and picture to be one, as opposed to you seeing just the style and cutting and filmmaking. He allowed the scene to play out in the fullest extent. He was probably the best director to evoke time.

He spent what he calls the "mature years of his life," about seventeen years, on it. He had ten hours of footage and a four-hour cut. But

because he was under contract, it was chopped up and put in chrono-logical order for the U.S. release—which, of course, bombed.
POLISH: James Woods still says to this day, it was the assistant editor on *Police Academy* who did it. He told me that before I even saw the DVD, on which he says that, too.

Isn't he being hyperbolic?
POLISH: James Woods being hyperbolic, that's an understatement.

In working with Woods, did he tell you any stories that were insightful or illuminating as to the making of the film?
POLISH: Any time I asked him about it, Woods was more than willing to say, "Hey, this is how you set up a shot; this is how you do it." Leone would walk everyone through it. Woods did one of his last scenes in high heels because the shoot was so long they would do anything to keep themselves entertained. He still has those high heels.

It was weird to hear it wasn't story-motivated by actors or by time sched-ule. It was set-driven. When a set was ready, they were chasing sets, which is weird to me. In *Northfork*, we were set-driven just because whenever the ark was ready, we'd go use it.

Leone biographer Christopher Frayling suggests that time is like the central character and theme of this film.
POLISH: That's the same with *Once Upon a Time in the West*, in particular, for which I discovered time is the central character. When Noodles [Robert De Niro] comes in and visits and the clock stops. And Leone starts the clock back up; it's a great little thing.

That kind of subtle detail means everything to the story. I hate to agree with that guy, but time is a theme. But you also have the theme of trust: the overall nature of trust, trust with loved ones, trust with a girl, trust with your best friend, trust with your family, and trust of faith.

There's a great story about director John Landis, who heard Sergio Leone made a film on Jewish gangsters. But, when he saw it, Landis breathed a sigh of relief because "it was about Italians after all."

POLISH: I always felt it was strange that it was about Jewish gangsters; I know pieces of it came from the book *The Hoods*, but I don't know if they were Jewish or not. I thought it was nice that they were Jewish.

But how Jewish do you think they were, aside from the odd Yiddish phrase?
POLISH: I know. The Star of David was everywhere. He had a different sense, and I don't know comparably how that plays out but there was a little difference to me—that Noodles didn't have this over-machismo. It wasn't totally over the top in any way. For some reason you had more innocence there; I felt there was more innocence in those younger boys and in Noodles. They were little street hoodlums.

Although the scene was cut out, there was a conversation about the difference between Jewish gangsters and Italian gangsters. According to Leone, the difference was the Jewish people didn't celebrate the fact that Jewish people were gangsters, whereas the Italians looked up to them with pride.
POLISH: You can see that in his film; they seem to hide it more. I'm not sure if that's due to Prohibition, when you really saw them flourish as gangsters, but it was something. They had respect, were proud of it, but it wasn't flaunted at all.

Leone hit it big in 1964 with *A Fistful of Dollars*—that was despite the prevailing opinion the Western genre was dead. He seems to face the same problem with this film. He was in the shadow of the first two *Godfather* movies, and he shared a flashback structure with *Godfather II*.
POLISH: I sympathize with him on that. Personally, I think he did Westerns better than anybody. I would never think *Once Upon a Time in America* would cancel out or be better than *The Godfather*, but those movies didn't speak to me like *Once Upon a Time in America* spoke to me.

I was also much younger when I viewed both of them. When I saw *Once Upon a Time in America*, I was twelve or thirteen, and for that movie I didn't have to make sense of everything to get an overall impression of it. Which, to me, if that film could do that at thirteen, and I kept rewatching it for twenty years—this was something very special. It evoked such great feelings in me.

I've heard it suggested that this is *Citizen Kane* retold as a gangster epic.
Polish: You end up having James Woods and Robert De Niro; there's just so much personality in those guys. It seems to divert your attention to a sort of *Citizen Kane* story just because they're so clear to what they want to be. When you watch those two, they end up being two brilliant actors who were so young at the time but each took a different path but so respectful of what they do.

That was one of the criticisms of this film: This is Leone's tribute to American cinema, but an America as seen through the eyes of a man who knows America only through the movies. [Spoiler alert:] Another was that you couldn't have a gangster disappear for thirty-five years, although some critics were willing to grant the film some operatic license on that point.
Polish: I need to disagree with that because people can disappear; gangsters can disappear. One of my answers comes from my favorite line of the movie, "No one is better in denial than an American." When Noodles comes back and says, "What have you been doing all these years?" that's as purely American as you can get; nobody knows it better than an American.

One thing Leone understood was America is made up of immigrants. He knows the people living here, the temptation. He understood that because you don't have to be American. At that time when he was talking about it, his relatives could have been here. I don't think he's that far removed.

His vision of America seems a little nostalgic, however.
Polish: I think that's a criticism his Westerns got. What's unfortunate about my viewing of it, I thought that's the way the West was. His interpretation of Westerns, I thought, was what the Western was really like. I was told much later that they were considered "spaghetti Westerns." I thought John Ford's Western was the opposite of what everyone else was getting. I thought what Leone did was really it.

Were they more real to you?
Polish: As a kid they played to me much better. If they were considered operatic spaghetti Westerns, I had no clue. They came to me easier; they

spoke to me better than other Westerns. They weren't as mature or serious as a John Wayne Western. They didn't speak to the America I knew, because I didn't know that stuff; I was just a kid watching Westerns.

Maybe it was because they are more cartoonish. They were framed differently, their particular way of close-ups. The music was more on top of the picture than any others, played so much into character that it identified certain instruments with people.

That's what I thought a Western should be. If someone asked me what my favorite Western was, I'd say, "Leone," and people were cracking a smile.

He was late in the game with the gangster epic and cowboy epic. Do you think that contributed to him not being taken seriously?

POLISH: Oh yeah, I think he wasn't taken seriously. That was unfortunate. He was going to be deceased before people would appreciate what he was doing. Probably one of the prime examples of this was Krzysztof Kieslowski. Another comparison of how genius his work was, but appreciated more after his death. His Three Colors Trilogy, *Blue, White*, and *Red*—when you look at *Red*, that was a real masterpiece. Everything he lived to do came together in that picture; it's just perfect.

Leone had more films to do before he passed away, but if any film was going to kill him, it was *Once Upon a Time in America*. You can't make a film like that, for that many years, and have it released at an hour and forty-five minutes and expect to have any reason to live after that.

He was preparing a film on the sieges of Leningrad when he died at sixty of a heart attack.

POLISH: He had a sense of widescreen and Cinemascope that probably nobody else had. His composition was unmatched by anybody else; his sense of close-ups and choreography is what separated probably *Once Upon a Time in America* and *The Godfather*.

Every scene was played to its fullest extent. How much of a challenge is it for a new audience to get into that rhythm?

POLISH: It hurts me as a filmmaker, and it doesn't give you much faith in people viewing cinema. This culture isn't conditioned to sit through certain aspects of filmmaking. There's just no patience, but with that being said, that doesn't mean it goes unappreciated. It just won't get mass viewings. Now it's considered one of the best films made. In the mid-'80s, when it first came out, it was considered the worst thing he's ever done. In the '90s, you're seeing it on top ten lists; by 2000 it was probably one of the best films made in a hundred years. So we're always fighting time and perception, and that's something Sergio did his entire life. We now know what Sergio was all about, but what a fight that guy had! His whole life was about fighting.

He was the assistant director on *The Bicycle Thief*, had a long career, but he was not well-respected possibly because he was a genre director. What sort of stigma comes with that, and is time the only thing that can remove it?
POLISH: If you start going up against what people perceive as your boundaries, you'll be fighting the wrong battle. You start fighting and answering the criticism, then you're not doing your work. You're spending time answering things that may not have any validity at the end of the day. They hurt you but you start answering your critics, and that's a battle you're not going to win because critics change, criticisms change. All you got to look at is Van Gogh, someone who didn't make a dime, was considered an odd painter who painted straight from the tube, who lacked technique, and now you can't touch one of his paintings. That's a cliche example, but it keeps happening over and over.

I think European films, in a way, are considered genre because they're shipped to us. They seem to love the exotic thriller, and we repackage it with exotic stars.

Let's talk more about the performances.
POLISH: James Woods has the goods. The reserved quality that De Niro possessed was just remarkable. He was able to carry the entire weight of the whole story without going above Woods's performance, which was great to watch—you compare and contrast. What James did was kind of be the emotion, the internal part of Noodles. They made such a great duo on-screen because I think Noodles always wanted to do what Max was doing.

Noodles ends up being a rapist. As a director how do you create empathy for such a morally reprehensible character?

POLISH: It's an uphill battle. It's already going to be tough, because he's obviously acting out serious pain that he feels. And all he feels is he can inflict pain on other people. That's the way he'll express it.

If you can accept his baggage, you'll be able to like him. I think he loses his moral compass when that young kid Dominic gets shot—that whole sense of watching that kid. That failure of him not being able to help him and seeing that kid go down. I don't think it's acceptable for him to go rape somebody, but yet his whole value system is askew.

There's been some critical commentary in this area that Noodles drifts from a fully conscious character to one blind of his own ugliness.

POLISH: Opium is one to take you there. What's amazing in *Once Upon a Time America* is what you don't see. You don't see a parental structure; you don't see any of their parents. So these kids, you're led to believe, are real street kids who create their own morals and Ten Commandments by what they do and how they act and what they believe is good.

The film takes place in 1922, 1933, and 1968. What do you think about the theory that once Noodles betrays his friends, he hides in opium, and the last third of the timeline is an opium dream?

POLISH: I love that interpretation. I love that people come to that conclusion. I'm one to believe that he really physically left because when you witness the death, or what you believe is the death of your friends, you'll leave the scene of the crime. Anyone smart enough is not going to come back. That's where serious guilt comes in. Whether it was a Jewish or Catholic saga, it was the guilt that drove him away.

17

Arthur Hiller
Open City

Roberto Rossellini's *Open City*, a World War II drama set in German-occupied Italy, caught Arthur Hiller at a sensitive time—just as he was leaving the military after the war. Its impact on him was palpable, partly because it opened him to an experience of war that he had not dealt with as a bomber pilot.

Though best known for his comedies (and the popular drama *Love Story*), Hiller talks about the power of *Open City* and its effect on him: "It just hit me. I think part of it was having come back from the war, so to speak, although I didn't face the kind of things the characters faced."

Arthur Hiller, selected filmography:
The Americanization of Emily (1964)
Promise Her Anything (1965)
Penelope (1966)
Popi (1969)
The Out-of-Towners (1970)
Love Story (1970)
The Hospital (1971)
Man of La Mancha (1972)
The Man in the Glass Booth (1975)
Silver Streak (1976)
The In-Laws (1979)
Author! Author! (1982)
The Lonely Guy (1984)
Outrageous Fortune (1987)
See No Evil, Hear No Evil (1989)
The Babe (1992)

Open City (also released as *Rome, Open City*)
1945
Directed by Roberto Rossellini
Starring Aldo Fabrizi and Anna Magnani

How would you describe *Open City* to someone who has never seen it?
HILLER: Well, you just get the strongest emotional feelings about what happened to people in Italy.

For those who haven't seen it, the film is set in Italy as the priesthood and the Communists team up against the occupying Nazi forces.
HILLER: Yeah. There's one scene that just couldn't have made me more emotional, when the priest is taken away in the truck and Anna Magnani is running after it, screaming. You see him in the truck, and that's still an emotional wallop.

When did you first see it?
HILLER: You see, when I first saw it, I had just come back from World War II. I was a navigator in the Canadian Air Force. I was over in Europe dropping bombs, and I decided to go to university in Toronto rather than back home to Edmonton. I was by myself, I'd just gotten there, and I had rented a room in an apartment above a shop, hardly the greatest. I was all alone; I didn't know anybody. It was the first Friday night I was there. I went down the street to the movie house, and I saw *Open City*. It just hit me. I think part of it was having come back from the war, so to speak, although I didn't face the kind of things the characters faced.

That was the wonderful thing about being in the Air Force. I'm not saying you weren't in danger; they would be shooting at us and indeed we did get hit. But basically you came back a few hours later to clean sheets and food. I don't know what I would have been like if I were in the trenches, having to put up with that all the time.

But it was all that neorealism; it just caught me at the right time. I can't even remember, but I know there were a few films at that time, neorealist films, that they were doing in Europe that we were not doing here. It just felt so real to me and so good. I didn't jump and say, "Oh, I want to make movies like that," but I guess I was feeling that without realizing it. The same as when I finally woke up and said, "I want to be a director."

So, obviously, something was going on inside me that I didn't know was going on. I mean, I knew how much I loved theater. I guess you just don't realize that, gee, you can do that for a living—that you can make a movie. Or that you can get into that business and work at it.

And how does that apply to neorealism? That you can use nonprofessional actors? Or political issues? What sort of epiphanies did neorealism open up for you?
HILLER: I think I leaned to that; I always thought once I started work, like I started in public affairs broadcasting. Through a whole set of lucky circumstances I ended up as a director in public affairs and doing talk shows. So again, because of my theater, I started radio documentaries or drama documentaries. It'd be a drama but about a social problem, a civic issue or something like that. And that's always appealed to me, that kind of reality.

***Open City*, for a lot of Americans, was the first movie out of Italy after the war. It was America's first look at Italy. What was that like, not only as a former soldier, but just an American, to look at that type of everyday life in another country?**
HILLER: It's funny, I knew it was in Italy, but the feeling for me was the reality and the feel of the people.

***Open City* started out as a documentary. They were going to film a documentary about Don Morisoni, a priest who had been executed by the Nazis.**
HILLER: I didn't even know that. All these years and I've not known that.

There was no film after the war, no studios. The story was that Rossellini scraped together 35mm film from street photographers and they spliced it together. Is that why *Open City* retains sort of a documentary-type feel?
HILLER: I think it's the way he shot it. But you're right, it may have been that it was lack of film. He couldn't go to too many interesting visuals and

keep playing the people. It's possible, but it may also be that that's the way he wanted to do it.

And Federico Fellini, he gets a writing credit on *Open City*.
Hiller: That's right.

One of the myths about this film was that it was a critical and financial flop and it was successful only later when it was critically reviewed. But it was well-reviewed in Paris two months after the Cannes Film Festival. However, for the rest of his life Rossellini carried around a negative review of this film. Can you conceive of doing anything that heartfelt or drastic?
Hiller: I have a phrase that I use all the time. If I said that every creative person I know is insecure, I'd be doing a disservice to very few people. It's just something about creativity, that you can't be sure. That's whether you're filmmaking or composing, or writing a book, or painting, or whatever— "Am I doing good?" You're so dependent on people that everything they say has such meaning for you.

Do you have or did you have a litmus test?
Hiller: No, not particularly. Usually it would be the writer, how the writer felt. Was I giving the writer what the writer was meaning? In fact, I always sit down with the writer just before and say, "Tell me what you wrote," just in case the writer might say something that I missed. It rarely happens, but it does, and then you think, "Oh, OK, then I know how to do that to get that." It's never been a major thing.

I remember when I first put together *Love Story*, and we were doing a running, and I wanted to bring Erich Segal out from the East, and the producer and the studio said, "What are you doing? What do you need trouble for?" I said, "It was his baby; I'm curious what he says." I might learn something; maybe I missed something. If he disagrees and I disagree, I'm a big boy, I can say, "No, I'm going to do this."

I feel a close affinity with the writer who sits alone in the dark room or wherever and comes up with the story. We must have something to work from. Which doesn't say that we're not original and come up with things. I hope I put in things that the writer didn't think of; I hope the actors put in things that I didn't think of, of course. I think that's what I love about movies. They are a group activity. All these creative juices come together, into the pot, and out comes this new little baby, the movie.

Do you think there is any specific lesson or idea that *Open City* left you with that you strive to bring into your own films?
HILLER: I think it's been there since I saw the film, but it may have been in me before that. It's what they call an affirmation of the human spirit. I've always liked that sort of realistic feel. When I did *Hospital*, I wanted the feeling that the audience was peeking around the corner.

So I did a lot of it handheld. I kept saying to the operators on certain shots, "Messy good, messy good." Which is very hard for the operator to hear. They're trained to be good and they can't be messy. Then you'd say, "But I want that." Deep down the camera operators were afraid that other operators would look at it and say, "You're messy." So I'd have to create shots that they couldn't do well, or I'd go handheld. And a lot of it is done that way. So I think it's always neorealism that has stuck with me. And even when I'm . . .

Even when you're what?
HILLER: I was just thinking that even when I'm working what I call the normal way, I'm not happy. I don't do farce. Now you may say *Silver Streak* was farcical or—

At least some of it was satire.
HILLER: Or *The In-Laws*. Yeah, but it's rooted in reality. As long as I could root it so that the audience feels it could happen, then I'm OK. Like when I was offered that film *Stir Crazy*, and I said I just didn't feel comfortable. Then they offered me more money, the whole thing, obviously because they were happy with *Silver Streak*. I just found it too loose for me, too farcical.

It did very good business, I think over a hundred million. When my wife and I saw it, I enjoyed it very much. We came out and she said, "Well, how do you feel now?" I said, "I feel the same." She said, "It made a hundred million dollars." And I said, "Well, I still feel the same." I thought if I had done it they probably would have lost thirty million of that, because I would have been so busy rooting it in reality. I would have spoiled what was working—it wasn't wildly farcical, but it was farcical.

Or like when they first did *Star Trek* as a film, they offered it to me and I said, "Don't even give me the script." Because I said, I can do it. It will have a beginning, and a middle, and an end. I'm not going to be able to do it better than somebody who loves that kind of thing.

One of the things I love about Rossellini is his little character moments. And the one that I think of and love the most is when the priest turns the statue of the saint away from the nude. What does Rossellini do, either in this film or in other films, that no other director does quite like him?
HILLER: That's the kind of thing. He sees little things about people that are meaningful. He shows you what their feelings are in an offbeat, yet visual way.

Why do you think the film had such an impact in 1945?
HILLER: It was just the horror of what was going on over there. One man, it was as if one person, what he was doing to people. What hit me hardest was that a friend in high school, her brother was killed overseas, and then a cousin of mine.

I'm also struck by the alternating tones of comedy and tragedy in *Open City*. Why does that formula work?
HILLER: It only works in the hands of very skillful writers. I think there are very few people who can do that sort of thing. Paddy Chayefsky was the only genius I ever worked with who could do that sort of thing. In *The Americanization of Emily*, we were doing the D-Day landings and people were being shot, and you were feeling that but you were laughing at the same time.

A wonderful scene is when they're supposed to land on the beach, and the first dead man is to be a sailor, when their little boat is not quite blown up but the waves throw it, and they're all thrown into the water. The James Garner character comes up and looks at the beach with all the shooting coming out and turns around and starts heading back to the boat. The James

Coburn character says, "Turn around! The beach is the other way!" And he says, "I know which way the beach is!" [*laughs*] You're laughing. You're also feeling, "I don't want to go be shot either."

What are the dangers of using laughter as a mechanism that helps us deal with the horror?
HILLER: Well, if you do too much, if your laughter is just for the laughs. It somehow has to be tied in and effective. And that takes unbelievable skill in writing.

And why do you think that today it still remains a powerful, influential film?
HILLER: That sense of making you feel that it was really happening, and getting you to see with your gut.

18

Pete Docter
Paper Moon

The connection between *Paper Moon* and Pete Docter's work isn't immediately apparent—until you get Docter talking. What Docter values and admires most about Bogdanovich's road movie is character, and the relationship between adults and children. *Paper Moon* left its mark in Docter's films, as he talks about how the relationship between Ryan and Tatum O'Neal in *Paper Moon* influenced unlikely friendships in both *Toy Story* and *Monsters, Inc.* (Unlikely friendships have become a hallmark for Docter, who won an Oscar for *Up*, which teams a curmudgeonly, childless senior citizen with an energetic Asian boy.)

Docter also expresses an ardent admiration for Bogdanovich's use of long, steady shots with complex interactions and caches of subtle storytelling. He says, "It has a similar kind of minimalism to camera theatrics. . . . [Bogdanovich] tries to make the camera as invisible as possible."

Pete Docter, selected filmography:
Monsters, Inc. (2001)
Up (2009)

Paper Moon
1973
Directed by Peter Bogdanovich
Starring Ryan O'Neal, Tatum O'Neal, Madeline Kahn, and Randy Quaid

How would you describe *Paper Moon* to someone who has never seen it?
DOCTER: It's a film about an orphaned girl who is stuck with a shyster and ends up doing a better job than he does.

[*laughs*] And of course it stars Ryan O'Neal and Tatum O'Neal, his daughter. It's Tatum's first role, which won her an Oscar. And so tell me, why did you choose this film? How did it change your life?
DOCTER: At the time I saw it, I had sort of gotten used to films being rather "cutty" and very much about action and what happens next. This film certainly has that, but to me, it just had such a high degree of control. Every shot was chosen; you could see that it was meticulously planned out. It was so deceptively simple. It's kind of like a haiku.

What we were taught in film school is: every shot has one point and then you cut and then you get another shot and that gets another story point across. And in this film, four or five things would happen, one after another—all so well-choreographed in each shot. It was really well crafted and very simple.

And do you remember, can you tell me the first time you saw it?
DOCTER: It would have been right after *Toy Story* came out. We were watching it in reference to *Monsters, Inc.*, which we were developing, so that would have been '97. I just was struck by it. To this day, it has a lasting effect on *Monsters*. I'm not trying to achieve what Bogdanovich did in that film. The things I admired about it I don't think really ended up in *Monsters*, other than the relationships.

This is what gets me about all films when they're about character. My favorite parts of *The Incredibles* are the bits where the family is sitting around the table eating dinner. In *Paper Moon*, the plot's not moving at a million miles an hour, it's not action adventure, but you just get to watch these great characters. And that to me, this whole film is like that. It's just chock-full of great character moments. The relationship between the two of them, there was so much that they mined there.

She's clearly searching for a father figure, and it's implied that he is actually her father although he doesn't want to admit to that. So there's a lot of great emotion and there's just some entertainment as well.

Am I wrong to make the connection between the character of Boo in
***Monsters, Inc.* and Tatum O'Neal's Addie in *Paper Moon*?**
DOCTER: No, not all. In fact, initially, we were even closer to Addie's age
with Boo. In our first draft, she was an older kid. And we really liked the sort
of the scrappiness of Addie. She can stand her own against this grown man,
intellectually but emotionally, too. She is just a force to be reckoned with.
She's a great character.

You said you watched it in reference to *Monsters, Inc.* How did that
process work? What were you looking for in particular?
DOCTER: Yeah, we do that pretty much on any film. As soon as we kind
of identify what type of film we're making—you know, a buddy film in the
case of, say, *Toy Story*—we start to watch as many as we can. Good, bad,
whatever. We just try to notice what other filmmakers do and don't do with
a similar subject. With *Toy Story* we watched *48 Hrs.*, *Midnight Run*, and
The Defiant Ones, which is pretty classic. We started to realize there are key
moments that each one of these hit.

So, with *Monsters, Inc.*, when we realized, "Oh, this is a film about an
older professional guy who's stuck with a little kid," we watched *The Professional*, *Paper Moon*, and *Little Miss Marker* with Shirley Temple.

We watched a lot of these films, again, just kind of looking for the bench-
marks that these kind of films hit. What are the things we like? What are the
things we don't like? I'm such an admirer of Bogdanovich, in this film especially,
and of his control. He'll have these shots that are, what? A minute long, two
minutes long? I mean, I think our average shot length is two seconds. It's just a
bold move, just lock the camera down on the front of the car and off they go.

They have this whole relationship. You can't save anything in the cutting,
which is what we're used to doing, not necessarily for animation but for
dialogue. You can use little snippets of stuff and piece it together in a sort
of Frankenstein way. The performance that we get was never really there
naturally, if that makes sense. Whereas in *Paper Moon*, it's either there or it's
not—and it certainly is there in this film.

Were you familiar with his other films? Because this was his third hit,
after *The Last Picture Show* and *What's Up, Doc*?

DOCTER: Yeah, I had seen *Last Picture Show* and what else? I had seen *Daisy Miller*, I think. Not a lot of his films, but this one certainly really struck me.

Is there some sort of through-line or some sort of common element that his films have?
DOCTER: Well, certainly with *Last Picture Show*, he definitely has a thing for that sort of bygone era and even the black-and-white thing, which is pretty bold. *Last Picture Show* has a similar kind of minimalism to camera theatrics. He tries to make the camera as invisible as possible and as simple as possible, which then makes it all the more difficult on everything else, including the actors.

I remember one shot in *Paper Moon*, where Ryan O'Neal is eating breakfast, and someone comes in from the back, then they exit, and somebody else comes in from the front. And there's all this choreography of people moving in and out of the frame. It's only one shot, and yet you're getting all this information out of it.

Do you have another scene in particular that made you a fan?
DOCTER: Well, the very opening shot is such a simple shot of the grave and of people standing around singing. And way off in the distance this car drives up. And again Bogdanovich is just holding, holding, holding, and it stops and he runs over and it's Tatum O'Neal. Just a great introduction; right away you're intrigued. What's going on? There are only three people there and there's this little kid. It's almost like: How much can I get away with not showing you or not telling you? I think that does a lot to make people intrigued and to want to continue watching.

So how did *Paper Moon* change your life?
DOCTER: I grew up liking *The Muppet Show*, cartoons like Warner Bros., and certainly the Disney films. Most people talk about *Star Wars* being this definitive moment. I saw *Star Wars*, but it didn't really have this huge effect. I like the more character-driven stuff, and *Paper Moon* brought that home to me in a way that I had not seen in live action, really focusing on the whole story just about characters. It was almost theatrical in the same way you might see a stage show because you're locked in a room. It's got to be about

characters, and yet it was so cinematic, a film that couldn't be done in any other medium. It just kind of blew my socks off.

Can you tell me what lessons you took from it? What lessons did you learn and adapt to *Monsters, Inc.*?

DOCTER: We went through the film and charted out relationships. In a weird way, it's almost a buddy film, as well. It actually had a lot of similarities to the Shirley Temple film *Little Miss Marker* where characters are metaphorically handcuffed together. For it to really work, you have this curmudgeonly guy who's got his own life, his own way of doing things, and then he's handcuffed with this kid. Story-wise, *Paper Moon* certainly did this really well—coming up with some social reason why he can't dump the kid or pawn her off on some relative. So I guess, long after your question, it was probably more story beats, if that makes sense. How the relationship progresses throughout the story. And this was probably more evident in earlier drafts because as it turned out, when you have a younger kid, that relationship is a little more of a one-way street. It's kind of like getting a cat or something. So that's kind of the way *Monsters, Inc.* turned out as the kid got younger.

There's this great line that kept coming up in pieces in 1973 and '74 when it was Oscar time for *Paper Moon*. Someone said, "You aren't a director until you directed children." I was wondering, how does that translate for voice-directing a child for animation? What are the specific challenges?

DOCTER: For us, we get off pretty easy. For *Monsters*, I initially thought, "Oh well, we'll stand her in front of the microphone, and I will say the line to her and she'll say it back." Well, she was two and a half, and she didn't want to do that at all. Basically what we wanted from her were real sounds, screams and yells, and giggles and things like that. She just started running around the room, and I thought, "Oh boy, this is going to be a disaster." Luckily one of the sound guys just brought in a boom mic and held it. We could play. So we had puppets, and we had quiet toys and candies and things like that. That's how we got the sound, by just goofing around, which is nothing that would be useful at all in a live action film.

Tatum O'Neal was older than two and a half, but even so, the amount of depth of performance that she's able to pull off is pretty astounding.

But it sounds like your directing bag of tricks is not that different because by most accounts, she hated filming this.
DOCTER: Oh, really?

Bogdanovich would bribe her: "I'll buy you shoes if you just get through this scene, I'll give you twenty dollars if you just get through this scene." On that level, she was really getting into the shyster spirit of the character.
DOCTER: Yeah that's true. It seems like, and to some degree this is true even of adult actors, but they're going along with you. Basically the whole thing about acting is kind of tricking either the actor or yourself (if you're acting) into experiencing these emotions that hopefully read as truthful.

With kids, especially, you have to be very clever about what you're making them do. They think they're doing this for one reason, but for the film it's actually giving what you need for the story.

Frank Marshall, the associate producer of *Paper Moon*, says Bogdanovich was "able to achieve a movie that is touching but not sentimental and funny but without using slapstick." As the viewer, how does it achieve that for you?
DOCTER: It was true to the characters. That's what I really admire about that film and the school of films we've be talking about too. It wasn't about gratuitous whacking people in the head with a two-by-four. It was funny because the moments were so truthful, and I recognized them as moments in my own life. Not literally, but in some relatable way. There are other films that do this, of course. I saw *The Station Agent*, which I think does the same thing. It's hilarious, but doesn't resort to slapstick or gags. It's about how characters react and the truthfulness of the characters.

I know having done a very minimal amount of improv in comedy classes as an actor, just to try to know more about how it goes on. They say the mistake that most people in comedy make is they try to be funny. Really the humor comes out when you're not trying to be funny, when you're trying to be truthful in the scene. And I think that's what's happening here.

On the commentary track for *Paper Moon*, Bogdanovich talks about advice he got from Howard Hawks that he applied to this film. It was something to the effect of, "Always cut on movement, so the audience won't notice." Do you have any sort of early advice that is still valuable to you?

DOCTER: After doing *Toy Story*, I got to know this wonderful guy named Joe Grant who did the story on *Dumbo*; he basically authored that and designed the Wicked Witch in *Snow White*. He had been working at Disney in the 1930s and was still working there just shy of his ninety-seventh birthday, when he passed away.

We would call each other almost every week and just talk about how things used to work, how things work today. He was very much a live-in-the-present kind of a guy. Whenever I would talk to him about *Monsters*, he would ask, "What are you giving the audience to take home?"

And I thought that was an interesting way of thinking about it—that the film shouldn't live just for that moment you are watching it. There's got to be some idea there, something that will stick with the audience. Something that they'll walk home thinking about and will pop in their heads the next week. That's what we're looking for, that films aren't just trifle and fluff. They have some deeper meaning and relationship to life.

One of the central questions in the film is whether Ryan O'Neal's character is, in fact, Addie's father. As an audience member, do you think he is her father?

DOCTER: I do, yeah. But I have no idea if that's intended or not.

Bogdanovich often talks about silent moments. He says, "It's those silent moments that often make stars. Those are the moments when the audience feels closest to the people, you're almost inside their heads." And as an animator, how does this translate? Are the rules exactly the same?

DOCTER: I'd say it's exactly the same. As we're starting out, young animators tend to think that the scene is the dialogue—that the dialogue is the meaning of the scene and we're illustrating that somehow. I've come to think of the dialogue as almost another appendage. It's what's coming out of the character's mouth, but it's maybe not really. In fact, most often in conversation, it's not really what you're thinking at all.

It might be as simple as when you come up and say, "Hey, how are you doing?" You're not asking literally, "How is your health?"

You're generally saying, "Hey, I'm your friend. Are you still my friend?" That's kind of the subtext of things. So there are these layers to things, and I think it's between the actual dialogue, as he pointed out, the space around them, that you really get to see inside the character's thoughts. And that was a lesson that we learned from the great Disney animators. They would always talk about what the audience wanted to see in the characters' thoughts, what's going inside their heads, not what they're saying. That's when it comes alive, when you can really see what's going on in there.

Why do you think *Paper Moon*—this a film made in the 1970s about the 1930s—still plays pretty modern? How do you think it achieves that?
DOCTER: To me, and this may be too obvious of an answer, it's because it's about relationships, which I don't think change from cavemen days to now. You get this very clear relationship dynamic between people, and it's infinitely entertaining and engaging. How many times do you go to the airport, and you're standing in line, and somebody starts talking or yelling? Some interaction is going on, and you can't take your eyes off of them? We're wired for that. I think, at the heart of it, that's what *Paper Moon* is about.

19

Atom Egoyan
Persona

In speaking to director Atom Egoyan, it's easy to become lost in interpretations of Ingmar Bergman's *Persona*. Even Egoyan admits it's impossible to decode everything in the film—which makes it so special for him.

Egoyan says, "It's not designed to be completely digested at a conscious level; it can't be. There are many sequences that may be taking place in the imagination. . . . That's what makes the film exciting. It both invites and resists interpretation. I think that there are certain ideas and themes in the film that are clearly at work, but the specific interpretation of a scene is left quite elusive."

Atom Egoyan, selected filmography:
Calendar (1993)
Exotica (1994)
The Sweet Hereafter (1997)
Ararat (2002)
Where the Truth Lies (2005)
Chloe (2009)

Persona
1966
Directed by Ingmar Bergman
Starring Bibi Andersson and Liv Ullmann

How would you describe *Persona* to someone who has never seen it?
EGOYAN: In some ways, it's the quintessential art movie in that it is, on first viewing, quite mystifying and yet, at some level, deeply seductive. It is both simple and impenetrable. And it's full of an unyielding sense of psychological complexity. It's one of the most astonishing films about transference ever made. It's probably the most self-referential work I can imagine.

How would you describe the basic plot, if we can even apply that word here?
EGOYAN: The plot is almost melodramatic. It's about a famous actress (played by Liv Ullmann), who loses her voice and falls into complete silence, and the nurse who is assigned to look after her (Bibi Andersson). The nurse finds that she has discovered an ideal listener in this silent actress. She begins to spill out the details of her life, and we understand that the dynamic between the two women begins to completely shift and blur, and eventually merge.

Tell me about your experience with the film. When did you first see it?
EGOYAN: I saw it at an extraordinary point in my life because I was raised on the west coast of Canada, and we did not have access to art movies at all. I was seeing a pretty steady stream of Hollywood fare. I was interested in theater as a kid, but I never really saw anything that would lead me to believe that film could be anything other than a very formulaic Hollywood product. And then, I stumbled upon *Persona* late one night on television; we had a French television station on the west coast. To be honest, I used to kind of troll that station for an occasional glimpse of nudity in movies. [*laughs*] I was fourteen at the time.

I was hooked on *Persona* from the first images: a projector being set off and the arc light coming to life and then a very fragmented sequence of very powerful images—Christ's hands being nailed into the cross and a strange puppet play. It was like nothing I'd ever seen. Finally, there was an image I remember identifying with: a young boy reading. He then turns around and faces the camera. The next shot was an unforgettable composition of him raising his hand over the projected image of his mother's face. I remember just being really moved by that, feeling that I was about to enter into an experience unlike anything I'd ever felt before. And certainly the film gave me that.

Here's where we get into interpretations, because a lot of reviews interpreted that character as the actress's son, when in fact, I think the actress's son is supposed to be younger, five years old. It gets into the meaning of symbols, especially in that whole montage. What was your first interpretation of that montage, if you even had one at that point?
EGOYAN: At that point, it seemed to be very fundamental. The film was using images that were iconographic. They were very portentous, inasmuch as they held a lot of meaning, which I couldn't even begin to analyze at that point.

Though, of course, the most enduring image was of the actual process of film being presented to you. And I don't know how relevant that would be to a contemporary viewer—the arc light being ignited, the film beginning to go through the gate, the shutter mechanism. That process made the idea of how I was watching the film and of the precarious nature of projection really clear. I think that notion of projection, obviously, works itself into the film in a number of ways. Not only the mechanical idea of projection, but also the psychological projection that happens, as well.

Because you are beginning inside the camera and working your way out.
EGOYAN: Sure. Now that being said, I wasn't really consciously aware of all of that at the time. I wasn't fully aware of what the mechanical process of filmmaking was. But I've always felt that when an image is made with a degree of clarity on the part of the filmmaker, it communicates its sense of urgency to the viewers, no matter what. Even if they don't understand exactly what it is they're seeing, they are aware of how invested that image is.

Part of that opening montage is an erect penis, which was cut from U.S. versions of the film. Susan Sontag wrote about it. Was that in the version that you saw?
EGOYAN: I don't remember, but I can't imagine it would have been. I don't think it was the European version because it would have left an impression on me.

It's been suggested, and we've sort of touched on it, that *Persona* is almost a pure reflexive film, about the audience's relationship with film—in fact the very film being watched. How did that feed into your experience?

EGOYAN: We were very involved in the construction of the film. It really tests our tolerances and our curiosity and sense of exploration as a viewer.

I think the film is also about the degree to which we tolerate the indulgences of other people. I remember feeling exasperated by Ullmann's silence and really identifying with the nurse. And in the scene with the boiling hot water—where she's about to scald Liv Ullmann, and Liv Ullmann cries out— I was there with the nurse.

More than the actual plot, you experience the film through the way the human face is used. The ability to hold on a face speaks to an absolute trust. There's an incredibly long shot of Liv Ullmann as she's listening to the Bach, which then uses a very slow, physical fade to black. It wasn't an optical effect; I believe they actually began to change the light. All of that was really impressive to me at the time. The sculptural sense of the film, and maybe the idea that the screen becomes an installation—Bergman's insistence on the screen as a sculptural device.

At age fourteen, did you have movie director aspirations?

EGOYAN: No, not at all. I was really more involved in theater. I think *Persona* was one of the first films that struck me as providing a theatrical experience, in as much as my imagination was working, and was as active as it would be in live theater.

And of course, the title of this book is *The Film That Changed My Life*— so how did this film do that for you?

EGOYAN: It gave me an incredible respect for the medium and its possibilities. To me, *Persona* marries a pure form and a very profound vision with absolute conviction. It's very inspiring. I felt that it was able to open a door that wasn't there before. At the time, there was the term Bergmanesque, and everyone knew what it meant. They would parody it and dismiss it in a way. Now, though, I notice there's a whole, younger, newer generation of filmmakers that doesn't know this incredible body of work. Maybe that says something about the way culture works.

After *Persona*, I began to watch the other films, films like *The Silence*, *Through a Glass Darkly*, and *Hour of the Wolf*. This whole, incredible body of work was very important to me.

I think film allows for tremendous exploration. It's made me an artist in a completely uncompromised way, a person who tests the limits of the form.

It's been said that the movie is not only a deconstruction of itself, but also Bergman's myth—that he had become sort of this stagey, mythic director. The *New York Times* reviewer wrote that it added to his myth and was "a film about loneliness." In breaking form, he seems to build his ivory tower as an artist. What do you think his intentions were?

EGOYAN: The whole notion of indulgence is very interesting. It comes up a lot in the movie—how indulgent the actress seems to be. At one point, the director of the hospital calls her game and says that it must be very nice to be an actress. But this is a performance as well and as an audience member, you also have control over this. You become really exasperated with her, and yet it's very compelling. In a way, maybe Bergman was reflecting on that fact.

The film is wildly pretentious at moments because it's presenting these images without any clarification. Like I said, there are really strong and almost laughably iconographic moments—like the crucifixion—that really have no rational explanation, yet they sweep you away with their power. The same is true of the atonal, fractured score at the beginning—the whole beginning is an affront, and yet it does have this cumulative sense of purpose.

I think the role of storytellers and the language they use is one of the latent themes of the film. With the incredible erotic monologue, the orgy that is described at a certain point—you're so aware of the process of the story being told. A lot of shots are of Liv Ullmann listening. It made me really aware of the device of the listener, the person who is encountering the story. A focus on that person is as compelling as the person who is actually speaking.

There's a great passage in the Susan Sontag piece. She writes about a reading of the film as a "parable of the predatory demonic energies of the artist, incorrigibly scavenging life for raw material." It's like that

**old quote about storytellers constantly selling their friends out. Did
that occur to you in later viewings? Did that theme make itself apparent to you at any time?**

EGOYAN: Yes. It's interesting, at a certain point, in her silence, Liv Ullmann's
character is aware that's she's drawing this history out of this other character, and there's this bemused smile that she has when she's listening to these
stories that's really unforgettable.

But I think that Bibi Andersson is really complicit in this process as well.
She's very aware and makes mention of the fact that the language she uses
may not be as developed as the theatrical language that Liv Ullmann exploits
to create her characters on stage, and yet she feels compelled to continue. I
think when someone is given such an audience, the question of who sets the
limits is really provocative. I think the responsibility is with the person who
feels she has found someone to whom she can entrust her story. She doesn't
then know what happens to that story.

Notions of indulgence come up again in the images that Liv Ullmann
sees on the television, and that was very impressive to me. It was the first
time I had ever seen anyone on-screen watching really horrifying apocalyptic . . . the image of the burning Buddhist priest, or of kids in the Warsaw
ghetto. What right does the dramatist have to use those images for texture?
Is it an exploitation of those images? And to what extent is the use of those
images an indulgence he gives himself as an artist? Does he have the right to
use those images vampiristically? I think that Bergman put it all in the soup.
That left an impression on me as well.

**Let's bounce back to the scene with Bibi Andersson talking about sex on
the beach. It's been said that without nudity or even physical closeness
between the women, with language Bergman creates one of the most
erotic scenes in film history. I was wondering for you, as a fourteen-
year-old boy, did it have that sort of erotic charge for you?**

EGOYAN: Yes, it was incredibly charged. And of course the scene right after
that in the bedroom. Liv Ullmann sort of appears behind her, and I'll never
forget the sound of the foghorn, and this incredibly, smoky, misty setting.

The fact that the monologue itself relies on the power to imagine something evoked by words actually makes the intention to tell it as erotic as

the scene it describes. Is she trying to coax an intimacy with Liv Ullmann? Why is she telling that story ultimately? I remember it seemed to be so constructed, and yet so overwhelming.

Now, this occurred to me after seeing your film *Exotica*. Did *Persona* help inform any notion of how one creates a sense of sexuality, or perhaps even sensuality on celluloid? What are the difficulties in doing that?

EGOYAN: I think so much eroticism is based on this need to find a connection. When I'm developing a relationship between characters, I think it's really exciting to consider what they're negotiating and establishing through their actual vocabulary. It's exciting to be involved in that mystery, trying to understand why someone is expressing a story and why he or she is acting a certain way. As the customs officer says at the beginning of *Exotica*, there's a wealth of possible reasons that could lead a person to that point. We are never more alive, I think, as when we are trying to ascertain our relationship to something which is completely mysterious to us.

This idea of people in grief losing themselves in another narrative—a narrative that they can construct and believe they have some control over—is also fascinating given that the world around them is swirling out of control. You're aware of a strong sense of need and an attempt to discover sensuality through a series of ritualized activities; yet, the form and intention eludes both the viewer and the person who is trying piece it together.

Do you have any insight about how to create an erotic space on film? Love scenes are hard enough, but to create something that is sexual and, at the same time, emotionally charged is even tougher.

EGOYAN: I think what Bergman teaches us in *Persona* is this idea of withholding: withholding information and withholding the expected reactions. As I said before, I think one of the most sensual moments in film is when that story is retold and you then apply the reaction that you've already seen from Liv Ullmann in the first manifestation of the story. The fact that you need to engage your own imagination in such an extreme way is just very exciting. Besides the obvious eroticism of the explained orgy, the fact is we're not seeing it—but rather the sensuality of the person who is listening.

That had a huge influence on a film like *Exotica* with the role of the person who is trying to navigate through someone else's mythology. It's also humorous as well. I think that when you think you have something figured out, and it's not at all what you expect—like the scene where Bruce Greenwood is driving a young Sarah Polley home after the club, you assume that Sarah Polley is a young prostitute. He's trying to pay her, and the pieces all connect in a certain way. And then later, you understand that she's a babysitter. All these things begin to compound as your mind is racing with possibility. To me, one of the most erotic experiences is when your mind is just racing with possibility: What might be happening? What could be happening? What's about to happen?

I remember as a fourteen-year-old kid, after the very erotic story, I expected release, I expected it to lead to something. In the next sequence, Bibi Andersson is in the bed, and Liv Ullmann mysteriously appears from another room, approaches the bed, and then turns away. Bibi Andersson then gets up, and there's this very famous shot of the two women's heads where Liv Ullmann caresses Bibi Andersson. I found that incredibly charged.

This is where Bergman bleeds himself into the film a little bit. He was just finishing his relationship with Bibi Andersson, and this was Liv Ullmann's first film with him.
EGOYAN: See, I didn't know that. That's fascinating.

Knowing that, does that add anything to the film for you?
EGOYAN: Yes, I think so. But, again, I'm thankful I didn't know that, in a way. It's fascinating, though, this idea of transference from one relationship to another, and that the actresses would both be involved. Does Bergman talk about that himself?

In his book *The Magic Lantern* he talks about the filming, because Bibi Andersson had been with him in *Wild Strawberries*. I think it was during that film that they were finding the end of their romance. But yes, *Persona* is the very time he becomes involved with Liv. It seems to telegraph his life, because *Persona* was filmed on Faro, the island he ends up retreating to for thirty years, and in fact lived on

with Liv Ullmann. His wish, or at least his fantasy for this actress in *Persona*, he ends up living. Do you think that's an impulse that a lot of artists share? That desire to be isolated? Brando had his own island as well.

EGOYAN: Yeah. I think that it's a result of feeling completely overwhelmed by other pressures and social responsibilities. If at that point the mythology of Bergman was such that he felt it was something he had to retreat from—I can understand that impulse.

I've never really entertained the idea of complete isolation. But I've never been exposed to the degree of scrutiny and speculation that those artists have. I need to be connected to the world. I was raised on an island, Vancouver Island, so I don't really have much of an island fantasy.

Especially if you were born on one. If you were born on the frontier, you don't go back to the frontier.

EGOYAN: [*laughing*] Right! But the fantasy that I certainly find compelling is having a small artisanal crew and a group of actors who are really committed. Also, the ability to dictate the means of your own production. That was made possible to Bergman because of the state funding of the Swedish film industry. That type of film is the product of a certain kind of support, and that was very inspiring to me. Up until recently, in Canada, we had some semblance of that, but I think that's changing as well.

Critic Andrew Sarris called Bergman "essentially an artist in an ivory tower in an isolated country." Do you think that's a fair statement? Or is he fundamentally misunderstanding something?

EGOYAN: I do think that's the way those films were made. They were not subject to the types of criteria held for most films. And I think that's great. It means that Bergman was able to act very impulsively. He was able to have a very intimate relationship to the form, and he was able to avoid other pressures or influences, which would've compromised what he was doing.

In the film industry, whether or not one is granted that freedom is a real issue. With the exception of experimental filmmakers who are working on their own, you're usually working in the dramatic form, and there are all sorts of people you need to convince and seduce to get your product made.

Bergman was working outside that for the longest period of time. He was a state-funded artist.

I think we tend to forget. When we look at an Andrei Tarkovsky movie, for all the huge difficulties he had in making those films, once they were approved he had a lot of freedom. And he had time. He could schedule the film's production over a much longer period of time than he would have been given in the West. Many of the films that I most adore are the product of a state-funded system.

Such as?

EGOYAN: I would say the films of Michelangelo Antonioni, all those Italian masters, and a lot of the Eastern films, although I suppose those productions were much more industrialized. I suppose the Japanese tradition was also very industrialized if you look at stories of the film studios there. I'm even thinking of the films of Robert Bresson. They were made with very small crews of people who were able to focus on their work without tremendous schedule pressures.

How did your interpretation of *Persona* change when you became a mature adult?

EGOYAN: I became much more aware of the actual grammar that it was reinventing. I sort of began to make images myself; I began to be able to dissect it and to see what the innovations were—what Bergman was actually reacting against and how he was able to change the form.

Liv Ullmann's story of having a child, because it was part of her artistic experience, was really horrifying to me. And maybe that goes back to what you were saying before, about the notion of artistic indulgence and the people who become the victims of it.

I also think it just taught me so much about the admiration I had for the performers, and their ability to contain and to completely trust their director. Interestingly, though, I've always felt that Bibi Andersson gave a most amazing performance, and yet we give a lot of attention to Liv Ullmann. But as I become more involved with filmmaking and film practice, I've really come to appreciate the specific innovations of the movie.

Elia Kazan said the adventure of the contemporary cinema is the adventure of film language, and perhaps that's indicative of an audience that has becoming more media-savvy. Do we lose anything by knowing how the magic works? What effect does that have?

EGOYAN: I think we've seen a huge change in film culture, in that there was something very mysterious about the process of projection itself. There was a magic behind it, and the film industry certainly did a tremendous amount to sustain the distance between the images we can make ourselves domestically and the images that we see on-screen. I think, though, those lines have become blurred and that perhaps the power of a certain type of film aesthetic has become diminished as a result.

I found it really interesting with the Toronto International Film Festival last fall—there were some films that I found really exciting, but the audience responses were so hostile in a way that they wouldn't have been ten years ago. For instance, I think the way people now respond to a long shot indicates that the viewer has become much more savvy about how images are made. And certain types of films don't have the same type of visual power they used to. I guess it's natural, though it's unfortunate.

I was thinking about that with *Persona*. I don't quite know how a fourteen-year-old watching that movie today would respond. I have no idea what it would be like to watch *L'avventura* now. I don't know if the mystery of those movies has the same effect on a contemporary audience. What do you think?

We talked about what has been lost. Do you think, in becoming more educated in film, we've gained anything as a culture?

EGOYAN: We're able to absorb images much more quickly and clearly. And I also think that, unfortunately, we're able to dismiss images much more easily. I think a sequence like the one I mentioned before of Ullmann watching the Buddhist priest burning—the power of having an image like that transported into a domestic setting is something that is not rarified anymore; it's not surreal to us. I don't think you can create a sequence like that in a contemporary film and expect it to have any significance.

I do think that there is a lot to be said about the effects of technology on the filmmaking process. I think Hollywood worked to ensure that people would always find that images and the making of images were something outside of their day-to-day lives, and that's obviously been completely reversed.

The unfortunate side is that not only is the image-making process completely available to us, but the marketing and the industry have also become very commonplace. People often discuss the success of a movie, and there's the whole idea of involving the viewer. That's the other crucial thing: Many of the films that I've adored would not be able to survive a preview process. There's absolutely no way.

This idea of clarity and that people should know at all times what's going on is obviously very attractive from a marketing perspective, but I think it would completely eviscerate the power of what these movies are about. Our conversation is a great example. We are still discussing what the opening sequence in *Persona* might mean and the wealth of possibilities that can be read into this piece of work. I believe that's why it endures.

Marc Gervais wrote that *Persona* subverts the notion that the nature of art is to communicate, and one of the reasons that it remains such a mainstay in film history, in film courses, is that no interpretation seems capable of including everything. As you look at it now, is it a complete picture in your head, or are there holes in your own interpretation of it?
EGOYAN: It's not designed to be completely digested at a conscious level; it can't be. There are many sequences that may be taking place in the imagination or in the possible imagination of one of the characters. That's going to change from one reading to another. That's what makes the film exciting.

It both invites and resists interpretation. I think that there are certain ideas and themes in the film that are clearly at work, but the specific interpretation of a scene is left quite elusive. For example, there's the question of who the boy is at the beginning; it could be any one of a number of characters, and, most compelling, perhaps it is the artist himself.

The way the child is described later on as being deformed and being repellent to the mother in a certain way would seem to resist the idea that he's the same character we saw at the beginning. Though we also understand that tense characters are fluid, that the actual visual identification of the characters is also up for grabs, and that it's also shifting at all times. It's part of the construction of the movie, which is part of the experience of it.

It's a supremely self-conscious piece of work. When I was watching it for the first time, I'd never felt that in a movie. I've never felt as conscious of the fact that I was watching something and having to make an assessment of it, and that my relationship was shifting it all the time. You were talking before about what is seductive. That to me is really erotic, that all my senses are engaged in trying to come to terms with something, trying to fix it in a certain place.

20

Gurinder Chadha
Purab aur Pachhim and
It's a Wonderful Life

Gurinder Chadha was the first director who couldn't just pick—in fact, refused to pick—the single film that changed her life. "I don't think that I can split them up. It's like children, isn't it?" she says. "I'd be splitting up the family because they both represent different sides of me, you see."

Gurinder Chadha, selected filmography:
Bhaji on the Beach (1993)
What's Cooking? (2000)
Bend It Like Beckham (2002)
Bride & Prejudice (2004)
Angus, Thongs and Perfect Snogging (2008)
It's a Wonderful Afterlife (2010)

Purab aur Pachhim (a.k.a. **Purab aur Paschim**)
1970
Directed by Manoj Kumar
Starring Ashok Kumar, Saira Banu, Manoj Kumar, Nirupa Roy, and more

It's a Wonderful Life
1946
Directed by Frank Capra
Starring James Stewart, Donna Reed, Lionel Barrymore, Thomas Mitchell, Henry Travers, and more

How would you describe *Purab aur Pachhim* to someone who has never seen it?

CHADHA: No one would have heard of it, but it's a fantastic Bollywood film and it means "East or West." I often put that in my top ten movies. It was made in 1970 by a man called Manoj Kumar, and it's one of the most wonderful Bollywood movies ever.

It's about an Indian who comes to England to study. When he gets to England, he's staying with an old friend of his dad's; they were both freedom fighters against the British. He's got a son and a daughter who have completely turned Westerners—they have very bad Western ways. Subtlety is not a big thing in this movie [*laughs*], like most Bollywood. The girl walks around with a glass of whiskey in one hand and cigarette in the other. And the guy is into flower power; he's got long hair and sort of hippie clothes. So, it's sort of on that level.

It's a magical mystery tour of the East and West from a very kitsch, '70s, resolutely patriotic Indian filmmaker. It's a complete joyride in terms of music, entertainment, cinema, and cultural politics.

But it was the first film, the first sort of Manoj Kumar film that I saw. And it's actually much cleverer than it sounds. Yes, on the face of it, it's very brash and very silly. There are sequences on the River Thames when they're all doing the Twist, and it's cheesy and over the top. But underneath it, there's a wonderful kind of yearning quality about what is culture and the perils of living in the West and the dangers of what could happen.

Do you remember when you first saw it, who you were with?

CHADHA: Yeah, I was a child, a small child, and I saw it in an Indian cinema in London. It would have been with my family. I was always watching Bollywood films, but this was the first one that showed England where we lived, as opposed to a set in India, so that's what made it striking.

Do you remember how your family talked about it when they saw it?

CHADHA: I think everyone in England was very entertained by it because it was so far from the truth. It was such an exaggerated version of our lives in England. As a young girl with two long plaits, with a mother who refused to let us cut our hair or anything, this girl was supposed to be like us, with long blond hair and cigarettes and miniskirts. We were like, "God, that would be great! But we're not allowed to be like that." I think it was the incongruity of what he perceived people like us growing up in Britain to be like, and what we were actually like. That incongruity—that was bizarre.

Was there a scene or sequence that you remember loving particularly?
CHADHA: As far as the characterization of the young woman: what she wore. And, actually, in my first film, *Bhaji on the Beach*, I referenced this film. In *Bhaji on the Beach* there's a character called Asha who had a video store. She kept going off into these fantasies and imagining what was going on around her, but she would experience those fantasies through Bollywood movies.

I would take elements of the story and make use of a Bollywood vignette. And one of them referenced *Purab aur Pachhim*. It's when she realizes that one of the young girls is pregnant and she's got a black boyfriend, and she's like, "Oh my God, this is what England is doing to our kids."

In my film, she walks into a temple in a miniskirt and a long blond wig, with a glass of whiskey in one hand and cigarette in the other. That was a complete reference to the film.

Did you ever work with or run into anybody associated with the film?
CHADHA: Well, as it happens, I was in India just recently for the release of *Bend It Like Beckham*, and I was on a TV program. They were asking me about films I had loved growing up, and I talked about this film.

Afterwards, I got a call saying the director, Mr. Manoj Kumar, wants to talk to you. The director of the film tracked me down and basically he was so thrilled that I talked about him in my interview, about influencing me, that he invited me over for dinner, for tea. And so I went over and saw him. He's an old man now, but it was a complete thrill for me. He's also the star of the film, so he's a very dashing man. And here he was this old man, in bed with dyed hair. He was great, completely focused and to the point, and still wanted to make very patriotic films. He was operating at a time when India was desperately trying to find an identity for itself after so many years under British rule and, prior to that, Muslim rule under the mogul.

So he used to make films that were all about rekindling and promoting a sense of Indianness, of Indian pride. And he loved the fact that he thought

I was doing something similar, albeit in a British context, that I had been touched by him. It was a very moving few hours I had spent with him.

What was the film's reception like in Britain?
CHADHA: Well, it was a huge hit in the Indian community. It's a gem, but, of course, someone who knows nothing about Indian film wouldn't know about it. That's why it's important for people like me to talk about it, because otherwise people would think the Indian cinema starts and stops with Satyajit Ray.

I was always taken to very populist films by my parents. And so, for me, it's about promoting this sort of work that no one knows about, but definitely was an influence on me, as was Ken Loach and all his early films of the '60s.

The actual film that I saw on a screen when I was young, and I thought, "Wow, I want to make movies like this!" was *My Beautiful Laundrette* by Stephen Frears, because that was a portrayal of my community in Britain in a very exciting way that I've never seen before. It tackled homosexuality and right-wing Indians, and it was just something different. Really political for that time—I just thought it was the most exciting movie on the screen, in terms of race.

Where I grew up, we had three cinemas that showed Indian films. But then down the road, there was an English cinema where I saw *The Wizard of Oz* and *The Sound of Music*, all those kind of movies. And on television every Saturday and Sunday afternoon, I used to love watching all the old British films by Ken Loach and people like that, where you'd get working-class girls getting pregnant and going for abortions, and all these kinds of really gritty social-realist movies. And, of course, the old evening comedies. I loved the old Alastair Sim, Margaret Rutherford comedies, so I had a very mixed diet of films when I was growing up.

Does your perception of that film change with subsequent viewings?
CHADHA: It gets better and better. Because as a filmmaker, I came to appreciate a bit more of how clever he was in terms of his message. If you look at it, it could be a very propagandist sort of message. It could have been very two-dimensional; he could have shown the West is bad and the East is good, but he did a very good job of making it human, making the characters human, making it work in a very human way.

My films are from a much more celebratory view to show that the nightmare Manoj Kumar saw was going to happen—actually didn't happen. It's like the opposite, you know. It's a film that has really informed me, and it's an absolute gem. If I had the power, I would take it and release it myself.

Why do you think it's stuck with you for so long?
CHADHA: It hasn't informed everything I've done. If anything, I would say *It's a Wonderful Life* is more like that. I think of it as something I watched at that time that had an impact because it was portraying people like me on the screen.

That's a good segue into *It's a Wonderful Life*. Why did you choose this film?
CHADHA: *It's a Wonderful Life* is one of the best films ever made. I can sit and watch it over and over. The other one is *Tootsie*. There's something about *It's a Wonderful Life*. It doesn't matter what generation, who you are, when it was made, what country you're from, whichever culture—it's so, so wonderful.

Frank Capra's *It's a Wonderful Life* is the film I come back to time and time again, which I think informs me and my work, if I could ever achieve an iota of what this film is really about.

Some context here for the three people on earth who haven't seen the film: James Stewart plays a man who wishes he was never born, then is taken around by an angel to see how the world would be without him.
CHADHA: It's about the human spirit and about what being alive means, what life is about. It's corny, but it's a masterpiece of cinema. It's a masterpiece of feel-good cinema. It's more than that. Ultimately, I think cinema is about exploring the human spirit. Capra just somehow manages to capture the essence of human life without making it schmaltzy. Try, if you can. You can watch that film, and you know what is going on. But I defy anyone who is able to watch that film, and the end when the table is cleared, and everyone is coming in with the money—I just cannot believe there isn't anyone with wet eyes at that point, or a big lump in their throat. I've seen it millions of times, and I'm just in floods of tears at that point.

This was Stewart's first film after World War II. A lot of critics and scholars have said that you can see him tortured by that experience, that he was a different actor after the war. Do you think any of that translated to the film?

CHADHA: Absolutely. I feel it. If you've been to war, you've seen people killing each other. War is about death and destruction. That's why it's even more of a remarkable movie, because it's about the human spirit and the willingness to survive. I think that it's actually what makes his performance so wonderful. Even in his face, that moment when all the money is being put on the table, holding that look of incredulousness without at any point it going schmaltzy. That's an incredible piece of acting. It's just really, really genuine.

The reason it's so powerful is: it makes you think. I lost my father a few years ago, and it had a profound effect on me. *Bend It Like Beckham* is dedicated to my dad. For me, it's a film about life and death. For me, it brings up grief and that whole side about losing someone. But it's also about an affirmation about what their life was about, and the pleasure that they gave in their life. For me, it's a great film when you're happy, when you're sad, when you're grieving. You can watch it any time, and it puts your feet back on the ground and reaffirms what it means to be human.

You mentioned that it doesn't matter which culture you're from to appreciate the film. Why do you think it reaches across cultures so well?

CHADHA: It's such a universal story, like the ordinary man against the corporation. It's about the human spirit versus dehumanizing forces.

What other scenes stick with you?

CHADHA: The whole thing about losing his hearing in one ear; I just think that's just so beautiful. That little bit of vulnerability, that constant reminder of his goodness to his brother. I think it was Jimmy Stewart's performance. I thought he was wonderful. I think that moment where he's trying not to fall in love with his wife, and he just says, "No, no, I don't want to do this, I've got so many things to do," and then he just succumbs. There are loads of moments in that film.

I think that one at the end, when everyone is coming with the money—there's twenty-five thousand dollars and he only needed eight thousand.

Even now, as I'm talking about it, I'm welling up. It's such a beautifully told story about a man making choices.

But the film flopped badly when it came out. No one went to see it. It only became a classic later on TV. Why do you think that is?
CHADHA: Well, I think it was after the war, and I think people were quite cynical. Many people had lost loved ones, and the world was being mapped out, and no one knew quite what was going on. There was a lot of insecurity and suspicion and the Cold War. People were all, "It's a cruel world."

I think we have better communication now. I was thinking the last time I was watching it, this film, if it had come out a few years later, it would have been totally massacred during the McCarthyism period. So it was a tough time when it came out, but I'm just truly grateful that I got to see it as an Indian girl in England, and it touched me.

Actually, here's a little story: When I was sitting with Manoj Kumar in his flat in Bombay, we were talking about how much I loved his film. He said that he was at a film festival in Delhi, and he ended up spending the night with Frank Capra, who loved *Purab aur Pachim*. Frank Capra actually spent all night talking about it. He actually wrote to Kumar telling him what a wonderful night he had, watching his film and talking to him.

And you talk about this film informing your work the most. Can you give me examples of how this film has impacted your work?
CHADHA: Well, *Bend It Like Beckham* has been sold to and seen in most countries around the world and appeals to people of all different ages and backgrounds and cultures. It's because it's a very human story about someone defying the odds and doing something they really want to do, but it's told in a very simple way in which you are hopefully emotionally involved with the characters. You understand the family's dilemma. You understand the parents, you understand the girl—you understand everyone's point of view. She's yearning, yearning to do something different. And I think both films have that sense of being universal, but I would never in a million years put myself on par with Capra's wonderful movie. I'm down below somewhere, trying to get up there.

21

Richard Linklater
Raging Bull

Linklater's career, spanning two decades, has alternated between art house fare (*Slacker, Waking Life*) and mainstream movies like *School of Rock* and his *Bad News Bears* remake.

It might be appropriate then, that the movie that changed his life straddles both worlds: Martin Scorsese and Robert De Niro's boxing masterpiece *Raging Bull*, often cited as the best film of the 1980s (even though it was released in 1980).

"At that point I was an unformed artist. At that moment, something was simmering in me, but *Raging Bull* brought it to a boil," says Linklater, paraphrasing Walt Whitman's praise of Ralph Waldo Emerson.

Richard Linklater, selected filmography:
Slacker (1991)
Dazed and Confused (1993)
Before Sunrise (1995)
SubUrbia (1996)
The Newton Boys (1998)
Waking Life (2001)
Tape (2001)
School of Rock (2003)
Before Sunset (2004)
Bad News Bears (2005)
Fast Food Nation (2006)
A Scanner Darkly (2006)
Me and Orson Welles (2008)

Raging Bull
1980
Directed by Martin Scorsese
Starring Robert De Niro, Cathy Moriarty, and Joe Pesci

How would you describe *Raging Bull* to someone who has never seen it?
LINKLATER: On the surface, it looks like a sports biopic. When it came out, that's what I thought it was. You get into it, and you realize it's this deep psychological portrait of this troubled, not-so-happy guy and how boxing is really a metaphor for his life. On top of it all, it's this deadly accurate period piece.

Under what circumstances did you see it?
LINKLATER: I remember watching the movie, and I was not a big movie person at this time. I was a writer. But living in East Texas, I had seen just the popular movies. I was more interested in the theater. I was twenty. I was an athlete, a baseball player. More than anything at that time, I really related to Jake. I was an athlete at the time and I agreed with him, even though most people see it and go, "OK, he's crazy. He's overly paranoid and he's suspicious, and he's out of his mind."

I saw very clearly that his wife was cheating. I thought he was correct in a lot of his assumptions, which seems almost embarrassing to say now.

It's a wild guy's view of the world. He was inarticulate. It was all feelings. He was this unleashed id. I was an athlete. That's no small connection. I felt the absolute dedication and focus you have to have to the detriment of everything in your life: normal relations, women in your life. For anybody to be at that level, you have to have made incredible sacrifices.

What other effects did it have?
LINKLATER: This film pulled me in so dark and deep. It was the boldness of the movie. In the era of feel-good movies, touchy feely stuff was all over the place, and man, this movie was unafraid. It was so brave to depict such a flawed, unlikable, scary guy.

There's a moment in the film where he's had a big fight with his brother Joey (Joe Pesci). Joey's sitting at home watching Jake take a beating from

Sugar Ray Robinson on TV. There's an ad, I believe it's a Pabst Blue Ribbon ad, but it's a transparency on the screen, and the ad flips down, but you can see a hand. It looks like it's been x-rayed. It's the slightest detail, a little bitty subtle mistake that probably happened on live television in that era, the '50s, but I thought, "Oh my God!" It sent a shiver up my spine. At that point, I was so enthralled.

How did it change your life?
LINKLATER: It made me see movies as a potential outlet for what I was thinking about and hoping to express. At that point I was an unformed artist. At that moment, something was simmering in me, but *Raging Bull* brought it to a boil.

I was on a college campus at the time, and I started thinking, well, gosh, movies are an outlet. It got me looking at a book on the history of movies. Every week, an English teacher would, in this little East Texas college, show a movie, and anybody could show up to watch the movie on a little monitor and would sit and talk about it after. Sounds like no big deal, but I would go to these things and sit and hear people talking about movies, and it was like throwing raw meat to starving beasts. I totally shifted to movies over the next six months, and I started reading everything I could. I still couldn't see that many movies. A little more than a half-year later, I was living in Houston where they had colleges showing these movies, and then I was really addicted.

That was the only film I had ever seen by Scorsese. I saw his stuff out of order. *Martin Scorsese: The First Decade*, the Mary Pat Kelly book, I read that very intently, and it talked about how he worked with actors and helped with loose, structured improv. I hadn't looked at that book in years, and I said, "Shit, that must have really left an impression on me," 'cause that's how I approached working with actors.

Scorsese wanted to direct what he called a "kamikaze way" of making pictures, pouring everything in and then forgetting about it.
LINKLATER: I do understand that—make every film like it's your last. He was coming off of financial failure and also, unfortunately, a critical failure, although *New York, New York*'s truly a great movie.

I've been in this position myself now, where you make a film you feel happy with and you realize no one's with you. Critics aren't with you, audiences aren't with you, the studio that made the film with you is not with you. I was in a similar position after *The Newton Boys*. You put everything you have into a movie. At that point you're tempted to make a commercial film, to get back into good graces, but it gave me this perverse desire to make a noncommercial film that you really don't give two shits what anybody thinks. That's really empowering yourself. You can come off a failure and not go back pandering, but actually go back further into your failure. I'm sure when they made *Raging Bull*, they had to have thought, "Oh, if this works it could be *Rocky*."

Scorsese thought this was going to be his failing, that he "would spend the next decade living in New York and Rome and making documentaries and films about saints."
LINKLATER: All filmmakers of his generation and all generations since have this specter of Orson Welles taking over everybody. He's the true Christ. If you think of Welles and *Citizen Kane*, he sacrificed for everyone, but you could be sacrificed, too. Your genius could go thwarted.

Scorsese said that the film was ultimately about a guy attaining something and losing everything and then redeeming himself spiritually. There's this undercurrent of finding redemption through pain.
LINKLATER: I'm not Catholic, but I could see that. Some of this stuff is hard to watch, but that's a total Scorsese theme. I've heard Paul Schrader say Jake La Motta wasn't redeemed; he was the same lug he was at the end that he was at the beginning. That makes me laugh. That's fine, and they're both right.

Even though he's in a slightly better place, he's dressed a little better. He bottoms out at that one place before he goes to jail. He's still got a long way to go, probably, in his life. Who knows what his relation is going to be with his kids? I would think that would be a big thing, but you gotta hand it to the movie not cheesing it out.

You feel like some of these bridges may be burned permanently, but at least you see him reaching at least a little bit. I see the slightest flicker of self, some kind of self, some kind of redemption in his mind.

One of the things that Scorsese said about the film was that he wanted to "take all the unsynthetic things from myself and throw them up on the screen."
LINKLATER: What about the difficulties of having what he called a loathsome protagonist? I don't think we're challenged enough with loathsome or questionable lead characters. Let's face it, it's like this dark theme, but it's funny as shit. That's what I truly appreciate and what redeems it on the entertainment value. *Raging Bull*, just like all Scorsese movies, is actually, it's very entertaining. It's funny. It's got a lot of these not-so-great heroic characters, or they are heroic in their own way, in their own mind.

La Motta himself said he took punishment in the ring as a penance of sorts because he believed that he had killed a mugging victim. How do you explain La Motta's masochism in the film?
LINKLATER: I took it as a lot of false pride, that whole thing about not hitting the canvas to take an extreme beating. It was weird because I'm not like that. Most people aren't. Let's face it—we all do things not in our best interests now and then, but in sports and boxing in particular, you can get your ass kicked by not performing well and someone beating you. In boxing, to lose is to get beaten, to get bloody but not to fall down. The ultimate zero-sum sports game is to take this incredible beating.

There are a lot of people in pain. An athlete is someone who willingly accepted the trade-off, that to be good, to be at the level you can reach, you're going have to push yourself to a place where your body is tested to the limit, where you might give out. A coach will scream at you, "No pain, no gain!" But it's true.

Why do you think we as a culture tend to romanticize the figure of the boxer, whether that's Rocky or in a song by Simon and Garfunkel?
LINKLATER: It's the modern gladiator sacrifice to all of us, someone who will go out there and suffer the blows, take the shots for all of us. Boxers get so many punches to the head. Everybody knows that that's unhealthy. They get their trade-off, their moment of glory. It's a weird pact they've made with the culture.

To see someone self-destruct, the moment where he's beating his belt to get some jewels out of it. It's the saddest self-loathing act you can imagine. It's unbelievable. It's stupid, and yet he can't help himself. It's painful to watch.

De Niro got an Oscar for his performance. He employed Jake La Motta as his personal trainer for the film, and he knocked out his teeth. De Niro famously gained sixty pounds for the role.
LINKLATER: He looked the part. Just in his looks, when he's in the nightclub performing, he's so sad. That's clearly one of the great performances, but it's such a great cast. Everybody—De Niro, obviously, but Joe Pesci is so perfect. Cathy Moriarty and Frank Vincent as Salvy, all those Mafiosi-type guys hanging around. They all seem so perfect.

It's hilarious, that milieu. Everything's so real you could feel it. I'd never been to New York, I didn't know any of that, but one of my boyhood friends' dad was this Italian guy from the Bronx, and he raved about the movie, saying, "Yep, that's exactly how it was."

Everything except the fight scene is pretty straight-up. Every angle, everything's beautifully, eloquently done. It's an ingeniously, perfectly edited movie, and not the fight sequences. I'm talking the rest of the movie, the way the first wife disappears. I thought it was bold that they didn't have to tell you everything; you could fill in some gaps. It pounds you. It didn't condescend at all to you on a narrative level. The first wife, she's gone; he's on to Vickie. You didn't have to see the scene that people would think was missing. We don't have to have that scene of her moving out. We know what happened; let's get on with the story.

The fighting stuff was so expressionistic. I remember Quentin Tarantino even said that. I asked him once. After *Pulp Fiction*, we were riding around and I said, "Did you ever want to show some of the fight when Bruce Willis kills that guy in the ring?" And he went, "How could you shoot a boxing scene after *Raging Bull*?" He's not even going to get in that ring. Why would you?

One of the things in this film that creates the tension is the traditional vow of celibacy before the fight.

LINKLATER: Jake got the best depiction of that mentality in athletes. It's the same as a crew cut and high-top black shoes for football players. Military, by definition, means no sex unless you're gay.

I remember this movie was on my offshore oil rig, and all these guys were sitting around and they hadn't seen it. He's got the girl in the room and then half the room empties. They'd been denied their sex scene.

How has your perception changed with subsequent viewings?

LINKLATER: I see Jake La Motta in different ways. I was, at the time, so identified with him. I remember I was more critical of Jake on subsequent viewings. Maybe it was getting older and finding my own equilibrium as an adult going through the world.

In your own work, are there any references or homages to it?

LINKLATER: A line here and there. I saw it nine years before I made *Slacker*. I started shooting in '89. This caught me at a real formative, early place. It got me thinking, but by the time I was making my own movies, I wasn't attempting to do that. The films you love the most, you're always a little sad to realize those aren't the kind of films you'll ever make. The die has been cast before you even know it, and you're making films. That's the sad thing about even starting to make films.

At the time, I remember mixed feelings. I remember telling people, some of my buddies, "Oh, you gotta go see this movie," and they're like, "Uh, yeah. Maybe." And even that girl I went with, we broke up shortly thereafter because she said it was boring. I was so mad. I'd had, like, this huge experience, and she walked out and goes, "Eh, it was kind of boring."

I was, like, "Who am I with? This is crazy!" That was the end of that. A guy wants his girlfriend to at least appreciate that part of him. It's every guy's fantasy to have a girl who, if she doesn't think that those films are great, at least can see why you like them, and tolerate it.

22

Jay Duplass
Raising Arizona

Jay Duplass, best known for his low-budget dramas on the Mumblecore circuit, got to *Raising Arizona* first. Among his age group—filmmakers in their early '30s—this Coen brothers classic was the most requested film to talk about in this book.

"I will be the first one to shamelessly admit that some of my peak emotional experiences in my lifetime have happened inside of movie theaters," Duplass says. "This was one of the top ones."

Jay Duplass, selected filmography:
Scrapple (2004)
The Puffy Chair (2005)
Baghead (2008)
Cyrus (2010; codirector, with Mark Duplass)
The Do-Deca-Pentathlon (2010)

Raising Arizona
1987
Directed by Joel Coen
Starring Nicolas Cage, Holly Hunter, Trey Wilson, John Goodman, William Forsythe, Sam McMurray, and Frances McDormand

How would you describe *Raising Arizona* to someone who has never seen it?

DUPLASS: Wow. *Raising Arizona* is . . . I've never even thought to describe this movie. It's like beyond a movie to me. A couple wants to have a baby and they can't for biological reasons, so they decide to kidnap one of, one of the quintuplets of a furniture store owner, Nathan Arizona. Then bad things happen. The most critical person in it is obviously Nicolas Cage. The best thing about Nicolas Cage in this movie is that I think he's about fifteen years old playing a thirty-three-year-old. I don't know how old he was, but—

He was twenty-two.

DUPLASS: He's twenty-two, and he's playing Holly Hunter's husband in the movie and you know, I don't even know the age difference. . . . I'm looking it up on IMDb right now. They're six years apart. She's twenty-eight. He's twenty-two. My brother, Mark, and I are obsessed with him in this movie in particular, but we like to refer to Nicolas Cage as the president of the Blown Testosterone Club.

What that means is there is a select group of males who blow out all of their testosterone in the first twenty years of their life. It's like they used it all up. So when he was twenty-two he seemed and looked like late thirties to us—the hairiest guy in the world. Then for some reason like five years later he was bald and chubby. He was just the image of virility, hopefulness, and male capability. That's just something that I enjoy thinking about. So he was fantastic in that. Holly Hunter is just absolutely adorable, and she is the cop he is just smitten with, and they get married and she can't have a baby.

Tell me about your first experience with the film.

DUPLASS: This is '87, I'm pretty sure. I would have been fourteen. We saw it on a family vacation in Hawaii.

We saw it in a tiny little movie theater on Maui. It was in a movie theater where we thought, this is the movie that will suck the least at this movie theater. We weren't too excited about anything going on over there.

It was one of those things, where all the movies before that were clear-cut; they were just movies. There was something intangible about it, and it didn't feel like other movies. It felt homemade. It felt—even though it's so superbly executed—it felt handmade on some weird level and it felt like us on some strange level.

It was the highlight of the entire trip, and I will be the first one to shamelessly admit that some of my peak emotional experiences in my lifetime have happened inside of movie theaters. This was one of the top ones.

Why do you think it resonated?
DUPLASS: Something that you need to know about me and my brother Mark is that we grew up watching very serious relationship movies our whole lives. Like when everyone else was watching *Star Wars*, we were obsessed with *Ordinary People* at the ages of, like, seven and four. I don't know why, but Mark and I have always liked movies about relationships and how people are treating each other, and how they're negotiating. It's just the weirdest thing now that we think back to it. It's like we would rush back from grammar school and watch HBO in the early '80s. So when this movie came up, it was a relationship movie that was incredibly stylized and amazing, and just so, so funny. It was one of the first movies that externalized the internal struggle that people have when they're trying to make their relationship work, and they're trying to make their dreams come true, and all the little things that they're battling with. After that experience we started stepping up our home video production from like cutesy little things to trying to incorporate some plot.

Tell me about your favorite line.
DUPLASS: God, it's an evolution is what it is. Right now, what we're obsessed with more than anything. There's this one guy, the husband of Frances McDormand. He's Glen, the wife-swapping guy. There's a line in there when he's talking about looking to adopt a new baby because "Dot says these here are getting too big to cuddle."

And: "They said we had to wait five years for a healthy white baby. I said 'Healthy white baby, five years? OK, what else you got?' They said they got two Koreans and a Negro born with his heart on the outside. It's a crazy world." I don't know why, but the "two Koreans and a Negro born with his heart on the outside" is probably my favorite line from the movie and nobody else probably remembers it.

And what about it?

DUPLASS: There are just so many layers of comedy and insanity and commentary on the state of America and Americans' self-entitlement. The fact that the character thinks *Negro* was a better thing to say than *nigger*, and just how ignorant that character is. I don't know. It was a ballsy ball of humor and just craziness. It's terrifying at the same time. That guy is terrifying, and you don't want to believe that he exists, but you know that he's out there.

What's your favorite scene? What stuck out to you the most, or what's been the most instructive or terrifying?

DUPLASS: My favorite scene is the eleven-minute montage that starts the movie. I've never experienced anything like that before or after, and it works so well, and it's so amazing. That being said, as opposed to being instructive, it has been completely destructive to our careers. Because of this movie, we spent—and I am not joking—thirteen, maybe fifteen years trying to be the Coen brothers.

We made our first successful film in 2002. We went to film school and, granted, a lot of those years were spent being a spastic teenager, some of them were spent being professional editors so that we could support ourselves within the industry. We, along with every other film student in the early '90s, wanted to be the Coen brothers. It took us fifteen years to figure out that you can't beat the Coen brothers at being the Coen brothers. They are so damn good at what they do. Honestly, for us, it took a really, really long time to figure that out. It's funny because what we do is so different from the Coen brothers. They're so specific, and I think their movies probably exist almost to a T in storyboards. And we don't know what the hell's going to happen when we get on set.

Is it as simple as imitation was the sincerest form of flattery? Or was it frustration for you?

DUPLASS: What made it click was a total accident. We kept making movies, and they weren't that good. They just weren't catching on, and we were completely depressed, and Mark basically was like, "OK, fuck this, we're making a movie." We were sitting in our south Austin apartment with seven items in it. One of those items happened to be our parents' home video camera, similar to what we used to use when we were kids. I'm like, well, we can't make a movie. We don't have any film; we don't have a crew. This is before making movies digitally was possible, or this was right at the cusp of it, in retrospect.

Mark was like, "Just come up with something, and we'll just do it." What we came up with was something that had happened to me the week before. I had tried to perfect the personal greeting on my answering machine, and it took me an hour, and I was so worked up I basically had a mini nervous breakdown trying to do this fucking thing. Because I was trying to get it right, and I couldn't get it right, and it was this horrid experience. Then we started laughing about it when we talked about the idea, and so we shot it—Mark did it. We spent three dollars on a tape at the corner store at the 7-Eleven and that movie got into Sundance. That three dollars and that one take of fifteen minutes did more for our careers than fifteen years of trying to be the Coen brothers. It was a total accident, and it was only by virtue of us being stupid enough to keep doing it when everything in the universe was telling us not to.

This was not a universally loved film when it came out. Janet Maslin called it "first-rate apprentice work." Vincent Canby called it "full of technical expertise, but has no life of its own." But Joel Siegel was in its corner. He called it "one of the most inventive original comedies in years." Why do you think opinions were so split?
Duplass: Like I had originally said, the movie feels completely different from all of the movies that came before. There's something about the way they put the images together that feels different, and anything that's different is going to be met with an antagonistic viewpoint. I don't know why it's polarizing, and you're right, when people think of the Coen brothers' catalogue it's not like that's even in the top five. I know that the people who love it are obsessed. It's one of those movies that elicits really, really strong opinions—probably not as much as *Barton Fink*. Certain people think I'm crazy when I tell them that's my favorite movie.

What images float to the surface when you think about it?
Duplass: The Woody Woodpecker tattoo and him realizing that the evil

man is himself. The guy on a motorcycle with a baby on the front handle-bars, picking off rabbits and lizards from miles away with his shotgun. I don't know, it had such a strong sense of place in Arizona. There was just a dreaminess to it. It just appealed to this deep part of my subconscious that had never really been accessed before by a piece of art. That's why I feel like a bumbling idiot, because I think that that's what the movie has done to me. It's working on me at such deep subconscious levels. The way it went in there was by making me laugh, by making me laugh as a dorky fourteen-year-old boy, and still now. It makes me laugh so much it just opens me up and gets within me.

How has it changed in your viewing experience from the first to the most recent time?
DUPLASS: I do know this—Mark and I did go see this movie together in Austin. The Austin Film Society had a 35mm print. We went to go see it, and we were scared because we didn't want it to not hold up. That's a big thing that we talk about, "Is this going to hold up? Do we have unrealistic expectations?" But we went, and we both walked out of the movie theater crying; we couldn't even talk to each other. It was just like, "I'll just talk to you next week because I can't even deal with it right now." In terms of how the experience affects me? The wild part to me is when I first saw the movie, all these guys looked like old, old men. When I watch it now the characters are younger than me, and it blows my mind. I don't know what that does to me, but it certainly feeds the frenzy that I've always had. I've always felt like I should be doing more, I should be accomplishing more. To think that these people could pull this off. I know the Coens were pretty young when they got it done.

Cage had tried to kick-start his career for years, and this is really kind of the second film that had done it. He was in *Rumble Fish* and *The Cotton Club*, which were both flops, and then he hit with *Peggy Sue Got Married*. This film made him a star, and he admitted that he based the character and the hairdo on Woody Woodpecker.
DUPLASS: Jesus, that's awesome.

And *Moonstruck* is the same year.

DUPLASS: Yeah. Where, I believe, he plays a forty-year-old or something? How old was Cher then and how old was he then? I mean, it's mind-blowing to me, and when I saw it I thought, man, she looks really young for him. I think he blew his testosterone out on that film; it was in between *Raising Arizona* and *Moonstruck*.

This film was the start of ongoing criticism about the Coen brothers in that none of the characters are ever smarter than the brothers themselves—that the brothers are oftentimes condescending to them. The other criticism is that a lot of their characters are cartoonish, and it's hard to care about a cartoon.

DUPLASS: Yeah, I feel love for all those characters, and I can only assume they felt love for all their characters in that movie, as ignorant as they all may be. I would agree with the statement that none of these characters are as smart as the Coen brothers. It's strange that you say that because that is something that Mark and I do hold ourselves to, is that we want our characters to be as smart as we are. The way that we feel is that we are smart enough to be aware of our problems, but that doesn't make them go away, and that doesn't make us suffer from them any less. In terms of the Coens and their characters being cartoons, I don't know. I am incredibly sensitive to overstylized stuff. It's very strange—I just feel that pure love for those characters. They're just distilling their own idiocy for us to share. That's just me projecting, because I don't know what their internal process is like.

Now when you saw this, and again I know you were fourteen, but did this make you seek out other films like it?

DUPLASS: It was exactly that. I didn't even know what it meant to be a director. I was very immature. Also, I have just a very microscopic, microcosmic view of things. I witness this phenomenal piece of art, and I couldn't quite even get my brain around what it was. And my fixation on it was just singular. I was just obsessing about that movie, watching it repeatedly, forcing my parents to buy it on VHS, breaking it, and getting another one. It was a very singular, microscopic obsession with that single piece of art. Then eventually I did branch out because it did make me obsessed with films. Then I started to learn what it meant to direct a movie, and then I dug back into *Blood Simple* and started following them to learn how to anticipate what it is they would do in the future.

And just ballpark here, how many times do you think you've seen it?
DUPLASS: I'm going to try to be really honest. I have a tendency towards hyperbole here. So I'm going to check myself. I probably have seen the film between thirty and forty times.

How do you think your life or your work might have been different if you hadn't seen the film?
DUPLASS: I probably wouldn't be making movies—seriously. It held over for so long. It really was the root of everything that Mark and I always hold ourselves to in making movies. That is to say that *Raising Arizona* is the most inspired movie that I have ever seen.

Inspiring or inspired?
DUPLASS: Inspired and inspiring, but mostly inspired. It's an inspired piece of art. I don't know how to quantify that or how to even talk about it, but I know that when they made this piece of art there was so much love, all pistons firing. Because they were creating things in ways that hadn't been done before, and they had to ignore the fears about why it may or may not hold up. Beyond that, the performances are inspired; it's hard to describe this electric thing that happens. I know it's probably cheesy for a lot of people to talk about or hear about, but—that really is the key element of that film. It's just an immensely inspired piece of art.

23

John Woo
Rebel Without a Cause and *Mean Streets*

John Woo was the second of two directors I could not get to commit to one film. No, he told me, *Rebel Without a Cause* and *Mean Streets* had equal but distinct impacts on his life and career. As any passing viewing of his films indicates, loyalty means a lot to him. He could not abandon one of them.

Woo on James Dean in *Rebel*: "I combed my hair like him, but I couldn't afford to buy wax, so I had to use water. I even talked like him. He was a very influential idol to me." Woo on *Mean Streets*: "If I hadn't have seen this movie, I wouldn't know what I was living for."

John Woo, selected filmography:
A Better Tomorrow (1986)
A Better Tomorrow II (1987)
The Killer (1989)
Bullet in the Head (1990)
Once a Thief (1991)
Hard Boiled (1992)
Hard Target (1993)
Broken Arrow (1996)
Face/Off (1997)
Mission: Impossible II (2000)
Windtalkers (2002)
Paycheck (2003)
Red Cliff (2008)
Red Cliff II (2009)

Rebel Without a Cause
1955
Directed by Nicholas Ray
Starring James Dean, Natalie Wood, Sal Mineo, Dennis Hopper,
Jim Backus, Edward Platt, Corey Allen, and more

Mean Streets
1973
Directed by Martin Scorsese
Starring Robert De Niro, Harvey Keitel, David Proval, Amy
Robinson, and more

**How would you describe *Rebel Without a Cause* to someone who has
never seen it?**
Woo: I truly love this movie. When I watched *Rebel Without a Cause*, I
thought I was James Dean. I always felt like there was a lot of misunderstanding between me and my parents. We were living in a very old system. I
tried to run away. I needed love, I needed someone to care about me. It was
pretty tough to do what I really wanted to do.

**Essentially, it's about a troubled teen trying to navigate a new town and
school. When did you see it?**
Woo: I was watching it by myself, in a theater in Hong Kong. I watched
that movie in a second-run theater. In Hong Kong, the first-run theater was
expensive. After a few months, it was in some kind of cheaper theater. That's
the only place we could afford to see it.

I had a very miserable life when I was a kid. First of all, I grew up in a
slum. It was a very tough way of living in a very tough neighborhood. It was
pretty tough to survive. I used to have to deal with the gangs; I used to get
beat up by some tough guys, wise guys. They wanted me to join them, but
I refused.

That's very close to the dynamic in film.
Woo: Yes. And my parents were pretty strict with me, and they wanted me
to go the right way, so I had to fight very hard to survive. I had to fight back.

I was pretty strong—every day, almost every day I had to grab something, some weapon, in case there was an ambush.

And our family was pretty poor. We were homeless for a couple years. The whole thing to me, it seemed to me—there was a system I didn't like. Pressure always came down on me. It just felt like a living hell. I always found a way to break through, to find myself. Since we were living in a pretty bad situation, my mother and my uncle, they were pretty tough on me. They were a very traditional family.

But that didn't mean my parents were bad to me. They were just so afraid that I'd go the wrong way. So they tried many ways to go straight. So when I watched the film, I found myself just like James Dean: I needed people around me who were more understanding of me. Giving more love and giving more encouragement.

The funny thing was, what James Dean did in the movie, it was the same as what I did. I had a couple friends who were in trouble, just like Jacky Cheung's character in my movie *Bullet in the Head*. I remember the reason I chose Jacky Cheung. He was a rebel in his eyes. His eyes have a similar look of anger, a similar passion as James Dean. Also, Leslie Cheung's character in *A Better Tomorrow* is pretty much like James Dean. It's a little bit of an homage to that character.

In our neighborhood there were the gamblers. They were pretty mean to their sons, like with a friend of mine. No one cared about him. He started to break the law, did some foolish things, taking drugs, and became a gambler. And he got in trouble with the police. I took care of him and tried to protect him. I took him in as my friend. It was a pretty sad story. When I saw James Dean, he looked out for his good friend, and I felt the same way.

You played a character similar to James Dean in high school. What was the production like?

Woo: The play was inspired by the movie. It made me feel like I should tell my story. The play's name was—how to say it in English?—something like *Parents' Hearts*. The story was about a rebel—he was really wild, and he never listened to his parents and did a lot of bad things. He just wanted to be himself, but there was not much of an understanding. I wrote the play, and I played the same character as James Dean in *Rebel Without a Cause*.

Was it just a stage adaptation, or was it an original?
WOO: It was an adaptation from another play, and I added some of my story into the play.

Did your parents see it? What did they think about it?
WOO: No, they didn't see it. By the time I did the play, my father had passed away. I respected my parents, but in that era, a lot of families were pretty poor. They were so worried about me; that's why they got tough with me.

On the other hand, my father was a traditional scholar. He never liked movies. He thought that movies were fake. But I loved movies; I was crazy about movies. When I told him that I loved movies and art, he would say, "You could never survive. In the arts, you could never make a living."

They wanted me to be a teacher—something stable, you know. But I didn't listen to them. I had so much anger. I wanted to fight with the whole system, the whole society—there were problems. There were not many people who cared about the poor, not many people who cared about young people. There were no good guidelines or education for young people, to tell them what to do or where to go. But the movies let us know. It gave me a lot of inspiration.

Before I saw the movie, I had so much anger with the whole situation, with my neighborhood, with the parents, with everything. But after I saw the movie, I changed.

What exact change did you make?
WOO: No matter what had happened, we had to find a way to understand each other. The parents and the kids needed to understand each other more and try to find a way to forgive and to love. The end of the movie, it really touched me. The father finally understands the son, and the son finally gets real love from his parents. That's a good way to do it, and the only way to do it. It really changed my life, made me feel that I shouldn't be angry about everything, to find a way to love my family.

When they originally adapted the book in 1947, Marlon Brando was attached to star—
WOO: Oh yeah, I remember that.

—but the role went to James Dean years later. Why do you think people put James Dean and Marlon Brando so often in the same sentence?

WOO: I think they both had the same thing, a very strong, independent character. They both had strong will against the system. I love James Dean. After I saw this movie, I began to dress like him.

Did you have a red jacket?

WOO: Yeah. I combed my hair like him, but I couldn't afford to buy wax, so I had to use water. I even talked like him. He was a very influential idol to me.

A lot of film acting, especially from the '50s and early '60s, can look stagey and very static. But even now, James Dean is so magnetic to a modern audience. His performance seems so raw. Why do you think he has such staying power?

WOO: He was so natural; I think he was just being himself. He didn't make you feel like he was acting. He makes you feel so comfortable, just like he was one of the neighbors. He was so real. Nowadays, some of the actors, they are too much into "acting." James Dean was just James Dean.

One of the odd bits of film history about *Rebel* was they started to film it in black and white—they even had James Dean wearing glasses. But the studio decided to make it color Cinemascope. I was just wondering how you think it might have been different in black and white? Or if it gains anything in color, aside from that iconic red jacket?

WOO: I think if that movie was in black and white, it would have been more powerful—the image would have been much stronger. In black and white, it would become a film noir. The movie was shot in color, and it looks like a Hollywood movie.

That was actually one of the criticisms, when Nicholas Ray moved to color—that it made his films less gritty.

WOO: Yeah.

Now, this wasn't James Dean's first film role. He was in *East of Eden* first. Did you know about him before *Rebel Without a Cause*?

Woo: I thought *Rebel Without a Cause* was his first one, because in Hong Kong, we saw the movie much later than in the States. In Hong Kong, we saw *East of Eden* second—and a lovely movie, too.

Do you remember what your reaction was when you found out Dean had died?

Woo: I was pretty sad. It was big news in Hong Kong—on the radio, TV news, newspapers—everywhere. It was a total shock. He was a lot of young people's idol. I could even say we worshipped him. He not only changed our lives, but he changed our attitudes. He changed the movies and how the movies looked.

I know you also want to talk about *Mean Streets*. Can you tell me why you chose it, specifically?

Woo: If I hadn't seen this movie, I wouldn't know what I was living for. Even though I was so in love with movies, I didn't see much hope. Even though I was active in school, I didn't have many friends. I was always looking for good friends, trying to find somebody who had the same goals. Since I loved art so much, I tried to find similar people, but I couldn't find any. I always felt lonely, extremely lonely. I needed to talk to someone. Even in the missionary school, I had so many friends, but all they could talk about was religion. I wanted something real, something that could happen to me. After I watched the movie *Mean Streets*, I found my friends just right beside me.

We should stop here and say that *Mean Streets* is about a neighborhood friendship. Charlie [Harvey Keitel] is constantly trying to keep his volatile friend Johnny Boy [Robert De Niro] out of trouble.

Woo: I had some friends like Robert De Niro in *Mean Streets*. Like I said, one of my good friends was the son of a gambler, and he had a drug problem. It made me feel sad. It made me have a lot of sympathy for my friend, and I tried to help him and took care of him. I also had another friend, and I tried to help him, but he betrayed me.

So, I found this in *Mean Streets*. The movie was so unlike a formulaic Hollywood movie. It looked so real; it was so touching.

***Mean Streets* came out in 1973, so you were already in movies.**
Woo: Yeah, but I saw this film before I directed my first movie. Even after I directed my first movie, I didn't have much confidence. I must confess, I think I started a little too young. I should have learned more. I started with some kung-fu movies and comedies. After I watched *Mean Streets*, it made me feel ashamed—"Why don't I make a movie like that? Tell a true story?"

But at that time, not many people liked to see true stories. Even in Hong Kong, they only liked kung-fu movies. That made me feel that I should make a movie like *Mean Streets*.

And you've said your character Jacky Cheung in *Bullet in the Head* was inspired by Robert De Niro's character in *Mean Streets*.
Woo: Yeah, that's true. Originally, *Bullet in the Head* was set up as a sequel for *A Better Tomorrow*, but the story didn't work. But I kept the idea, and I kept *Mean Streets* as a sample. I tried to tell part of my story. In the movie, Tony Leung Chiu Wai portrayed me. And Jacky Cheung's character was an homage to Robert De Niro in *Mean Streets*. At the end of the movie, when he goes crazy and gets a bullet in the head—he holds his head walking in the dark alley—he was just like Robert De Niro at the end when he gets shot in *Mean Streets*.

Just to be clear, he gets shot in the neck.
Woo: Yeah, in the neck. He's holding his head, walking in the dark alley, and in the background they are playing opera. That kind of strong image was always in my mind, and I used it in *Bullet in the Head*.

About the friendship, Tony Leung Chiu Wai is just like Harvey Keitel, and the young guy who got so greedy was like the other friend who betrayed him. When I watched *Mean Streets*, it looked just like a Greek tragedy. Of course, in *Mean Streets* there are strong themes of friendship, like people in my life and people in my movies. When you really love a friend, and he betrays you, it becomes tragic.

Critic Pauline Kael suggested that Charlie is the good side of Martin Scorsese, and Johnny Boy is the negative part.
Woo: [*laughing*] Oh yeah, that's interesting!

[Spoiler alert:] What do you think that means then, when Martin Scorsese plays the gunman at the end who shoots Johnny Boy?
Woo: [*laughing*] I don't think he wanted to kill himself. But that's very interesting. I think Marty had portrayed himself in all of his movies. I think he's more like the Robert De Niro character.

I find that we have similar backgrounds. His first dream was that he wanted to be a priest, and my first dream was that I wanted to be a minister, a reverend.

And he was kicked out for roughhousing, and your friends told you that you didn't have the discipline.
Woo: Yeah, yeah. [*laughing*] And my friends suggested that I go into arts.

Do you know Scorsese pretty well?
Woo: I've met him two or three times.

What makes you think he is more like Johnny Boy?
Woo: Well, he's a great artist. He's like a rebel in art, to me. He changed so many things. His movies broke the system. He made the movies like going into a brand new world. He gives it a lot of honesty. I think he's a man who changed the film world quite a lot. When you're doing something like that, it's really hard to make people understand you—like Robert De Niro in *Mean Streets*. But not many people know deep inside his heart what he's thinking.

One of the other similarities between you two is the use of music. In *Mean Streets*, there's a whole fight scene in a bar room set to "Be My Baby." It reminded me of *Face/Off* in which the big shootout is set to "Somewhere Over the Rainbow." Did you take that cue from Scorsese?
Woo: Not only music; I also learned so much from his editing. His editing is so sharp and so precise—and sometimes too raw. He doesn't play by the rules; he just edits the scene by his own feeling. Of course, he's very, very in control of the whole rhythms. The way he was using music was very unique, like the scene you mentioned. It really inspired me to use music the same way, in *Face/Off* and in all my movies.

Scorsese's violence is usually very quick and bloody. But your violence, like you say, is like dancing. It's slow motion, a stylistic thing. So how do you come to use music the same way, even though the action is very different?

WOO: I think we have the same idea of using music. Of course, I got the inspiration from his movies, but that thing is—my kind of violence or action, I try to make it a little more romantic. But sometimes I try to get the message out from the action scenes. In *Face/Off*, I was using a bloody shoot-out scene set to music as an antiviolence message. In some of my Hong Kong movies, sometimes I was using music to qualify the behavior. But I got other things from Martin Scorsese films, like the way he uses slow motion. He only uses a little slow motion in a dramatic moment, so I use that skill in some of my drama sequences.

When I watch a Scorsese movie, every movie has some kind of a new experiment. Even when I watched *Casino,* and the way he was using the camera work, it was amazing.

I can see why you're drawn to Scorsese, because you guys have many of the same themes. Scorsese, especially in *Mean Streets*, uses a lot of Catholic imagery—almost the exact same imagery you use in your films. But the difference is: he's Catholic, you're Lutheran. How do you reconcile the use of Catholic imagery?

WOO: Well, in the opening of *Mean Streets*, we see Charlie—Harvey Keitel—going into a Catholic church. He goes to confession, and that scene was always in my mind. Because I loved Scorsese movies so much, I love to use the Catholic church in my movies. And I can tell you honestly [*laughing*], I wanted to be a Catholic. After high school, I really wanted to be a Catholic—because I loved the songs. I love the hymns, they are so beautiful. So sometimes I use the songs in my movies. To tell you the truth, it's because of *Mean Streets* and the parade scene and the scene in the church.

Are you telling me that Martin Scorsese almost made you a Catholic?

WOO: Well . . . [*laughs*]

Tell me about the first time you met Scorsese.

WOO: I was so shy when I met him. I didn't talk much. It was so exciting when I met him. After I made *The Killer*, I overheard that he didn't see many Hong Kong movies. And he's a great friend of Jay Cocks, a cowriter with him on several movies, and also a film critic. And he asked Marty to see my movie *The Killer*. Jay loved *The Killer* so much, and Scorsese went with him. Jay told me when Marty saw my movie, he didn't say a word. His eyes didn't move from the screen, he liked it so much. After that, I wrote him a letter. I really needed to know what he felt about the movie. I also told him the movie was a tribute to him and Jean-Pierre Melville. I told him that I got so much inspiration from his movies and his style that I hoped he didn't mind.

He wrote me back a letter saying how much he loved the movie. When he watched the fight scene in the church, he was pretty shocked. He wrote about one or two things he liked in the movie. I flew over to New York to meet him in 1991. I went with my business partner, Terence Chang. I didn't know what to say, because I was shy and very, extremely nervous. It was the first time I had met a real master. Marty talked pretty fast, and he was smiling. He was so nice to me. After dinner, he invited me to his house to take a look at a picture. We talked about movies. And then he also said my movies had inspiration from Samuel Fuller and Douglas Sirk. I loved them, but I didn't quite remember their movies, and he told me he hadn't seen many of Jean-Pierre Melville's movies.

I brought some LaserDisc movies for him to sign for me, and he asked me to sign *The Killer* tape for him. After we separated, I was so happy. When I came back to Hong Kong, because I had quite a lot of Jean-Pierre Melville's collection, I made copies for myself and I sent him all the originals. He also sent me a lot of Douglas Sirk and Sam Fuller's movies. I was very touched. He wanted me to watch all these movies again. It really fulfilled my life. Not only did I have a chance to meet him, but also I found he was a very nice man. After that, we have met a few times. We tried to work together, he tried to produce a movie for me. He had a project, a story from a Lou Reed song . . .

"Walk on the Wild Side"?
WOO: Yeah, something like that. Unfortunately, the project didn't work out, but hopefully I'll have a chance to work with him again. Learn from him.

That's one of the perks of this business. You get to grow up and meet your idols.

Woo: Not only that, but before I came to this world, I didn't know much about filmmakers from here. I always felt they were very high—hard to reach. We can touch their movies, but it was very hard to see and talk to them in person. Like David Lean is a god to me. Stanley Kubrick, Hitchcock—they are hard to touch. After Scorsese, it was Oliver Stone—and I found that they were very easygoing, very easy to talk to, just like friends. It made me feel so happy, and I know it's not a dream.

***Mean Streets* came out in 1973, the year after *The Godfather*. Can you tell me a little about the climate this movie came out in?**

Woo: Well, at that time, the audience loved *The Godfather* the most. It had a great impact. It made the gangster movie a high art form. It was very successful and made a lot of people, filmmakers, think they could never make a movie like that. It was so perfect. And also, it made the gang world change. It made a lot of people feel like all those gangsters were also human beings: they had family and love and conflict. The cinematography, the design, everything in the movie was so perfect. It changed the look of our movies. There were a lot of imitations. It made Hong Kong movies follow his step. *The Godfather* became a classic.

After I saw *Mean Streets*, I still loved both movies, but *Mean Streets* was kind of an art film. It didn't have the wide-open distribution. It was only in art houses in theaters.

Here, it won all sorts of awards and critics loved it, but few people outside of New York saw it. How did it play in Hong Kong?

Woo: For the movie lovers and intellectuals, they loved it very, very much. Francis Coppola became the great master. Martin Scorsese became the new symbol, the New Wave. We admired him. We admired him just like Jean-Luc Godard and François Truffaut. He was that kind of director. I must say, *Mean Streets* gave us more impact. The movie is so free, so natural.

Why do you think that Americans and the citizens of Hong Kong love the gangster genre so much?

Woo: In the early '50s and '60s, we already had so much fun with American gangster movies with Humphrey Bogart and James Cagney, and Howard Hawks movies. So we had seen a lot of that, and we were amazed by those gangster movies. In Hong Kong, especially in the early '50s and '60s, the whole society was tough. Everybody had a tough life. So that's why when we watched a gangster movie: it was easy to find ourselves. We knew that kind of life. We know how they are feeling. People like to worship the hero. Sometimes when they watch the gangster movie, we know they are all bad guys, but they are also the heroes. The gangster movies are tragedies.

24

John Landis
The 7th Voyage of Sinbad

Talking to John Landis about movies is like trying to stop water from boiling. His enthusiasm and joy for movies is both infectious and informative, making him one of my favorite people to interview.

He best encapsulates the spirit of this book when talking about *7th Voyage*: "The reason it changed my life, and it really did—I had complete suspension of disbelief. Really, I was eight years old, and it transported me. I was on that beach running from that dragon, fighting that Cyclops. It just really dazzled me and I bought it completely. All my energy and efforts were to be a filmmaker, and it was because of that film."

John Landis, selected filmography:
Schlock (1973)
The Kentucky Fried Movie (1977)
Animal House (1978)
The Blues Brothers (1980)
An American Werewolf in London (1981)
Trading Places (1983)
Spies Like Us (1985)
¡Three Amigos! (1986)
Coming to America (1988)
Beverly Hills Cop III (1994)
Mr. Warmth: The Don Rickles Project (2007)
Burke and Hare (2010)

The 7th Voyage of Sinbad
1958
Directed by Nathan Juran
Starring Kerwin Mathews, Kathryn Grant, Richard Eyer, Torin Thatcher, Alec Mango, and more

How would you describe *The 7th Voyage of Sinbad* to someone who has never seen it?
LANDIS: The movie is about Sinbad the Sailor, and it's very *Arabian Nights* fairy tale fantasy. He is bringing his fiancée, who is a princess, back to the kingdom where she's from, and they stop at an island for fresh water and supplies, the island of Colossa. While they are there, they encounter the Cyclops, who are these spectacular stop-motion figures done by Ray Harryhausen, and a magician, Sokurah (played by Torin Thatcher), who is running from the Cyclops. He's carrying a lamp, but in the escape at the beginning of the film, he drops the lamp. The Cyclops walks away with the lamp, and Sokurah is desperate to get the lamp back. It's terrific. It scared me, it thrilled me, it excited me, I loved it.

Do you remember where you first saw it?
LANDIS: I saw it in 1958 at the Crest Theatre on Westwood Boulevard, which is still there in Los Angeles, where I grew up.

In literature, it's called "suspension of disbelief," and I had complete suspension of disbelief—really, I was eight years old and it transported me. I was on that beach running from that dragon, fighting that Cyclops. It just really dazzled me, and I bought it completely. And so, I actually sat through it twice and when I got home, I asked my mom, "Who does that? Who makes the movie?"

And my mother, she was pretty smart—we didn't have any relatives in the business or anything—she said, "The director." So I thought, "Ah ha! The director!" That's what I want to do; I want to make movies. From the time I was eight, that was my whole focus. I dropped out of high school, became a mail boy at Fox, and went to Europe to make movies. When I was twenty-one I made my first movie. All my energy and efforts were to be a filmmaker, and it was because of that film.

That's funny, because in a lot of Harryhausen films, he ends up overshadowing the director.

LANDIS: Well, he doesn't overshadow the director so much as he is in a unique position as a craftsman, because Ray is probably the only special effects technician who has his own body of work.

He is the auteur of his films—not the director, not the producer. He did a lot of pictures with producer Charles Schneer, but nonetheless every movie that Ray has ever worked on (except a couple where he was a hired gun, like *One Million B.C.*), he generated. They were his conception; he did lavish storyboards that sold the properties. When they built the sets, the art directors copied the storyboards. Ray always directed any sequence that involved any of his puppets. It's interesting—the best Harryhausen film is probably *Jason and the Argonauts*, because it is by far the best written and wonderfully cast, for the most part, except for the lead.

It really has the best Hercules in movies, Nigel Green. It's just a really smart screenplay, as is *Clash of the Titans*, although there's some horrible shit in *Clash of the Titans* where they were trying to compete with *Star Wars* to keep up [see Bubo, the mechanical owl —ed.].

When I made *An American Werewolf in London*, I actually went to visit Ray, and he was shooting *Clash of the Titans*. He was animating the Pegasus. He and Jim Danforth—I remember them in this little garage animating away with their little puppets.

Ray has become a really good friend of mine and has acted in three of my movies. Ray is a great artist, and when I was twelve I wrote a letter to "Ray Harryhausen in care of Famous Monsters in Filmland Magazine," which Forrest J. Ackerman actually forwarded on to Ray, and he sent me back a signed 8x11 glossy of him animating the dragon from *7th Voyage*. He wrote on it: "To John Landis, Best wishes for your success—Ray Harryhausen." And it really meant so much to me, that thing. That's why whenever anybody ever asks me for an autograph, I always give it.

Where is it now?

LANDIS: In my library. It's between my signed photos of Billy Wilder and Groucho Marx. And above them is my autographed Stan Laurel and Oliver Hardy photo.

In this film, was there any one sequence that cemented you into the fantasy?

LANDIS: The film itself just made a huge impression on me in its creating a completely different world. Instead of being this little kid in a theater in west L.A., being transported to this magical place, really going on these adventures. I think it's similar to what *Lord of the Rings* does to younger people now. It's what *Wizard of Oz* can still do. There are only certain movies—*Wizard of Oz, 2001*—there are very few movies that can do that to adults.

Everything about a movie, and I mean this sincerely, is who you are and where you are when you saw it. Because it's hard just to say, "This movie is a piece of shit," because depending on who you were and where you saw it, it can be a great and important thing. There are great films that are completely misunderstood because the people weren't ready for them. Or they were seeing them under bad circumstances. There are too many wonderful films that people disregard.

I actually met Ed Wood. Forry Ackerman actually brought Ed Wood to the cast and crew screening of *Schlock*. That was in 1971, and he was so amazed that I knew who he was. When Tim Burton made *Ed Wood*, Wood's movie *Plan 9 from Outer Space*, which had always been a fringe movie that was known to certain people who enjoyed its camp value, became more profitable than *Ed Wood*. It sold all these copies.

Harryhausen called his handcrafted animation "Dynamation." As a director, what is the difference in seeing physical effects versus computer animation?

LANDIS: The big breakthrough, the big revolution that was really demonstrated the first time in *Jurassic Park*, was not the computer-generated animation so much as the new digital technology that allowed the animation to be placed in a way that looked *in* the picture instead of *on* the picture.

Some of Ray's stuff is hampered by the old sodium screens and the superimposition of things. Ray's brilliance was to make things interact between the animation and reality and make it seem so seamless. Now, with the new digital technology, you can put these things in a picture and have them run around you in a much more convincing way.

People have a misunderstanding of CG; they think that in CG somehow the computer itself does the animating. That's not what happens. People do the animating. It's just that they are using different tools. As evidence of Willis O'Brien [the animator behind the original *King Kong*] and Ray Harryhausen's geniuses, if you look at the most successful animals or creatures that have been done in computer animation so far—dinosaurs in *Jurassic Park* or that big monster in *Lord of the Rings*—if you look at them, they move exactly like Harryhausen animals.

What's remarkable about that is, how were Willis O'Brien and Ray Harryhausen able to animate dinosaurs in a way that has become accepted as the way dinosaurs move? It's quite something. If you look at the King Kong/Tyrannosaurus Rex battle in *King Kong*, it's incredible. No matter how sophisticated computer animation becomes, it just copies those movements. And often those sounds.

One of the interesting things about Ray is he puts an incredible amount of personality into his creatures and the way they move. In *7th Voyage*, a spear is thrown at the Cyclops's back—and that reaching back trying to grab that spear, the Cyclops trying to get at it, it's so extraordinarily sympathetic or empathetic. His characters have a real sense of life. And it's handcrafted, literally frame by frame.

One of the interesting things I read about him was that he didn't take notes. In the Hydra scene, he did it all by instinct.
LANDIS: Not only that, but stop-motion animators now use video playback. Ray did all his stuff without this advantage, keeping place in his head.

When you see things flying and realize not only were there wires, but those wires had to be hidden in the lighting. Now, everyone uses wires. In *Spider-Man* it's all these stuntmen on wires, and it doesn't matter because you can just erase them. Whereas in *War of the Worlds* and Harryhausen's movies, they were on-screen. You had to camouflage them. The amount of work and physical labor involved, it's quite overwhelming.

Ray has said that he's never made a horror picture, that they were all fantasy pictures. From your point of view as an eight-year-old, how did that fit into your sense of genre?

LANDIS: Ray Harryhausen saying he never made a horror film is very much like Boris Karloff and Christopher Lee and Peter Cushing and Vincent Price—they always objected to that name: horror film. Because the truth is, to horrify is pretty easy. [*laughs*]

If I want to make a horror film, if I show you a person who's been shredded up, it's pretty easy to get a horrified response. It's not hard to horrify. It's difficult to generate suspense, or terror, or suspension of disbelief. Karloff especially used to hate the word "horror," because that meant just gruesome. There are many horrible things: starving children. It's not difficult to make a horrible horror film—it's difficult to make an elegant, terrifying, suspenseful picture that keeps you on the edge of your seat because of your concern for the characters' welfare, as well as the filmmaker's ability to make you believe something not real is real. A fantasy picture.

For me, probably the best fantasy film ever made is *The Exorcist*. Now people say that's a horror picture, because it's so horrific. Well, in fact, I totally do not believe in the devil—at all. I think that *people* are what's scary. But nonetheless, the devil is something I emotionally and intellectually reject as a bad excuse people have for their own behavior. Having said that, the genius of the *The Exorcist* is while you're watching the movie, William Friedkin manages to make you believe that this little girl is possessed by the devil! And it's really scary.

Now, for me, having been raised liberal Jewish, as soon as the movie was over, we went out to eat, we had dinner and talked about it, I was very excited, then we went home to bed. Didn't scare me. But my Catholic friends were tormented for months.

My mother, too. It messed with her pretty badly.
LANDIS: All those kids who were raised Catholic, all those altar boys and stuff—it scared the shit out of them! [*laughs*] Because it touched something in the brainwashing of their youth. However, my point is, that film genuinely created suspension of disbelief. While you were watching that movie, you had—yikes!

And in terms of creating fantasy worlds, it's something many people have done. Probably for me one of the most successful fantasy films is also the most blatantly artificial, which is *The Wizard of Oz*. That movie completely dazzles me. I think it's genius. No matter how stage-bound it is, I believe all of it.

And I think Ray is right. He makes fantasy films; he deals with the fantastic.

The reason I asked about its horror status is that the film actually ran afoul of the British Board of Film Censors.
LANDIS: Everything runs afoul of the British Board of Film Censors. Censorship, by definition, is arbitrary, because it's consistently changing. What is shocking one year is not shocking another year. And standards change all the time.

Well, they cut out his skeleton bit—the one thing that people remember from that film.
LANDIS: They cut that out for England?

And they cut out some of the Cyclops sequence.
LANDIS: Well that's completely silly. It's ridiculous.

But his longevity hasn't been impacted much. There's a bar in *Monsters, Inc.* called Harry Hausen's. In *Spy Kids 2* the skeletons show up.
LANDIS: Well, those are acknowledged homages. I would say that the rip-offs are far greater! [*laughs*]

Speaking of homage, I know that Ray is in a couple of your films, *Beverly Hills Cop III* and *Spies Like Us*. But do you have any homages to his work in any of your films?
LANDIS: Gee, that's a good question. I'd have to look back on it. I was doing an animated Sinbad feature years ago, but the funding ran out. My animators went over to Disney and made *Aladdin* using our characters. I was pretty pissed off about that.

But, I don't know. I have used stop-motion photography because I love it. The opening titles for *Oscar* are quite beautifully animated by the great Dave Allen, who has since passed away. Have you ever seen *Oscar*? It has an amazing cast, a comedy with Sylvester Stallone, Chazz Palminteri, Kirk Douglas, Peter

Riegert, Harry Shearer, Eddie Bracken—it just has this astonishing cast, but the lead is Sylvester Stallone and people went, "Oh shit, it's some stupid movie." It's very different from what people were expecting. Stallone fans were disappointed that he didn't kill anyone, and people who would have enjoyed it didn't go see it because of him. In any case, it opens with a beautiful puppet-animated sequence by Dave Allen. And then in *The Stupids*, I have a dog and a cat done in traditional stop-motion animation by the Kyoto brothers.

What impact has Ray's work had on your films? Any lessons that you take away?

LANDIS: The way that Ray's work impacted is it made me understand the power of film. It made me want to make films—that's how it impacted me directly. And that's pretty profound. Because I have to tell you, when I wanted to be a filmmaker—I was born in 1950—and filmmakers, they were the audiovisual kids in school. They were the ones who ran the projectors. And they were the nerds. Steven Spielberg, George Lucas, Francis Ford Coppola, Brian De Palma, Marty Scorsese—these guys are *Revenge of the Nerds*. It was a very unhip, uncool thing to do, to want to be a filmmaker. It was downright strange, until sometime in the '70s it became kind of hip. Now there are film festivals and film schools—it's a huge thing. But before, people really didn't celebrate directors; it was all about the actors.

First of all, in terms of Harryhausen, his films directly influence *all* of the filmmakers today. If you look at Sam Raimi, *Evil Dead* and *Army of Darkness*, those are just Ray on steroids. Everyone. All the filmmakers, from Spielberg's *Close Encounters* to *Jaws*—and especially *Jurassic Park* and *The Lost World*. How's that for balls? Not only did they rip off Sir Arthur Conan Doyle, they stole the title!

And Bernard Herrmann (*Citizen Kane*, *Vertigo*) composed the score.

LANDIS: Bernard Herrmann did a marvelous score. And, for instance, if you listen to Max Steiner's score for *King Kong*, that is the score for *Jaws*. Bump, bump, bum-bum—bah! You'd be surprised.

We talked about people who Ray influenced, and when Tom Hanks gave him the Gordon E. Sawyer Award, he said, "Some people say

Casablanca or *Citizen Kane* . . . I say *Jason and the Argonauts* is the greatest film ever made!"

LANDIS: I can't speak for Tom Hanks, but I know that's not entirely with tongue in cheek. It was a low-budget picture made in Spain. I know all the production history because I knew Nathan Juran fairly well, who just passed away; he directed several pictures for Ray and also directed a Harryhausen rip-off called *Jack the Giant Killer*. And one of my favorite movies, which he shot in five days, was *Attack of the 50 Foot Woman*. Juran was a lovely guy; he was an art director who worked for John Ford for many years. He won an Oscar for *How Green Was My Valley*. A lovely, lovely guy. He was just a crafts guy. Whatever was thrown at him, he did. When I was a mail boy at Fox, he was doing all those terrible Irwin Allen things: *Lost in Space*, *The Time Tunnel*, and *Voyage to the Bottom of the Sea*.

He went on to do *Land of the Lost*, as well. As I talk to more filmmakers about the films that changed their life, one of their great joys is casting their heroes. Ray has been in a few of your films. What is he like?

LANDIS: Ray? I've known him for years; he's a lovely guy. He's a very sweet man, and he still has all his boyish enthusiasm. Peter Jackson flew him to New Zealand to show him all their stuff for *Lord of the Rings*. Ray is a terrific person. He's spent the last fifteen years just traveling the world being lionized.

He really is one of the great, old-time crafts people. He's an artisan. And a lot of that stuff is being lost. He was in a unique position in motion picture history, he and Willis O'Brien. They have their own body of work that is unique. He never made a big-budget picture; he only made B-pictures. He has a great imagination.

How has your perception of *The 7th Voyage of Sinbad* changed now, when you see it as an adult?

LANDIS: Well, now when you see it, you see how low-budget it was. I'm a little more sophisticated in the process, so it's like *The Wizard of Oz*: "Don't mind that man behind the curtain."

But I think that Torin Thatcher is great. The costumes are silly and the genie is kind of stupid, but it's just got a wonderful sense of fun and adventure. I think it's a wonderful movie. Even now, with some of the monsters, people say, "Look how silly they look!" But they work for me. I think *Jason* is probably a better film, because it's based on the Greek myths and there's a history. But I've got to say, there are some terrific moments in *Sinbad*—when they go in that cavern, and the way that dragon is chained up. And that giant crossbow!

How do you think you'd be different if you hadn't seen that film?
LANDIS: I don't know, I really don't know. I do know that I was very lucky. I had the advantage, which I now understand, which is I knew what I wanted to be from the time I was eight. I was able to seek out filmmakers, and I met everybody. Hitchcock, Capra—everybody. George Stevens, William Wyler, Billy Wilder—I really wanted to meet these people. But I wanted to meet them and to know them and to learn from them. That was a big advantage because most people don't know what they want to do, even when they are in college. So I had an advantage.

It's extremely important to know, and this includes movies now, that how you appreciate a movie has everything to do with your life experience at the moment when you see it, how you see it, and where you see it.

People who see *2001* on DVD, on an eighteen-inch TV, letterboxed or not, that movie is not going to have the impact it did when you saw it in a Cinerama theater in 70mm. It's just not, it's a different experience. So many of the things in *2001*, because of the dating—Pan Am doesn't exist anymore, there's a close-up in the movie of this stewardess's slippers because there is *Velcro* on them. Like in James Bond, where they have a close-up of a *digital watch*. That stuff dates, but that space station set to "Blue Danube" is still one of the most powerful images ever. And it's just, how old were you when you saw it? Where were you? How did you see it? Movies are subjective.

25

Kevin Smith
Slacker

For director Kevin Smith, Richard Linklater's *Slacker* was the spark. Quite simply, seeing *Slacker* was the encouragement he needed to believe in and pursue his own career as a filmmaker. Smith, of course, would add his own classic to the indie canon with *Clerks* just three years later.

"I viewed [*Slacker*] with this mixture of awe and arrogance, where I was amazed at the movie, because I'd never seen anything like it and it was so original," Smith says. "The arrogance comes in when I'm sitting there going, 'Well shit, if this is a movie, I could make a movie.'"

Kevin Smith, selected filmography:
Clerks (1994)
Mallrats (1995)
Chasing Amy (1997)
Dogma (1999)
Jay and Silent Bob Strike Back (2001)
Jersey Girl (2004)
Clerks II (2006)
Zack and Miri Make a Porno (2008)
Cop Out (2010)

Slacker
1991
Directed by Richard Linklater
Starring Teresa Taylor, Rudy Basquez, Jean Caffeine, and many more

How would you describe *Slacker* to someone who has never seen it?

SMITH: It's kind of a stream-of-consciousness journey through the Austin, Texas, underachieving set.

You saw this film on your twenty-first birthday, right?

SMITH: I did.

And how did you find out about it?

SMITH: I had gone to a screening of a movie with Judd Nelson and Bill Paxton called *The Dark Backward* the weekend or two prior to that, at the Angelica Theater up in Manhattan. It was the first time I ever left New Jersey or Monmouth County to go see a movie. It was Vincent Pereira and I.

So we trekked up into the city, and we went to this movie chiefly because in the *Village Voice* an ad said Bill Paxton and Judd Nelson were going to be at the midnight screening of *The Dark Backward*. And they were offering something called Pig Newtons, which were props in the film, this bizarre alternate-Earth-dimension food that they ate in the movie. So we were like, "Holy shit, they give out Pig Newtons! Let's take the trip."

Bill Paxton and Judd Nelson introduced the movie, and these theaters, they're no more than 200- maybe 220-seaters, right below Houston Street, and you can hear subways go past periodically. Before the movie began, there were trailers, and one of them was for *Slacker*, and one of them was for Hal Hartley's *Trust*. They both kind of struck me because they didn't look like movies I had seen before.

A week or two weeks later, I'm at the Quick Stop reading that week's issue of the *Village Voice*, and there's a review for *Slacker*. And I read it and it just sounded cool; the Madonna Pap smear scene sounded pretty funny. [In this scene, an Austin native attempts to sell a sample from Madonna's Pap smear.]

So Vincent and I decided to go see it, and it was my twenty-first birthday. I had nothing else going on that night, so we headed back into the city again for a midnight show, 'cause that's when the Quick Stop closed, and took in *Slacker*. It was a pretty full house, and I was enjoying it. And everybody around me was *really* enjoying it, insanely much, a knee-slapping, gut-busting humor. I didn't quite see the same movie they did. I thought it was very clever, very funny—humorous more than anything else. But I wasn't dumbfounded by the comedy.

And I was sitting there thinking, "God, if they think this is funny, I think I could give them a funny movie." And *Slacker*, I've always said I viewed it with this mixture of awe and arrogance. I was amazed at the movie, because I'd never seen anything like it and it was so original. What a great idea: a movie that has no plot, just goes from character to character, just drifts for ninety minutes and change. And the arrogance comes in when I'm sitting there going, "Well, shit, if this is a movie, I could make a movie."

Vincent had always been the one who wanted to be a director, talked about being a director, and so at that point I had never really considered it seriously. I wanted to be a writer, but not necessarily a screenwriter. I wanted to write for *Saturday Night Live*. But that night on the way home, I started talking about the possibility of making a film and how I could get my head around doing it, and maybe that's what I was meant to do, or give it a shot at least. So from that moment forward, I wanted to be a filmmaker.

And as I talk to more and more filmmakers for this book, the epiphany moments are of two types. The first is, "Wow, that's amazing, I want to make films, but I could never do that." And the second is, "Hey, I can do that!" This sounds like your experience. Were there other films that gave you confidence to think that you could direct?
SMITH: Yeah, that would be *Trust*. A few weeks later I went to see *Trust* at the Angelica. It was very basically shot, but what really struck me about the movie was the dialogue. The dialogue was very stagey, almost surrealistic dialogue. Very clever, but not very realistic. And I said, "Oh my God, so you can flout convention in films." They don't have to speak like most characters do in the mainstream stuff I've seen or in TV shows or even like people in real life. You can craft the ideal, the way you would want characters to speak.

So that was another linchpin. Off the heels of those movies, I started getting knee-deep in indie film and trying to get my hands on anything I could to watch. Back home we had a great video store near us called Choice Video, which carried a lot of tapes. That's where I first found the Jarmusch stuff, which I'd read about in some film book. Watching *Stranger Than Paradise*, that was the movie that made it seem absolutely possible—"Oh my God, this movie, they just turn on the camera and let things happen in front of it." So when I started shooting *Clerks*, it was with *Stranger Than Paradise* in mind, in terms of the mise-en-scène approach.

Circling back to *Slacker*, one film critic wrote that the film was an "anthology of eccentricities without a guide or even sort of a table of contents." To me, it's one of the few American films that consciously and determinedly has no plot. Linklater doesn't come back to characters, and certain things aren't even explained, like a character's black eye. Were you prepared for this by the review you read? What was that experience like?

SMITH: I was used to watching pretty mainstream stuff at that point. So here's a movie, kind of looks like a movie, and we're watching it in a movie theater, and it's populated by nonactors who are acting. I was not prepared going in. It was one of the most wonderful and pure filmgoing experiences I've ever had.

When I was sitting there, I wasn't prepared for it at all. But it was amazing, because it was such an insane, wonderful, and fresh experience. But at the same time, the film was very mundane. It's not like Richard Linklater took us on a journey to space, but he might as well have because the people were very strange. The idea, the whole idea behind the movie, was very strange but insanely liberating for me and very inspiring. Because it was like, "So you can make a movie about *anything*, apparently." You don't have to adhere to the three-act structure, or it doesn't really have to be a story. When I was writing *Clerks*, I was very aware of the fact that I didn't need a plot. There is no plot. It's just a series of stuff that kind of happens there, loosely hung on the framework of a dude who doesn't want to be at work.

A lot of the pieces first written about the film tried to describe or define the title—what is a *slacker*? What did that term mean to you at the time?

SMITH: The only other place I had heard it was in *Back to the Future*, where Marty McFly is referred to as a slacker and his father is referred to as a slacker. And then in *Back to the Future, Part II*, a teacher fires a shotgun at some off-camera hooligans and screams, "Eat lead, slackers!" So that was the only other place I'd really heard the term before. And then suddenly here it was as a title of a movie. I at least had a working idea of what the term meant.

After the movie, did you glean any deeper meaning of that term, if there is such a thing as a deeper meaning of that word?
SMITH: After the movie, I kind of walked away with an excellent understanding of what he was going for. In that film, everyone seemed to have finished college. But *Slacker*, to me, encapsulated that group of people who knew a lot about useless things that didn't really provide a living. It also kind of encapsulated, for me, the overeducated and idle. Or even the people who are just too smart for their own good, which kind of felt like me a little bit at that point when I was working in the convenience store.

I didn't really go to college at that point. I dropped out—didn't even have enough credits for an associate's degree. I had enough of an education where I shouldn't have been working in a convenience store. It felt like that applied to some degree to the term *slacker*: to take refuge in not actually joining the workforce, the serious workforce, take refuge in sitting around and bullshitting with your friends and talking about, oh, I don't know . . . pop culture. There's not a lot going on in *Slacker*, but there are moments.

It was the movie that got me off my ass; it was the movie that lit a fire under me, the movie that made me think, "Hey, I could be a filmmaker." And I had never seen a movie like that before ever in my life. I mean, you sit there watching *Die Hard*, it's not like you go, "Man, I wanna make that." Or at least I don't. I'm sure somebody does, but that wasn't me. Some movies are made to solely be watched, and *Slacker* had the benefit of being one of those movies that you could watch, but it was almost the movie that just kept telling me, as I was watching it: "You can do this. You can do this. Give it a shot." It had possibility written all over it.

As I read all the reviews around *Slacker*, I was fascinated by how polarizing it was.
SMITH: Really, there were people who didn't like that movie?

Kenneth Turan wrote that *Slacker* "does not offer much to anyone who likes to stay awake." But the *New York Times* said, "*Slacker* is a

fourteen-course meal composed entirely of desserts." What do you suppose sparked those diverse emotional responses?

SMITH: That film had the possibility layered throughout the movie, that if these dudes in Bumblefuck, Texas—at that point I didn't know Austin was a cultural fuckin' epicenter—could make a movie, I could.

Linklater is one of the few directors who have been able to harvest a local film scene. He's stayed in Austin. When you and I first met and talked years ago, you talked about wanting to do the same thing for New Jersey. But what obstacles exist for directors wanting to film in their home state and nurture a film production industry?

SMITH: New Jersey is so close to New York that most people just gravitate there. Who would want to hang out in Red Bank, New Jersey, when an hour away they could just go to Manhattan, where there's a much bigger film center?

Also, I was kind of a victim of my own success at a very early age. It was impossible to get people to work for nothing after a certain point, because we were backed by Miramax, and Miramax is backed by Disney. So it was kind of like, "Hey, man, can you come in and pitch in, give it the old college try, put on a show?" And at a certain point, people would just be like, "Dude, you have Miramax money. Clearly you can afford to pay people."

I also didn't live in a college town, so I wasn't surrounded by young energetic zeal. Those were the kinds of hurdles for me and my group. Some movies just completely dragged us out of state. *Mallrats* was cheaper to shoot in Minnesota, so said the studio. So off to Minnesota we went. With *Clerks* nobody gave a shit, nobody knew who we were, and *Chasing Amy* was following the failure of *Mallrats*. So we'd been pretty written off at that point. There was no expectation, and we were so low-budget that we could stay in our hometown and shoot the movie. When we get to *Dogma*, ten million bucks, suddenly we can't stay in New Jersey because to shoot union would have been more expensive in Jersey. So if we go out to Pittsburgh, or western Pennsylvania, it's not nearly as expensive, and you could shoot nonunion.

Both you and Linklater have used nonprofessional or first-time actors, and for your second films you both worked with professional actors. What are the benefits of both?

SMITH: The benefit of nonprofessional actors is that you've got people who are hungry. You can never discount a hungry cast and crew, because, man, they'll fully give it everything they've got. You know, 120 percent, or some other cliche. Because this could be their shot, right? They don't really have much else going on, so they haven't arrived yet. They're working to get to that point, to that arrival point.

When you're working with a professional cast, they've already been to the circus. They've already seen the trapeze act and they're just not as impressed. And just a little bit jaded. So you're pulling more teeth at that point.

So is there something to that adage that great films or great ideas in film are formed against the odds—the odds of a budget—so filmmakers are forced to be more creative?
SMITH: It certainly seems so, but if you go to like the IFFM [Independent Feature Film Market, an indie talent showcase] every year and see the hundreds of movies that aren't gonna go anywhere further than the eyes in front of them, and you know they were all made under duress/stress and under limited budget circumstances and they're not even watchable—it doesn't really apply to every film.

How would your life have been different if you hadn't seen the film? Do you think something like *Trust* or *Stranger Than Paradise* eventually would have inspired you?
SMITH: I don't think anything else would have done it. Because even *Trust* looked good. And it's not like *Slacker* didn't. *Slacker* had this kind of grainy quality to it. But *Trust* seemed too accomplished for me. I think it was *Slacker* or nothing.

When you saw this film on subsequent viewings, how did your relationship with it change?
SMITH: It still really takes me right back to that moment, where suddenly I could see myself doing that. I think it's still an insanely original film. It's still very clever; it's still the movie that I recommend to people when I do college Q&As.

I get the next generation saying, "Hey, when I saw *Clerks*, it's the movie that made me want to get off my ass." And I always hit 'em back with, "Thanks, I appreciate that. But, a movie you gotta watch is *Slacker*."

When did you first meet Linklater?
SMITH: The first time I met him was through John Schloss, my lawyer, who was Rick's lawyer first. And he was going to see a movie, it was the Wim Wenders's follow-up to *Wings of Desire—Faraway, So Close!* So Schloss is like, "Me and Rick are going to catch this movie. Do you wanna catch it with us?" I really liked *Wings of Desire*, and of course I wanted to meet Rick, so I was immediately, "Yeah, of course, I would love to."

And so we all went out to eat first, and then we went out to the movie. So we chitchatted in the beginning—he had already seen *Clerks* at that point through a tape with John. But we didn't really have that much to talk about, oddly enough. He seemed very old to me—not old like, you know, forty, but he's just a much more centered, calm, quiet personality than I am. And so after about ten minutes, we didn't really have much to say.

I remember being a little disappointed, not so much in him, like he let me down, but just like, oh, man, I imagined it would be like a couple of dogs—we would sniff each other's asses and then run and frolic, 'cause we had something in common, we were filmmakers. But it wasn't until years later that I did feel that I was finally on the same level with him to some degree, that I was a peer.

Once you met him and got to know him a little bit, did that make you understand his film differently, or did it make you view that experience differently?
SMITH: It kind of made the film make more sense. Because it is kind of Rick's personality. He is kind of whimsical and artistic, and so is that film on many levels. His discussions aren't mired in pop culture and the here and now and humor like my stuff, the way my conversations tend to be. His conversations lean more toward art and concepts and trying new things. When I met him, I was just like, "Yeah, it makes sense that this is the guy that made that movie."

What was your reaction to *Waking Life*, *Slacker*'s unofficial sequel and sister movie?

SMITH: This is horrible: I've never seen it. And part of the reason I've never seen it was, someone was like, "Hey man, it's the perfect companion piece to *Slacker*." And to me there will never be a perfect companion piece to *Slacker*. So I almost didn't want to taint the *Slacker* experience on some level. On the other level, I just found that kind of animation grating and hard to take. Because I watched a five-minute sequence of that stuff, not necessarily from that movie but of that type of animation, and I just found it a little hard to take.

You should give it chance.

SMITH: I will totally give it a chance. I also bought *Tape*; I really wanted to watch *Tape* and I've never gotten around to watching it. I loved *School of Rock*, though.

I saw that at a midnight screening, and it was one of the few movies I've seen where people spontaneously applaud. That's when you have something.

SMITH: Something special. What was really weird was watching the effect that that film had on the next generation of Smiths. I took my kid to see that movie three times in the theater, and each time the movie got her off her ass, into the aisles of the theater, dancing and pretending to be onstage, pretending to be in the kids' group.

A Linklater movie got her off her ass and really kind of inspired her to do something.

It was weird. I was always kind of charmed by that, 'cause I was like, "Man, like father, like daughter."

26

Chris Miller
Sleeper

Somehow, it all comes back to giant food.

Chris Miller made his move from TV (*Clone High, How I Met Your Mother*) to the big screen with *Cloudy with a Chance of Meatballs*, which he directed with Phil Lord. Below, he talks about the film that turned him on to directing: Woody Allen's *Sleeper*, which also features massive, out-of-control food.

He says, "It was a middle phase for Woody Allen. Those were two things I was very interested in: having something interesting to say in a movie but also not taking yourself too seriously and really making the kind of gut laughter that you get from pure physical comedy."

> **Chris Miller, selected filmography:**
> *Cloudy with a Chance of Meatballs* (2009; codirector, with Phil Lord)
>
> *Sleeper*
> 1973
> Directed by Woody Allen
> Starring Woody Allen, Diane Keaton, Mary Gregory, Don Keefer, John Beck, and many more

How would you describe *Sleeper* to someone who has never seen it?
MILLER: It's a 1973 Woody Allen movie in which he is cryogenically frozen, wakes up several hundred years in the future, gets into a bunch of mayhem, and becomes involved in a plot to overthrow the government.

When did you first see it?

MILLER: I was a freshman in college when I saw it, and it really did change my view of film and comedy. For me, *Sleeper* was a great balance between physical comedy—slapstick humor—and clever savvy social satire.

At that point I'd never really seen a film that has really balanced both of those elements. It was kind of like—you know how *Rubber Soul* and *Revolver* are the best Beatles albums because they're somewhere between "She Loves You" and "I Am the Walrus"? They have elements of catchy pop songs, but with experimental stuff in them.

I felt like *Sleeper* was not just a silly, goofy comedy like *Take the Money and Run* and not like *Hannah and Her Sisters*. It was a middle phase for Woody Allen. Those were two things I was very interested in: having something interesting to say in a movie but also not taking yourself too seriously and really making the kind of gut laughter that you get from pure physical comedy.

It's interesting that you had that reaction. Allen told biographer Eric Lax that *Sleeper* was the first film in which "I started to get interested in my profession." It was the first movie that wasn't a series of sketches and was his first full narrative.

MILLER: Yeah, I like *Annie Hall* better as a movie and so does everybody in the universe—no big whoop there. But again, this was near my heart, *Sleeper*, because it was one of the first movies that I've ever seen where he was just unabashedly funny but still caring about things like art direction and what kind of shots he makes.

I took a lot away from that movie as far as cinematography. I still believe that long, wide setups are good for physical comedy. And when you get too tight with too many cuts, it often ruins the joke. It was definitely the case in *Sleeper*. There were lots of big wide shots where he just lets himself do all sorts of physical antics.

What scene sticks with you when you think about the film?

MILLER: I think about the whole series of things when he is impersonating the robot. It's the first thing I think of. Then, there's the giant food and slipping on a banana peel—a really classic, old-timey, cartoony gag.

And it's kind of interesting now, thinking about how we just made this film also with giant food and lots of physical comedy in it. We don't have a banana peel guy; we probably should have. It would've been a rip-off of the rip-off.

Also, when they are reading off the ingredients for his breakfast and it's like wheat germ, organic honey, tiger's milk, and his doctors in the future say, "Oh yes, those were the charmed substances that some years ago were thought to contain life-preserving properties."

And the other doctor says, "You mean there was no deep fat? No steak or cream pies, or hot fudge?"

"Those were thought to be unhealthy, precisely the opposite of what we now know to be true."

I always think about that moment because it has borne out to be true again and again. Seems like every few months scientists come back and say, "Oh no, we said this was good for you but actually it's bad for you."

How did *Sleeper* actually change your life?

MILLER: It was a real inspiration with me doing my earliest student films. I made a student film that was called *Sleazy the Wonder Squirrel Goes to France*, in which I had this comic strip character that I drew for my daily paper in college called Sleazy the Wondrous Squirrel, which is already, obviously, not the most pretentious thing.

He had a talk show with an Ed McMahon–like hamster, and they had talks about film that I want to say were not that great. Ah, the wisdom of several years. But the idea was that he had booked Godot to be on his talk show and he never showed up. And so they said, "We'll go to France to find him and kick his ass."

And it was all about the adventures they had in France. And so for me at the time, I was trying to do what I felt was being done so well in *Sleeper*, which was trying to make some commentary about America and France. There were a lot of people getting hit by giant toilets and that sort of thing, as well. I was really trying to marry the high and low of art. That's been something that, to the less obvious extent, I've been trying to do ever since with *Clone High*, with *How I Met Your Mother*. Especially with *Cloudy with a Chance of Meatballs*, where we really wanted it to be a really emotionally compelling and very cinematic movie. We also wanted it to be a silly cartoon at the same time. That constant tug-of-war between silly and meaningful is something I've always been intrigued by ever since I saw *Sleeper*.

Let's talk a little bit about the performances in the film. It's one of the early pairings of Diane Keaton and Woody Allen, who may have been dating at the time.
MILLER: She's quite foxy, especially back then. Yes, they had this sort of bickery romantic comedy thing going on in the middle of this terrible sci-fi movie. That was charming and rat-a-tat, which I really enjoyed. You know, there were a lot of cringey side jokes that Woody or she would make, but it would move so quickly that it didn't have to linger and make you think, "Wow, they really thought that one was a real home run." But even if only two out of every three worked, it was still a great batting average.

It also was a really fun like Billy Wilder or Bogart and Bacall, sort of fast-talking, packing-a-lot-of-clever-lines-and-hope-that-you-catch-half-of-'em style that I really liked. I'm sure that he was referencing that stuff, as well, but you know it was Woody Allen being Woody Allen. For most of his movies he plays exactly in character, which is a great comic character.

On subsequent viewings of the film, how has your perception of *Sleeper* changed?
MILLER: I started caring more about things like cinematography and story. I look at it through that lens now as an imperfect movie, and it kind of ends abruptly. It's not as lovingly crafted from a shot-language standpoint as some of his later stuff. The later stuff gets more talky. But he was such a gifted physical comedian. I would put him up there—not quite as athletic or amazing as Buster Keaton—but he is up there in the canon of great physical comedic actors, and he doesn't really do that as much anymore, which is too bad. That movie still makes me laugh.

How do you think your life would be different had you not seen that film?
MILLER: [*laughs*] I would be penniless and drunk on the corner, begging for cash, if I had not seen the film *Sleeper*. I guarantee you.

27

Neil LaBute
The Soft Skin

Neil LaBute's appreciation for one of François Truffaut's darker, often over-looked films makes a kind of sense. There's LaBute's penchant for somber tones, but the influence goes deeper. He points out that *In the Company of Men* and *Your Friends & Neighbors* pay homage to *The Soft Skin*. LaBute says even *The Mercy Seat*, a play he worked on, also contains clear evidence of Truffaut's effect on him.

For LaBute, *The Soft Skin* was a new and different approach to portraying both reality and New Wave filmmaking. He says, "I've never been one to love the camera or even to be as drawn to it as I am to the human front of it. . . . I think [*The Soft Skin*] was a film that speaks in a very simple way of here's a way that you can tell a story on film in human terms. It was the kind of film that made me go, 'I could do this; I want to tell stories that are like this and told in this way.' And so it was altering for me in that way, in its simplicity or deceptive simplicity."

Neil LaBute, selected filmography:
In the Company of Men (1997)
Your Friends & Neighbors (1998)
Nurse Betty (2000)
Possession (2002)
The Shape of Things (2003)
The Wicker Man (2006)
Lakeview Terrace (2008)
Death at a Funeral (2010)

The Soft Skin
1964
Directed by François Truffaut
Starring Jean Desailly and Françoise Dorléac

How would you describe *The Soft Skin* to someone who has never seen it?
LaBute: It's a fairly distinctive approach and certainly at the time, a very modern one, to a classic love triangle. It's a dissection of a marriage and an adulterous relationship, as well as a study of a man who ultimately is unable to choose between the two.

And do you remember when you saw the film? Did you see it in the theater?
LaBute: I didn't see it projected—I don't know that I've ever seen it projected. And that's a real shame. I think it's a film like a lot of the films that I admire. They're not driven so much by, "Oh do you remember that one shot?" so much as, "Do you remember the feeling the film left you with?" or "Weren't you impressed by the incisive character? The detailed character analysis or the dialogue?" They're really driven by other concerns rather than purely visual, although I think it's visually a quite striking film.

Do you remember the details of when you saw it and what initial effect it had on you?
LaBute: I think I saw it in a film class years ago. Brigham Young University had a great program where they showed films constantly. All the arts that they had were, I think, to keep students from dallying with one another, to keep them busy. So there was always a plethora of music and theater and film, so I took great advantage of that rather than my fellow students. And so constantly I saw a number of films, and I may have seen it first there.

Previous to watching *The Soft Skin*, it was described as a film that was a lesser known piece of work, and at the time of its release it was seen as a disappointment, because of the artistic high of the first few films—*The 400 Blows, Shoot the Piano Player*, and *Jules et Jim*. By comparison, *The Soft Skin* seemed fairly straightforward, slow, and dour in some ways, and cold.

And I think it's all of those things, and I think that's what makes it so great. I think Truffaut, from what I understand, he wanted to make something that was quite modern. In its own way it's as modern as *Alphaville* because it's set in a very real Paris, but one that is filled with the cold, everyday things that make up life. You know, the elevator just outside the door, and the bars and the cars and the pushbuttons of the machines that take us to and from the people that we love or have lost love for. I like that juxtaposed with a man who's quite chilly, who's far more a man driven by his mind than by his heart, who suddenly has that fall in such a remarkable way. I think it's a great performance by Jean Desailly.

I have a gift, the latest Truffaut biography; it's a few years old now. And I can remember reading about the film because at that point I'd seen it and liked it, and it appeared that he was unhappy ultimately with his choice of the lead male character.

And I couldn't disagree more. I think it's such a strong piece of acting. If you approach it from the way that I do, that it really is about this man's indecisiveness that brings him down, and the impassivity of this intellectual mind trying to become emotional. So I think Desailly does a wonderfully incisive, to-the-point performance. The fact that it is so chilling is what makes it so heartbreaking. He wants to be this great intellectual, and all of a sudden he's just this scared kid.

In his letters, there was a lot of turmoil in Truffaut's life at this time. He wrote of Desailly, "He doesn't like the film, or the character or the story or me." At the time, Truffaut had announced that he was breaking up with his wife, and there was some reading that this was a self-portrait.

LaBute: It very well may be, because you look at the tale and think it's so marvelously acute, and he does seem to understand. And there's a fairness there, for all parties concerned, which I think someone who hasn't gone through that wouldn't portray. Even though he could carry a film like *The Man Who Loved Women*—which is essentially the story of a man filled with great love or a cad—it depends on how you read it.

But because it's a small number of people that he's dealing with, I think he's able to give them nearly enough time. I think the wife (Nelly Benedetti), if anyone, is shortchanged a bit; her character Franca has the least amount of time, and we understand her as a person the least. But we understand certainly how she is motivated, because it's fairly broad strokes of desire and hurt and revenge and those kinds of things. But I think that, for me, is all the better because I didn't have to suffer through it, but I get to reap the benefits of his emotional understanding of that story.

How then did it change your life?

LaBute: It exposed me, probably in the earliest way, to "Hey, I could do that." I've never been one to love the camera or even to be as drawn to it as I am to the human aspect of it, and I think it was a film that speaks in a very simple way of here's a way that you can tell a story on film in human terms. It was the kind of film that made me go, "I could do this; I want to tell stories that are like this and told in this way." And so it was altering for me in that way, in its simplicity or deceptive simplicity.

It reminds me of something from roughly the same time, Godard's *A Married Woman*, and subsequent films that I saw after that, films by Rohmer, who I'm a huge fan of. Another one who you never say, "Oh what a great tracking shot, what a great this and that" but "How incisive!"—I'm using *incisive* too often—but how close to the bone this guy understands people, what great understanding into the mind, into the heart.

What's interesting for me is just the arc. When he was a film critic, Truffaut embraced films that talked about bringing about a new morality or a new way to look at human relationships. By the time he gets to *Jules et Jim*, he's turned that on its ear with a modern three-way relationship and explains why that doesn't work and how it still falls into the same problems. By the time you get to the fourth film, *The Soft Skin*, he's very contemporary in his morality.

LaBute: Although, in a way, it's probably much more bourgeois in that film, even though it's got a more modern feel than, say, *Jules et Jim*, because it's a radical approach. It's a radical story, especially for the time that the story's set in. It's a very freewheeling ménage there that those three are executing, compared to this story. It plays out in a dalliance; then there's the decision really to go back to it, if at all possible.

It's really that striking denouement of the gunshot that makes the difference that people kind of can't help but remember. But it really is conventional in its day, and perhaps that's what people reacted to, that it was both cold and modern and yet the morality of it was fairly conventional.

The *New York Times* called it "a curiously crude and hackneyed drama to come from Mr. Truffaut." *Sight & Sound* wrote, "There have been plenty of films about adultery, but few have ventured to take the mechanism so methodically to pieces."

LaBute: I would embrace that. I didn't see it as hackneyed at all, but that's the beauty of it. It's subjective, and they can very well think that, and I can think something different.

This was also the first film in what is called his "Hitchcock cycle." There were four films that he was working on while he was interviewing Alfred Hitchcock for his famous book.

LaBute: I think that's quite evident in the work, just the appearance of this woman who's somewhat unattainable and the kind of voyeuristic side of it—there are great passages of silence in the piece punctuated by some of the most beautiful music, a great score. One of Georges Delerue's best, I think, and he made so many.

I think the influences are kind of obvious, and yet less so than say, *The Bride Wore Black* or *Mississippi Mermaid*. There's the use of unexpected humor, that distinctive second act, where it's almost farcical—there's running back and forth between hotels, and his desire to be with her, and yet having to uphold this rigid code of civility with these people who are essentially paying the tab for him being there. That's that kind of great section, and it stands out from the rest of the piece. But there's absolutely a layer that is shellacked over that kind of proceeding, the tawdry aspect of essentially a decent guy, and a guy who wants it to be romantic and for no one to be hurt, and yet he's running around like a bumbling fool. I think that's an important aspect, if that wasn't there, that kind of deft handling of that passage. Without it, you would have a much more conventional film.

The least electrifying aspect of the whole thing of course is the actual physical contact. Truffaut shies away from that continually. Probably the most passionate moment comes between the husband and wife, surprisingly. There's a kiss early on, even though they go back and they have that fantastic moment where she begins unrolling that crazy wool painting that hides the bedroom, and the nurse sees that and shuffles the child into the next room. But that's not nearly as strong, I mean physically, as that one kiss that they have, and there's nothing like that on the other side that we see, and I think that's really a shrewd move on his part. It's another thing that makes it really quite modern, and de-romanticizes the tale and really gets down to the messy mechanics of love.

This is shot very differently from all his previous films.
LaBute: Well, it also gives more of a nod to his fellow New Wave directors. There's more of a sense of Godard there and more of a sense of Rohmer, although he hadn't done work by that point, aside from his short films.

The 400 Blows probably owes more of a debt to neorealists than it does to the New Wave. But Chabrol's *Le beau serge* couldn't seem further from *Breathless* to me. It's kind of an old-throwback well-made piece, but I love that.

But, yeah, I think there is a different shooting style. One of my favorite moments is that freeze-frame when Lachenay [Desailly] is walking out of the plane. He starts to walk past Nicole [Françoise Dorléac], and they start to look at each other. And they stand and look at each other, and Truffaut literally freezes the frame but cuts to the other side. There's a straight cut to her, which is frozen as well, and then it starts again, like that moment when time stands still when you're with this person who takes your breath away. And it's just really a gorgeous moment you can almost miss, but it's really incisive in terms of technique and emotion. It just all works together right then.

There's a great quote from Truffaut in which he says, "The critics say I changed my style, but not at all. I had merely changed my subject." So, from your perspective as a director then, how does subject inform style?
LaBute: You kind of erase the board every time, and you let the piece speak to you. I think he was one who could do that, although you could look at almost all of his work, more so than many people, and feel it fit within his hand.

His work ripples all the way from *400 Blows* through, perhaps not the last film, *Confidentially Yours*, a black-and-white throwback, Hitchcock-y kind of a lark. Which is fine, but it's certainly not my favorite. But *The Soft Skin* has direct parallels to something as late in his life as *The Woman Next Door*, even down to the fact that his wife looks remarkably like Fanny Ardant, and the movie ends in roughly the same way, although she this time kills herself as well. But killing the hero with a gun makes it another quite Hitchcock-y thriller in its own way.

So I think his preoccupations were there throughout, but I think that each time he approached the material anew and said that it's as much at least, if not more, about the material, about the story, telling that truthfully, than it is about me. I think there were times that, as much as I like Godard, it became more about Godard than it did about the film.

So I prefer that about Truffaut—that he always seemed to be true to his characters and true to his story, rather than true to himself or true to the audience.

But his love stories were always tortured and just difficult to embrace. *The Soft Skin* isn't one you just cozy up to and go, "This is fun." *Two English Girls*, that's very distancing. And then the obsessional things like *The Green Room*, which I've seen only recently, and again I don't think of as the same quality as some of his films. But that kind of absolute measured, distanced approach to things, I really admire. So this movie just sort of distilled those themes that I've been interested in.

One of the things, and you mentioned before how this theme resonates throughout his career—Have you ever seen *Day for Night*?
LaBute: Yes.

I'd just seen that, and do you remember that they re-create a scene from this film? It's when the lovers are in the cottage, and they have the kitten who comes to drink the milk.
LaBute: Oh, yes, of course.

It's sort of a very strange, surreal, insiderish thing to do, so much later in his career, in a color film.

LaBute: Yeah, well, and not at all strange for the New Wave, but something he didn't do for the kind of freedom that someone like Godard did. You look at like *A Woman Is a Woman*, and he has Jeanne Moreau walk through and break character, and the character talks to her as herself, not as a character who's walking through the movie, not as a character who's walking through the movie saying, "Hey, Jeanne, how's it going? What are you working on?" She's like, "Oh, I'm working on this film called *Jules et Jim*, you know, isn't that great?" And you know, very self-referential, that whole movement may be. And I think he was either late to jump on the bandwagon, or he just thought of it right then because he was making a movie about making movies.

But it's funny that I didn't remember that it was from that particular film, but yeah, that's another great moment in that film, the cat climbing on top, looking for something to eat or drink.

In his letters Truffaut wrote, "*The Soft Skin* was painful to make and because of the story I now have a loathing of marital hypocrisy and on that point I feel a total revulsion at present." And again, it suggested that much of this was at least thematically autobiographical. From your perspective, what are the dangers of exorcising your demons on the screen or on the stage?
LaBute: The dangers are pre-evident, that it's hard to get any distance, to get the aesthetic distance that one needs to. Because I always think—this is an easy catchphrase—"It's theater, not therapy." And I love the one, "Just because it's true doesn't mean it's interesting."

I think the danger is that you can't get back far enough to really see if you've got a dramatic story, one that works on-screen. You live out your own life, and it happens whether you like it or not, but you have more control over cinema. And I think that if you begin to use it as a sounding board, as a therapist, then you run the danger of getting in too deep and to not being able to tell a proper kind of dramatic story. I mean proper for my taste.

That said, you can't speak with any more authority than about something that you know. He obviously had those qualities, when you look at his work overall. You look at *The Man Who Loved Women* and then read anything about him, you know that this was one of his great obsessions, women, and this inability to ultimately choose between them and to be faithful and all of those things. So he obviously could pull from that wellspring and did quite well, in terms of choosing material and making films that have some lasting impact. But I think the danger always is that you can get too close, that you lose sight of what it is you're trying to do rather than what it is you're trying to say. It's all about the why. Why do you need to make this? Is it for anybody else, or is it merely for yourself?

A movie can cost a hundred million dollars or cost two million, and you pay the same amount to go see it. It doesn't matter what *Master and Commander* cost. I don't know what he had to live through, this accurate portrayal of relationships unraveling. I just get to sit back and say whether I think it was worth watching or not. And happily, I think it was.

Do you think it resonates within the film, though—is there that extra element? *The Soft Skin* **was inspired by a newspaper story of a true-life event. Parts of it were shot in Truffaut's actual apartment.**
LaBute: Well, no doubt. I'm sure that the battlefield, the landscape, being that close to the director's life, couldn't help but pepper his judgment and his choice of shots. Just the number of times that you see the guy walk up and down the stairs. And that's what he does the whole movie, and he's constantly climbing toward somewhere else. There are some very obvious kinds of motifs like that. After he's met Nicole, the airline hostess, there's this wonderful shot of him walking around his hotel room and turning on lights. It's literally like a lightbulb going on over his head.

It's nice when somebody's actually so bold as to do something so obvious. We're always so worried about being so subtle, and "Oh, is this a cliche?" I think life is often a cliche; you find yourself in moments where you go, "If this was in a movie, people would say this is ridiculous, this is too much." And yet, it happens all the time.

For you, what does the title mean?
LaBute: Well, I think it's kind of lovely and ironic because it's a beautiful title in and of itself. So that's enough for me. But I think there's precious little time devoted to the physical aspect of the story, and I think that's true in life.

Such a small portion of our life is dedicated to really physically expressing ourselves, to really investing in a hug, to holding someone's hand and thinking about it while you're doing it. It's much easier just to have that distance between someone and say, "I love you" or "I've been thinking about you" to your child or to your wife or to your friend.

But rarely, and especially outside the immediate circle of your family, do you physically show someone how you care for them. In Europe, you see the tendency to kiss on the cheek. There's the tendency for two men to hug. I think in this country in particular, we're still quite Puritanical about the physical side of things. And I think it suggests sort of the beauty of that, the beauty of the skin and that kind of longing for that physical element in a relationship—and yet how little time we actually spend enjoying it when it's happening. So I think that's a huge part of the title, at least in my translation of it.

It's interesting that you bring that up, because my next batch of questions is about the role of language. One of the critics wrote that in this film, language is used to hide emotion rather than to convey it, and all the passions and tensions are portrayed visually.
LaBute: I think that's true, but it's not only seen with the spoken word. It's the written word as well. There's this moment where he runs back into the airport. He's in a panic; he's driven out to the airport and is kind of wild. Even at that time in Paris, are you going to just drive out to the airport in order to run into this person? And, of course, he does.

You know, love is that way. It's sort of an insane proposition at times. But he writes out that kind of desperate telegram to her, and he ends up slipping it into his pocket when he sees her. Rather than giving it to her and saying, "Hey, this is what I was thinking about you," he destroys it; he throws it in a wastebasket, embarrassed by this kind of display. Instead it's just like, "Oh, hey, gosh, I saw you, that's so great; I thought you'd be on that other plane," when on that piece of paper in his hand is "I love you, you've changed my life." And his first impulse when she's there is to toss it in. It's a difficulty that we have in person, that closeness, that place where you can actually feel skin, the softness of it we're very embarrassed by. What we're embarrassed by is opening up, being vulnerable.

But those statements are constantly being underscored or betrayed by the look of longing on this guy's face, or the wife is understanding what's going on, or the indecisiveness of this young woman who probably isn't ready for these kinds of feelings. She has a very telling monologue when they're on their short vacation, saying, "I like this, I like love, but I can go without it for months. I was too young to understand it when it first happened."

There's that amazing moment near the end where a guy comes up to her and propositions her, and she doesn't just walk away; she grabs him and screams at him and puts his face in the mirror and says, "Look at yourself. You think that people are going to be interested in you?" It's like everything that she's been feeling explodes in this guy's face. Of course it's not enough; she stills goes off into this other trajectory. It's unstoppable.

A lot of Truffaut's love stories—whether it's *Jules et Jim* or *Antoine et Colette*—it's been written that those women demand all or nothing. "Perfect love or death," I think was the quote. Do you think traditionally that women characters have been boxed in by that perception, or is it just a metaphor for how differently men and women view love?

LaBute: Probably a bit of both. I think some would find that very limiting and some would find it very freeing. And it just depends on where you are in your own life and how you interpret that. You could be on either side of that triangle and feel very differently about that film. You could watch that film at two different times in your life and feel very differently. I think that's what lasts about it, and what's perfect about it in its own way—it's very much of its time and yet it's quite unbound by its time as well.

I think it's pretty classic in that way, and I think the portrayal of women is quite modern—they're quite free to make their own decisions, and I think there's still the rigidity of convention there, but I think you're seeing people who are kinda breaking free of that, sometimes so forcefully, like what Franca ends up doing. And in a simple way, just kind of awful, brutal indifference. "Indifference" is probably too strong a word, but the way in which Nicole breaks up with him: they're looking around that apartment; she's kind of, "Eh, I'm probably not really ready for this. We could still meet every so often." You know, it's such an unemotional moment, really. And even on his face, he realizes what a mistake he's made.

If I remember right, that's from a construction site. He's buying an apartment that's not even finished.

LaBute: Exactly. It's literally exposed to the elements.

How has your perception of this film changed on subsequent viewings?

LaBute: I've seen it at different times of my life and in different stages, and I think it is fresh each time. But I haven't lost my initial respect for it. And it's true that I probably admire more than love it. I think that's partly due to its construction, that kind of distance; there's sort of Truffaut's hand on your chest, he doesn't let you in completely.

He keeps you, he forces you as an outsider—you don't choose an allegiance with one character or get so deeply involved that you can't see the whole. If you've seen Godard's *My Life to Live*, there are thirteen or however many chapters of that film that chart this woman's downfall, but it's always, it's quite chilly in that distanced way. And I think there's a bit of that here. It's not as inviting, although it's so wonderfully juxtaposed with as rich a score as there could be. I mean it's such beautiful music, and yet the proceedings are icy at times. You're thinking, "Wow, this is really moving, and what I'm being moved by is the music. It's kind of inappropriately romantic, what I'm watching."

I was interested in how you see this film informing your own work and if you've had any references or homages to it.

LaBute: Turn my own work on and you'll see the direct influence. I mean those are almost the same kinds of words used to describe *Your Friends & Neighbors* or *In the Company of Men*—the ones that have come directly from my own work.

The Mercy Seat, the play, hasn't been a film, but my theater work is as much of a part of me as my film. And that's absolutely the same thing, the story of a man who has the inability to choose. The themes have directly influenced my work and that clinical approach of something like *Carnal Knowledge*. So it's hugely influential, as are a number of other things. But absolutely, this film was.

Are there any homages to it in your work at all, overt or otherwise?
LaBute: No, I don't think so, not in the way like there are in *Friends &*
Neighbors, where there are literally scene cards from *Chloe in the Afternoon*
on the wall of the restaurants and the posters on the wall of one of the apart-
ments. That era of film has been influential, but there's nothing directly
lifted from this.

Have you ever met anybody connected with the film?
LaBute: No, never have, no. Never had any direct connection. You know,
Françoise Dorléac was lost really early in her life, in a quite horrible way. She
died in a car accident somewhere on the road between Nice and Cannes. It
was a quite horrible, fiery crash, where she couldn't get out of the car, that
kind of thing. And she was like twenty-five. She was twenty-two when she
did *The Soft Skin*. She looked older than her years, I think.

Yes, yes she does.
LaBute: I think it's the time and the makeup and everything; everyone sort
of looked older than they were. In a good way, you go, "Gosh, twenty-one,
it's hard to believe." But yeah, I don't know any of those people beyond just
admiring their work. [Director of photography Raoul] Coutard, beautiful
cinematography, he's still out there. I don't think he works anymore, but I
have seen interviews with him fairly recently.

But yeah, I think everybody was just at the top of their game there, and
Jean Desailly in particular, he was primarily a theater actor. He did not do
a lot of film work. I think Truffaut wanted truly to have someone who the
audience would not know, and he could then much more easily fall into the
story. And I just thought he was a great choice.

As an adult, what do you see as your initial attraction to it?
LaBute: I think all the things that attracted me are still there, but I have
a greater understanding of life, of love. And one of the great aspects of it,
and we didn't touch on it at all, is Lachenay's feeling for his child. You can
see how much he loves his daughter, Sabine. Some of the freest moments,
the film really slows down; it's amazingly crisp, just even the pace at which

Lachenay moves around in his literary world. The opening scene is him rushing home to get his things and head off to the plane. He's constantly rushing from place to place to be adored briefly by this group or to say his important thoughts on Balzac.

But there are moments where he stops, and he listens to Molière with his daughter and one of his questions is "Before I go, can I see my daughter?" He has a definite love of his child. He understands that pure kind of love; he's able to comprehend. And that having children, you understand how important they are, and that's something that you leave behind—far more important than these papers he's writing or these lectures he gives.

28

George A. Romero
The Tales of Hoffmann

Romero began his career as a director of commercials and educational films; notable among them were short segments for the children's program *Mr. Rogers' Neighborhood*. His first feature, *Night of the Living Dead*, was released in 1968. It became a cult classic and continues to spawn sequels and remakes.

But the film that changed his life is an unlikely one for this master of horror: the 1951 opera-to-movie adaptation of *The Tales of Hoffmann*. Moviemaking team Michael Powell and Emeric Pressburger reimagined Jacques Offenbach's opera as a dreamlike stage/screen hybrid that tests the bounds of narrative. The story follows Hoffmann (played by Robert Rousenville), a young man from Nuremberg, Germany, who recounts the stories of his three great loves, depicted in operatic flashbacks.

Of the movie, Romero says: "I love watching the film as much as I like going back to a favorite piece of music. It never diminishes for me."

George A. Romero, selected filmography:
Night of the Living Dead (1968)
There's Always Vanilla (1971)
Hungry Wives (1972)
The Crazies (1973)
Martin (1977)
Dawn of the Dead (1978)
Knightriders (1981)
Creepshow (1982)
Day of the Dead (1985)
Monkey Shines (1988)

The Dark Half (1993)
Bruiser (2000)
Land of the Dead (2005)
Diary of the Dead (2007)
Survival of the Dead (2009)

The Tales of Hoffmann
1951
Directed by Michael Powell and Emeric Pressburger
Starring Robert Rounseville, Moira Shearer, Ludmilla
Tchérina, Ann Ayars, Pamela Brown, Léonide Massine, Robert
Helpmann, Frederick Ashton, Mogens Wieth, Lionel Harris,
Philip Leaver, Meinhart Maur, and more

How would you describe *The Tales of Hoffmann* to someone who has never seen it?
ROMERO: It's a version of the Offenbach opera with some added music and some ballet. It's about a guy and his unrequited love. He's in love with a ballerina, and there's a villain who's almost vampiric who appears in all the tales.

Hoffmann gets drunk in a tavern telling the three tales, and the same guy walks away with the ballerina. It's a fantasy. He falls in love with a mechanical doll. I like to call it the first music video.

You were twelve when you first saw it?
ROMERO: I was at the Sutton Place Theater in Manhattan. An aunt and uncle took me to see it, and I was just blown away. I was in a great theater with terrific projection, a really big screen, and it was just beautiful. I was knocked out. I noticed even then the colors and how they were used, and I just thought it was gorgeous. It was beautiful, and you just don't see it anymore today.

I was expecting to be bored to tears by this movie. It wasn't a *Tarzan* movie; it wasn't a war movie; it wasn't John Wayne, John Ford. I expected, "Oh God, I'm going to get some culture here!"

First of all, I love the music. I thought the music was better than any score I had heard. It turned me on to classical music, and it turned me on to the piece itself. It was the filmmaking, the fantasy, the fact that it was a fantasy and it had a few frightening, sort of bizarre things in it. It was everything.

It was really a movie for me, and it gave me an early appreciation for the power of visual media—the fact that you could experiment with it. He was doing all his tricks in-camera, and they were sort of obvious. That made me feel that, gee, maybe I could figure this medium out. It was transparent, but it worked. It didn't bother me in those days, nothing bothered me. I thought *King Kong* didn't look fake.

And do you have a particular scene that you are drawn to?
ROMERO: The duel. I thought it was beautiful. The music is slow; the action is very fast. It's just a well-described scene. And I like the shots of one of the characters walking down statues, like stepping on lost souls.

You've called this film a constant metaphor for the transforming power of imagination through art.
ROMERO: It really is very heady. Powell was able to take whatever ideas came at him. The basic storylines are in the opera, so he wasn't inventing the whole thing. But he was able to visualize it and imagine things the way he thought they should look and the way they could never be done on a stage at the Metropolitan or anywhere else. It's like painting. Even though it's not literal, it's not abstract. I think it was referencing painters in the overhead shot of everyone at the table at the tavern. I think he was able to really use his imagination to pull these wonderful ideas out and execute them.

There's a scene in which a life-size mechanical doll, whom Hoffmann falls in love with, is torn apart. I couldn't help but think of a similar scene from *Dawn of the Dead* in which your zombies tear apart one of their victims. Do you have any conscious homages to Powell and Press- burger in your films?
ROMERO: No, not really. I generally don't play around with that. I don't try to think of how to emulate. I generally try to just serve whatever I'm doing the best I can think of. So, if anything, I think there might be some subliminal stuff.

I've never had a budget to work with color the way Powell did, to take the time and the care to develop a color palette or anything like that. I've never been in a position where I could absolutely control something to be able to do that. I think the one thing I might try to do is really work with color.

It's been suggested blue is the predominant character.

Romero: I don't know about that. One of the shots that I remember vividly is the shot in the opening sequence, when the actor Robert Helpmann comes in, and he does that little gesture with his finger across his mouth. I thought he was the greatest Dracula there ever was. When he does an overhead shot where he walks around with his cape with a tassel on the end, and he walks around three chairs, and it's just beautiful. It's a symbolic shot of him walking through this place with just three chairs. The ballet is more blue and aqua when she's doing the firefly dance.

He uses hot red to indicate passion. The cooler colors are more subdued emotions. It's very emotional, and yellows are very bright and sunny. It's sort of very obvious, but it's very deliberate, and the chaos of color in the tavern is beautiful. It's a chaos of color.

I read when you met Michael Powell, you mentioned *Hoffmann* to him, and he said, "Oh well, there's a film no one saw." Why do you think no one saw it?

Romero: It wasn't a narrative. I really think it was just a little out of reach for people. It was very bold. It was an experiment, and without a narrative story it is hard for people to get with it. It's all sung, and it's very difficult to hear some of the dialogue unless you hear it over and over and over. I have an old vinyl soundtrack, and gosh, I've listened to that soundtrack over and over.

An editor whom I work with when I can named Pasquale "Pat" Buba was a longtime friend of Thelma Schoonmacher, who married Michael. She's Martin Scorsese's editor. When I was still living in New York, there was no such thing as video, so if you wanted to watch a movie at home you actually had to go rent a 16mm projector, go rent a movie, and there was a place called Janus Films that used to have *Tales of Hoffmann*. It was the only place in New York you could get it, and if I went down and it was gone, I knew that Marty had it, and if he went down and it was gone, he knew I had it. So we knew of each other back then, but we hadn't met. Pat knew that I was just a huge fan of Michael's, and he knew that they were married, and it just so happened that we were all in New York at the same time, so he arranged for us to go have dinner, and we all went out to a restaurant, and it was just wonderful.

Powell was this wonderful old British gent. The way he talked about the business, when he was making propaganda movies for the war, the influence of the producers and studios and the rank organizations—great old war stories. It was like sitting down with Dr. Watson. Absolutely droll, really calm, spoke in complete sentences and not at all impressed with his own stuff, wishing that he could do more, wishing that he had had the benefit of some of the new technologies. He was a real craftsman.

Critics have noted that *Fantasia* might have been one of the influences on *Hoffmann*. Do you see that?
ROMERO: Powell talked about loving *Fantasia*. If in any way it was an influence, I think maybe it gave him the idea of taking classical music and trying to visualize it. I don't think he was trying to imitate or emulate it stylistically at all. I think he was just taking music and translating it from whatever ideas come into your head. I mean, I've often sat and listened to classical music and imagined visuals for it, imagined little stories that could go with it. Maybe that's what he meant. I don't see any visual parallels.

Powell made his name in literary movies and ballet, and ended with one of the first psychological horror films, *Peeping Tom*, and other kinds of movies. You began with horror and went to other genres. Is there a parallel?
ROMERO: I've been typecast. I wouldn't just stick with this genre if anybody would hire me to do something else. I don't do films about men with hockey masks with knives. I try to put some content in there, at least express my opinions or do some social satirizing. I think that is what fantasy is supposed to be used for, as metaphor. I think the influence is there, and I think that it made me, rather than just do some slasher thing, want to use it more for social commentary.

Pressburger and Powell are credited with expanding British eroticism. Did *Tales of Hoffmann* have an effect on you this way?

ROMERO: The Russian (Ludmilla Tchérina)—I don't know if she was a ballerina or not. She's trying to do it, and sort of kneeling in front of Hoffmann trying to come on to him. He had her throw her head back and forth in the throes of passion, but really, he was trying to get her downstage so you couldn't see her mouth.

Our eroticism was much more obvious and much more voluptuous, like everything American. We had all those bombshells. I think, maybe, in the earlier days with Ingrid Bergman, even in the silent days, we were closer to classical, subtler forms of eroticism.

Hoffmann, when he comes back to Giulietta's room and he sees the hunchback wallowing in a clam-shaped bed, it really evokes passion, a longing for something. That one shot is very provocative. That scene where she walks down that statue barefoot is very seductive, sort of misogynistic. I don't know that he liked women very much. I think he enjoyed them.

How has your experience with it changed?

ROMERO: It still recalls the same sort of wonder. Of course, you see some of the flaws and you can appreciate their production problems. You can see some jump cuts, but the overall experience doesn't hurt it at all. Some films that I remember really loving, on repeated watching, lose some of their allure. I love watching the film as much as I like going back to a favorite piece of music. It never diminishes for me.

29

Frank Oz
Touch of Evil

Frank Oz knew Orson Welles, so he felt comfortable calling him "Orson" in this interview about *Touch of Evil*. It is strange, however, that in their friendship he never talked to the filmmaker about this "ode to the B-movie" that changed his life.

In this interview, he describes Welles's performance as the villain in the film: "Orson was a raconteur. When he spoke, it was like poetry and it was a performance. I'm not so sure that it wasn't completely all thought-out all the time, you know. [*laughs*]"

Frank Oz, selected filmography:
The Dark Crystal (1982; codirector)
The Muppets Take Manhattan (1984)
Little Shop of Horrors (1986)
Dirty Rotten Scoundrels (1988)
What About Bob? (1991)
The Indian in the Cupboard (1995)
Bowfinger (1999)
The Score (2001)
The Stepford Wives (2004)
Death at a Funeral (2007)

Touch of Evil
1958
Directed by Orson Welles
Starring Charlton Heston, Janet Leigh, Orson Welles, Joseph Calleia, Akim Tamiroff, Joanna Moore, and Ray Collins

How would you describe *Touch of Evil* to someone who has never seen it?

Oz: It's about the dissolution of a decent man, Quinlan (played by Orson Welles), who was not a bad cop, not a bad guy when he was young. It stars Charlton Heston, Orson Welles, Marlene Dietrich, Dennis Weaver . . .

Essentially it's about two detectives, one American, which is Welles, and one Mexican, which is Heston. They're warring over a case in which Quinlan frames a young kid. And Janet Leigh has bad luck in yet another hotel room. [*laughs*]

Oz: Exactly. It's amazing seeing that thing; it looks so much like the Bates Motel. That's striking to me.

So tell me about the first time you saw the film.

Oz: I don't remember the first time I saw it. All I remember is every time I look at it I am never ever bored with this thing. I always find new things that Welles did. I don't remember the first time that I saw it. Isn't that funny?

You must have seen the original cut.

Oz: Yes, I did.

Tell me your initial reaction to it. Tell me about why it stayed with you so long.

Oz: Well, I think it stayed with me so long because of the wonderful emotional history between Marlene Dietrich, who plays a madam, and Quinlan. I think that's very strong and what could've been between the two of them. I think that emotional core is very strong to me. It's not about Janet Leigh and Charlton Heston. It really is about when they were younger. Also, of course, just what he's done. From the blocking to the lighting, to the depths, creating your own close-ups, going off with these long scenes, the overlapping dialogue, the dark and light values, all the upshots, rarely at an eye-line. Every time I look at it, everything is just amazing to me.

Let's back up and I'll just start it off here: Charlton Heston as a Mexican. [*laughs*]

Oz: Yeah, but you know the story behind that. Heston really was the one who wanted Welles. And they wouldn't do it without Heston, so he said, "OK, I'll do it, but Welles has to direct." That was a good thing he did.

Oh yeah, but still . . .
Oz: It's lousy that he's a Mexican, lousy that a Mexican can't play a Mexican, but if they didn't do it, there wouldn't be a *Touch of Evil*, either.

How does he do?
Oz: Well, I don't believe in him as Mexican for one second. I see some dark makeup and that's it. And some lousy Spanish. No, I don't see him at all. I think he is Charlton Heston and that's what he is. I think he was courageous at that time to push for Welles. As far as a Mexican, no, I didn't believe him for a second.

There are two different stories about Heston coming on to the project. Universal wanted him for it, and they had told him that they had cast Welles, but I interviewed Charlton a couple of years ago, and he told me that he misunderstood. He thought that they had cast him as the director.
Oz: The director, huh?

Playing on that ignorance they hurried up and called Orson right away and offered him the job. It's been recapped in a couple of different places.
Oz: Isn't that something? You never know.

It turned out to be Orson's last Hollywood film.
Oz: Yeah, and it's certainly a B-movie, but it's more than a B-movie to me. It's almost like an ode to B-movies. It's just so extraordinary. I'm just amazed by it every time I see it.

Heston said his favorite quote about the film is, "*Touch of Evil* is not a great film. It is beyond question the best B-movie ever made."
Oz: It was like a valentine to a B-movie, it was like an ode to the B-movie. It was a very self-aware B-movie.

Tell me about that distinction. To me, great film is great film, but what makes it not a great film but a great B-movie?

Oz: Let's see, what makes B-movies? It was melodramatic. He didn't have much time to shoot and you could see that. B-movies have melodrama as opposed to honest drama. But I think he pushed that in every way. From the lighting to the shots, everything was overly dramatic. He pushed the envelope of B-movies even further to make it an ode to B-movies. The melodramatic aspect of B-movies to me is what makes them unique.

There's this great opening sequence that was restored—a three-minute-and-eighteen-second tracking shot.

Oz: Yes, true. Here I go dropping names—Orson invited Jim Henson and me to dinner at Mon Maison years ago, after *The Muppet Movie*. It was amazing to hear him, but he was saying that the take they used was the very last one, because the guard kept on fucking up at the end.

He said, "Don't say a fucking thing; just move your mouth. I'll dub it in later."

Oz: [*laughs*] So that was staggering. If you look at that whole front section— that shot and the shots afterwards, a couple scenes later and scenes throughout the movie—it's very bravura filmmaking. With all these cars and the lights and the movement and the people and the streets. I mean, that's really bravura. He took major chances.

On your commentary track for *The Score* you talk about the direct influence—

Oz: Absolutely. Essentially, I said to my DP [director of photography], "Look, I want to make this as close as possible to the *Touch of Evil* lighting because I felt that would make this really work." And so we couldn't really do it because it's color. The value of color and black and white is all different, but we got close to the *Touch of Evil* kind of feeling. That's exactly what I wanted.

How did that manifest itself?

Oz: Dark and light. Not being afraid of black, about not seeing people's faces. If you look at some of the scenes, my God, the ideas you got. The traditional thing with DPs is you've got to see their eyes, and the eye light and everything. Orson just said, "Fuck that," because of economics, I'm sure. He had people in complete blackness. I was saying to Rob Hahn, "Let's go for that, let's have dark and light," which Rob does very well anyway, but to really push it as much as possible with the knowledge that we can't because it's color. It's about not being afraid of taking big chances, not worrying about seeing people's faces.

Tell me about your favorite scene.
Oz: My favorite scene, without question, is one of the five-minute scenes. It's when they're in the room and there's about eight people. Quinlan is there, and they're talking to the Mexican kid. The Mexican kid is supposedly being used by this woman, and then Vargas goes in and sees the shoebox in the bathroom.

That whole five-minute scene is absolutely amazing to me. Trying to block eight people in a room with all the dark and light, the depth, and the foreground, the background, the close-ups, the wide shots, and shooting up. I mean just one shot, five minutes. Now, it's not unusual that there's one shot that's five minutes. I mean, Christ, Kubrick did a ten-minute shot, and Orson did another five-minute shot, in the same room the second time we were there. That is the most staggering scene to me. I can't get over how he had to, economically, you know. He couldn't keep on cutting and having a new deal and shooting in a different direction and relighting. He just kept the camera steady and moved everybody around and created his own close-ups and wide shots. It was fantastic.

Welles, in talking about his style and vision, said that editing was the most important element. He goes into this great hyperbole about how directing itself is "not an art, or at most an art for a minute a day."
Oz: I think he's right, except if he was here I'd disagree with him. Look at what he did in those two scenes. You've got to have those scenes blocked. In a way, he's editing as he's shooting. He edited that five minutes because he created his own close-ups, his own wide shots, his own mediums, his two-shots, his eight-shots. So, in a way, it was editing. He didn't just cut the film. He moved people around to create the editing as he's shooting it. Just the fact that the scene exists belies what he says.

There's a story about Heston and Welles toasting one another after the film. Heston says, "You know, Orson, I think we're gonna have a great film, except for the fact that you hid the fact that you gave yourself the best part."

Oz: [*laughs*] It's very funny because if you look at the entrance to Quinlan, he gave himself this monster. He gave this monster such an amazing entrance, that upshot in the car. Then the predeath scene where he kills his friend and he's in a stupor. The end, the whole death scene and also his dissolution, which is what the movie is about to me. He really gave himself a hell of a part.

Film writer Joseph McBride has said that the actual guilt or innocence of the young Mexican kid is the red herring. For me the bigger red herring is that Charlton Heston is even in it, when it's obviously about Orson Welles.

Oz: It really is about Quinlan and what happened to this man that Marlene Dietrich knew younger, twenty or thirty years ago.

Welles said, "I'm a natural for big characters. I've always been bigger than life. It's a fault in my nature." He says this led to him having no ambiguity in any of his characters, which I'm not so sure I buy.

Oz: Orson was a raconteur. When he spoke, it was like poetry and it was a performance. I'm not so sure that it wasn't completely all thought-out all the time, you know. [*laughs*] He was so amazing in his speaking. Not to say that he was lying or anything, but it's possible the performance got to him. I did see ambiguity in certain characters. I tend to disagree with his statement.

This is Welles in a pre-Falstaff role as well. It's him becoming, as you perfectly say, the monster.

Oz: What a great monster he created for himself. He was amazing. He was as corpulent as possible. [*laughs*] He was amazing. It was obvious: the cancer in that character, the moral cancer in that man. It just came out physically.

Welles talked about his preoccupation with the moral dilemma in this film, namely: "Is it better to see a murderer go unpunished or have the

police being authorized to abuse their power?" From the finished film, do you think he ever reconciles that?

Oz: Boy, that's a dilemma, isn't it? I wish I was smart enough to answer that. I don't think there's a yes or no. A complex question needs a complex answer, and there are shades of gray. I don't know.

Orson was emphatic. He said better that they go unpunished, because—

Oz: No, I'm sure, I'm sure that Orson said that. There's no question in my mind.

Heston would argue that the crux of the story hangs on the line that comes from Vargas's mouth, "A policeman's job is only easy in a police state."

Oz: It's interesting. He said to me and Jim Henson that he hated the word *professional*. He didn't like being called a professional because he thought *professional* seemed like a soldier's title, and so he was very much against that police state and the soldier. But it's interesting. That five-minute scene that just blows me away, I think—wasn't there a story there?—the studio was on to him saying, "You're gonna be late, you're gonna be late, you gotta cut."

It happened a couple of times. He would do a great, five-minute-long scene and then say, "Okay, wrap and print the last three cuts. We're ahead of schedule by two days."

Oz: There's the first five-minute scene, then you go away for several scenes, then you come back to the same room—that room must have inspired him.

Let's talk about the Henry Mancini score a little bit.

Oz: It was very interesting. Right now it's very dated, the bongos, a very Beat thing. At the same time, it's almost as if it was an ode to B-films because it was such a melodramatic score. Maybe on purpose, maybe not, but it felt that way to me. There was a dissonance, and it wasn't something that was melodic or very inviting because that tune isn't very inviting, but it still seemed melodramatic to me.

I remember the bongos, when Tamiroff is climbing and breaking that window, and then Quinlan takes him by the neck and Tamiroff is dangling. The bongos were kicking in there like crazy; I felt like I was in a Beat coffeehouse. That was very dated and funny to me, but nevertheless, it was B-movie effective. Tamiroff was such a funny bad guy. He wasn't really evil like Welles's character was evil.

One of the things that's interesting about it is that in the 1998 version, they move things around a little bit and they make use of Welles's track where he overlaps dialogue. It's not just cutting together shots; it's also layering in soundtracks and creating geography.
Oz: Postproduction is a slave of production there. You've got to plan that ahead of time and allow the actors to do that; otherwise there's nothing to loop later on. I'm sure he cut the whole movie in his head, and as a result the overlapping made it much more believable in the B-movie sense because it's still a B-movie. It's a wonderful B-movie.

How did the film change your life?
Oz: Well, I think I learned about all the depth and all the light. It harkens back to *Citizen Kane*, no question about it. So it's not just that. I would probably have chosen *Citizen Kane* really as the first thing that changed my life, but everybody was choosing that so I didn't choose it.

The techniques, what he did in both of them, just opened it up visually. The ceilings, the upshots, the dark and light values, use of extraordinary depth, the overlapping. I think it opened up my view of film—that there's so much more that could be done. Actually, by breaking so many rules, he allowed other people to say, "Hey, I can maybe think of some stuff, too!" He just opened up the possibilities more for me. That's what he did.

Did these encounters with Welles make you perceive *Touch of Evil* differently?
Oz: I never asked him about *Touch of Evil* or *Citizen Kane*, because I know what it's like when people talk to me, and people want to ask me about what I do. It's usually not as much fun as listening to other people. With Orson, I didn't want to start asking him about *Citizen Kane* and *Touch of Evil* like a fan because I was a co-worker at that time and I didn't want to bug him. So, no, I don't think it affected me.

To me, I thought a lot about the childlike innocence that Jim Henson and Orson had. Certainly, they're both iconoclasts, but in that there's this child-like innocence in both of them, and that struck me. I don't think it has any bearing on *Touch of Evil*, but it struck me that two great men like that had that same kind of feeling.

We were talking about people who were naturals for big characters. Welles was lucky in the fact that he was always the most forceful, charismatic guy in the room. He was the one who could drive the train. But I know you had disagreements with Marlon Brando on *The Score*. What did you learn from that? Is there something that you took from that experience about dealing with big personalities on the set?

Oz: Yeah, I learned how to be a better director. I learned that even big personalities like Marlon were scared, and I should've nourished them, that Marlon needed support and I was trying to be ultrastrong because I wouldn't let him do in my movie what he did in *The Island of Dr. Moreau*. I was not going to let him do that. He tried but I stopped him. Unfortunately, I stopped him in a way that was adversarial instead of supportive. I certainly learned from my mistakes from Marlon there. Not to say that he was the nicest guy in the world. [*laughs*]

Yeah, we're saying big personalities and all that that implies. . . .

Oz: Nevertheless, he taught me that even the biggest of actors are always scared. I learned to be more supportive as a director.

Do you think, and we're getting a tad off topic, but do you think ultimately that served the movie, that tension?

Oz: No, he wouldn't let me really direct him. I think it was one scene he let me direct him. I had to really make choices; I had to have different camera angles and make the choices in editing. That's what I had to do. Thank God De Niro was there. Bob was a tremendous help. I unfortunately kinda had to break Brando down. I mean, in the sense of, "Stop playing a character."

I went over to Marlon during the scene with Bob and I said, "Gee, I really like that." I knew he couldn't give a shit what I thought, and he said, "I don't know what I'm doing." That's kinda what I wanted. I didn't want a big bravura performance, I just wanted the character. To me the big mistake would have been, "Oh, Marlon Brando, Robert De Niro! First time together on film! You gotta have big explosives, like Al Pacino and Bob!" Well, sorry, that's not my job; my job is to make a believable character in the moment. Because the producers and I wouldn't let him do what he wanted to do, he kinda only did himself. What you see on the screen is Marlon, which is what I wanted.

In dealing with big personalities you talk about nurturing people, and Welles was known for doing this. He would never necessarily pit people against one another. He was one of these guys that thought that film was a family.

Oz: Well, yeah. On the other hand, he asked Jim Henson and me to sell a filmed talk show. He asked Jim and me to dinner, and a few days after dinner we went on his set and he was absolutely effusive in his caring for Jim and me, but he was miserable to the crew. [*laughs*]

So I guess he changed later in life then?

Oz: [*laughs*] I don't know, but he was absolutely wonderful to Jim and me. It's not that he was miserable; he just had absolutely no patience with the crew whatsoever. Maybe he got a crew that was not very good. I'm sure his outlook would still be the same, but that particular instance—and who knows, you wake up in the morning, you're grouchy, who knows—but I do believe that the family thing does make sense with him.

Did that ever surface? Is that in the archives someplace?

Oz: Yeah. It's embarrassing because I'm the young kid who's trying to make a name for myself, and I'm the one who talks a lot and Jim doesn't. It's just embarrassing. It's around somewhere. I try to avoid seeing it. It's in an archive someplace in the Muppets studio.

Let's come back to *Touch of Evil*. There are a couple of things we didn't mention, and maybe they're not important for the conversation, but it was originally called *Badge of Evil* . . .

Oz: I didn't know that.

... and Orson hated that, so they called it *Touch of Evil*. They changed it because I think in the way he wrote the script, it's obvious that the story is about Quinlan ...
Oz: Absolutely.

... and *Touch of Evil* makes it more ambiguous. [*laughs*]
Oz: Yeah, yeah.

The story of this film is great because forty years later they recut it. How do you feel about that notion in general? This is huge in DVDs, and it's being done theatrically. You worked with George Lucas on both *The Empire Strikes Back* and *Return of the Jedi*, which got rereleases. How do you feel about rereleases and extended cuts in general?
Oz: As long as it helps the story, I don't care. The key thing with any filmmaker is to help the story, you know. With Orson's stuff it's wonderful that they recut it the way he wanted it, as close as they could. That is great. As far as other people recutting their stuff, you know, there is a lot of pressure in movies during the previous stage, where the studio wants to do *this* and you want to do *this*. Fortunately, I've always been in the position where, except for two times, the studio has agreed with me, but those two times I wish I could put those things back.

Well, that was my next obvious question: are there any prints of your own that you would like to revisit or have revisited?
Oz: I would probably like to revisit *Little Shop* for a few small things. I would love to use digital on the color on *Little Shop*; I wish I had the opportunity to do it, but it wasn't available.

Is there anything specifically, or is it just little things? I just saw that the other day, and it holds up really well.
Oz: Yeah, I've always wanted it to have more of a Technicolor look, and it didn't quite have what I wanted, but in general it worked well. I think *Dirty Rotten Scoundrels* is pretty tight. I do know that whenever I make a movie and I finish a cut, I think, "That's great, fine, done." Then a year later, every single movie I've made I've had to take five minutes out because of TV sales.

It's amazing how you can do that without hurting a movie. So I'm sure some of the movies that I've done move slower than they should, and if I looked at them again I'd probably take something out.

There's nothing overwhelming that you say, "My real cut of _Bowfinger_, _The Stepford Wives_, or whatnot"—is someplace?
Oz: No, no. I've been fortunate in that. Oh, _Stepford Wives_ is a whole different deal. That's the only movie I'd go back to and not recut, but I'd reshoot. The other movies I'm pretty satisfied with. When it got down to making decisions about things, I'd either fight for them very hard, or I'd acquiesce because they weren't that important. I've never had a real bad situation with the other movies. _Stepford_ was a whole different deal.

But in that case, and we don't have to go into it, it's not the case that your vision or your print of the film exists someplace else; it's just that there—
Oz: No, my vision does exist someplace else. It exists in my head. It never got up there. It got way too complicated and way too big.

Oh, one other thing I wanted to bring up: Remember the scene in the hotel where Janet Leigh and all the Mexican hoods are in there?

He says, "Hold her legs." All of a sudden, it turned truly evil. I mean, it raised the level for a second there. That was like a rape moment and I don't think she was raped, but it really elevated the evil. It evoked that nightmarish feeling. It had a touch of _The Trial_ there.

That's always been my one reservation about the film, and I think Stephen Hunter points this out in his review of the '98 version: What happens to her? They blow marijuana smoke in her face?
Oz: Really, it's like a setup for a major rape. And it really is. It's almost if he wanted to get a sense of evil there but at the end said, "Well, this is not the movie where she really is raped."

Well, and what do they do? They play bebop music until she goes mad. [_laughs_]
Oz: Yeah, yeah. [_laughs_] That's what I mean. That's really B-movie. There's a lot of little things. I love Marlene Dietrich when he goes to her place. What's

wonderful is he goes back to this woman that he probably knew thirty years ago and she can't even recognize him, he's so dissolute. Great line, he says, "To read my future for me." Then she says, "Your future's all used up." That's a great line. [*chuckle*]

It turns out to be true.
Oz: Absolutely. She knew it. And he knew it. He knew the game was up when Vargas accused him of planting. He knew the game was up and he started going downhill immediately. To me that movie was about him, the dissolution, and what he used to be or could've been with her. I think that was pretty great.

How has your perception of the film changed over time?
Oz: I just love it. Every time I see it I never get tired of it. By seeing this, really studying it, yes, I did realize more. What struck me this time was how the relationship between him and Marlene Dietrich was so key. It's almost that she represented the youthful core of him when he was not a bad guy. I think that this viewing really hit that home to me.

30

John Waters
The Wizard of Oz

The Wizard of Oz keeps haunting John Waters.

It pops up in at least three of his films and accounts for the only time Waters found himself in drag (as a child, at a birthday party). At first when Waters told me he wanted to talk about *The Wizard of Oz*, I was skeptical—this was the filmmaker William Burroughs christened "the Prince of Puke" for extreme comedies such as *Pink Flamingos* and *Mondo Trasho*.

But as we talked, Waters's affection for *The Wizard of Oz* seemed to fit right in with his misfit-with-a-camera image. He tells me about a favorite scene: "When they throw the water on the witch, she says, 'Who would have thought a good little girl like you could destroy my beautiful wickedness.' That line inspired my *life*. I sometimes say it to myself before I go to sleep, like a prayer."

John Waters, selected filmography:
Mondo Trasho (1969)
Pink Flamingos (1972)
Female Trouble (1974)
Desperate Living (1977)
Polyester (1981)
Hairspray (1988)
Cry-Baby (1990)
Serial Mom (1994)
Pecker (1998)
Cecil B. DeMented (2000)
A Dirty Shame (2004)

The Wizard of Oz
1939
Directed by Victor Fleming
Starring Judy Garland, Margaret Hamilton, Frank Morgan, Ray
Bolger, Bert Lahr, and Jack Haley

**Although it's unnecessary in American culture, how would you describe
this film to someone who has never seen it?**
WATERS: Girl leaves drab farm, becomes a fag hag, meets gay lions and men
that don't try to molest her, and meets a witch, kills her. And unfortunately—
by a surreal act of shoe fetishism—clicks her shoes together and is back to
where she belongs. It has an unhappy ending.

Do you remember how old you were and where you saw it?
WATERS: I probably saw it at the Senator Theater in Baltimore the first time,
which I still have my movie premieres in. I probably saw it there and then
on TV every year. But certainly I saw it at the movies as a kid.

I don't remember how old I was, and it wasn't the first movie I saw, but
it was close to it. It was a complete, complete obsession from the very, very
beginning. Now, today, you have video. We couldn't do that, so you had to
wait once a year to see it. That's that sadness about the magic of movies: you
can watch it over and over, and you can rewind it, see how everything is
done. Still, is there a better tornado scene? To me, all these really expensive
digital effects are very uninvolving. That tornado scene is as good as *Twister*
to me, and I think it's done with a nylon stocking.

It's a great surrealist scene, too.
WATERS: And how radical—the black and white to color is almost like an
LSD effect. It is a drug movie almost.

**I know there are homages to *Wizard of Oz* in your films, specifically
Mondo Trasho.**
WATERS: In *Mondo Trasho*, she clicks her heels to go home.

And then, the seldom seen *Roman Candles*.
WATERS: Oh yeah, they are reading the book!

Are there any more overt ones?
WATERS: I'm trying to think. In *Desperate Living* there's a Wicked Queen. Well, every day of my life I wear striped socks a lot. Actually, Commes des Garçons this year had women's shoes that looked exactly like that. They were curled up, so if you wore them, they stuck up in the air. Remember how the witch's shoes shrink? That's one of my favorite shots, and the close-up of her hands with electricity.

Still, to this day, that's creepy.
WATERS: That's a great shot. And talk about an entrance, my God! "Who killed my sister!"

One of the things I'm always amazed at is the range of films that this has had an effect on. From David Lynch's *Wild at Heart* to—
WATERS: That's so great, and Tim Burton's films as well. Oddly enough, it's way more influential in America than in Europe. They know the film in Europe, but not like here.

What is it then, in America, that makes the movie stick as such a huge influence?
WATERS: Because it was surreal and it was magical and it was trippy. We saw it when we were young, and it had good villains and one of the most famous songs in a movie ever. And great surrealism: "How about a little fire, Scarecrow?" When the winged monkeys fly, and rip out the straw! It's surrealistic.

My mother, to this day, is still scared of those monkeys.
WATERS: I think kids are the most scared when the trees grab back the apples. Kids *freak* when that happens; they cry.

Why do you think it's become associated with the gay community, as being a "gay classic"?

WATERS: See, to me, I don't think it's that much of a gay movie. Judy Garland is, but I don't think so much of that movie. Of course, this is her first one, but she wasn't tragic in that movie, except later they found out she was on diet pills when she was singing.

I think it's only a gay movie, if it is, only because of Judy Garland's later suffering in her life and melodrama. I love Judy Garland, but did she ever marry a straight man? I don't know. Did anyone in the family? It's a tradition. But basically, I don't think of it as a gay film. I know "Friends of Dorothy," but I think it's because of Judy Garland's later career.

Well, it might be a gay children's movie. I don't think it's a gay *adult's* movie. I know drag queens do the Wicked Witch, but I never saw one. It's not a drag role.

I read somewhere that you once, as a kid, dressed up like the Wicked Witch at a party.
WATERS: The only time I've ever been in drag in my entire life was once, at a children's birthday party. I was a witch. I'm sure a few eyebrows were raised, but not really. And once was enough. It ended my drag career. [*laughing*] I don't even think I thought of it as drag. It wasn't like being a woman in that outfit—it was being a villain. That's what I wanted. Of course, I also loved Captain Hook [Cyril Ritchard, in the 1955 NBC television production of *Peter Pan* with Mary Martin]—he was more a woman. Look at him. And Patty McCormack in *The Bad Seed*—that was the Holy Trinity of my youth, and they were all villains.

I was always lookin' for somethin' that other people didn't like, or people were frightened of, or didn't care for. I was always drawn to forbidden subject matter in the very, very beginning. *The Wizard of Oz* opened me up because it was one of the first movies I ever saw. It opened me up to villainy, to screenwriting, to costumes. And great dialogue. I think the witch has great, great dialogue.

It's always held up as one of the quintessential American films. Why?
WATERS: Because it takes place in LSD Land!

Maybe it's because—and what I do believe—in America, anything can happen. The great freedom of living in America, compared to many other countries—maybe this could happen; you could be home one day and be really just transported to another world, learn everything, and come back. To me, it is American because of the values with friends, and how people save each other and expose fraud—the person behind the curtain is really bullshit that has no power. All those are very American subject matter, but I don't know why they aren't European really, either.

To me, it's about one person, the whole movie: the Wicked Witch of the West. She inspired me. When I first saw the Wicked Witch of the West, I was completely obsessed by her. I didn't know why Dorothy wanted to go back to that smelly farm, with that badly dressed aunt and black and white, when she could live with gay lions, basically, and magic shoes.

Tell me about a favorite scene.
WATERS: When they throw the water on the witch, she says, "Who would have thought a good little girl like you could destroy my beautiful wickedness." That line inspired my *life*. I sometimes say it to myself before I go to sleep, like a prayer.

Her outfit, what a great outfit, it was a Commes des Garçons outfit years ahead of its time. Her makeup, the music around her—that one little shot where you see her in the tree before the Tin Man. It's my favorite little hint of her, because you're missing her.

I can still, with my nieces and nephews, just say, [*menacingly*] "Who killed my sister!" and they break into tears. They were young. It really scares most kids. If it scared me, I loved it. And it made me appreciate villains in films.

I never met her, Margaret Hamilton. But she did, before she died, send me an autographed picture. And my favorite thing that's made me obsessed to this day is she signed it, "Margaret Hamilton," but then "WWW" for Wicked Witch of the West. It was like her monogram. What a great, great thing to have all through your house. Those three letters were so amazing to me.

But she led to my whole belief, in all my movies that I made, that basically my heroes and heroines are sometimes the villains in other people's movies. Everything was backwards: The fat girl gets the guy [*Hairspray*]; the good killer is *Serial Mom*. It's always the reverse character in other people's movies that are heroes. I realized that I was never going to be like the other kids, that I wasn't going to fit in, but it didn't bother me. It was a secret society to know that the villains were just much more fun.

But with Hamilton, the witch was a part she could never break away from. WATERS: I never felt she minded. I felt that at the end of the day, she wouldn't sign a picture "WWW" in her old age if she was uptight about that.

I love that movie *The Making of the Wizard of Oz* by Aljean Harmetz, because there's a lot of great stuff about her in it. I think she even went to pose for Andy Warhol when he did the "Legends" thing. She embraced it, and she was really made a legend from that part. How many other villains are *that* famous from a movie, that can make a kid scream?

Although, and I said this line in a speech at the Independent Spirit Awards this year, but it's true: Last summer, I asked this kid I was talking to who was about seven, "Did you like *The Wizard of Oz*?" And he said, "Naw, basically that's just about *walking*." It was a great line!

I was stupefied: What do you mean about *walking*? It really shocked me. It was the only time a young person said something that was great, in a way, because they are just so into special effects. It was basically walking. But I asked him about the witch, because you've never seen a kid who has a neutral reaction. They all basically remember her.

And I have this great poster. I didn't have it as a kid, I bought it later, but it was this great marketing. It's this really scary picture of the witch for a kid's bedroom, and it says, "The Wicked Witch wants you to clean up your room—right now!"

Acknowledgments

First, thanks to the filmmakers and their staffs who so generously gave their time and passion to this project. Some directors I pursued for years, waiting for a gap in their schedules. This is really your book, so thanks.

Among the people who introduced me to filmmakers or otherwise helped facilitate an interview include the directors themselves, plus Nicolette Aizenberg, Brian Andreotti, Terry Armour, Jan Blenkin, Lara Bogenrief, Julian Brooks, Mark Caro, Charles Coleman, Morgan Harris, Larry Jakubecz, Ziggy Kozlowski, David Lee, Sharon Lester, Sally Madgwick, Meghan McElheny, Rusty Nails, Will Rowbotham, Richard Ruiz, Brittany Smith, Gail Stanley, Tim Sika, Milos Stehlik, Leo Thompson, Jill Wheeler, and Brenda White.

Second, thanks to my agent—the undaunted David Dunton—for believing in this book. Ditto to Yuval Taylor, my editor, friend, and most excellent poker host. None of this, of course, would have been possible without the encouragement from people at my various journalism jobs, so many thanks to Marcia Parker, Tim Bannon, Maureen Hart, Scott L. Powers, Sherry Skalko, and James Warren.

The Film That Changed My Life would not have been possible without the eagle eyes and research mojo of Shay Bapple, Gina Brown, Lilian Bürgler, Sheila Burt, Lisa Cisneros, Alexis Crawford, Marcella De Laurentiis, Kasia Dworzecka, Michelle Edgar, Jenifer Fischer, Drew Fortune, Megan Frestedt, J. Scott Gordon, Constance Grady, Jay Grooms, Kelin Hall, Jina Hassan, Matthew Hendrickson, Michael Hirtzer, Laurel Jorgensen, Sharon Kim, Alison Knezevich, Rikki Knutti, David Lanzafame, Samantha Leal, Gabriel Mares, Kevin Meil, Nomaan Merchant, Theodore Noble, Caroline Picard, Ryan Ptomey, Nate Radomski, Kristen Radtke, Angie Rutkowski, Zack Seward, Benjamin Summers, Chelsea Trembly, Mia Umanos, and Eugenia Williamson.

Special gratitude goes out to Devon Freeny, Jessica Galliart, Joey Kahn, Daniel Peake, and Sofia Resnick for their detailed final edits of the manuscript.

Thanks also to the staff and management of the Bentwood Tavern in New Buffalo, Michigan, who hosted me for long afternoons while I edited this book on a would-be vacation.

The Film That Changed My Life is partly the fault of Lawrence Grobel and David Breskin, whose own interview books have provided years of inspiration for me. So, thank you both.

Finally, thanks to my wife, Betsy, and our twins—who are two years old as I write this. New fatherhood + book deadlines = lots of late nights, early mornings, and working vacations. So thanks for all your love and support. To Eva and Dylan, I can't wait until you're old enough so we can watch these movies together.

Index